T]

"The international community and the next United Nations Secretary-General will have a chance to initiate meaningful, transformative reforms in the way the United Nations addresses twenty-first-century social, political, and security challenges; the road map is provided by John Karlsrud in his new seminal treatise *The UN at War*, highly recommended to all international peace and security academics and practitioners."

—José Ramos-Horta, *Chair of the High-level Independent Panel on UN Peace Operations, Special Representative of the UN Secretary-General for Guinea-Bissau, Nobel Peace Prize laureate, and former President and Prime Minister of Timor Leste*

"This is the most current, up-to-date assessment of UN peace operations available. It addresses the new challenges of violent extremism and terrorism, and how to confront them without resort to the UN's use of violence. Karlsrud proposes sequencing tasks (rather than trying to do everything at once); devising long-term political strategies; burden-sharing between the UN, African Union, and other partners; and proposes 'people-centered reforms' that protect 'civilians, not governments.' A must-read for both analysts and practitioners of peacekeeping."

—Lise Morjé Howard, *Associate Professor, Department of Government, Georgetown University*

"John Karlsrud's book is a true state of the art on contemporary UN peace operations. Among its many strengths, it addresses two critical challenges head on: how peacekeepers can protect civilians in places where terrorism is a threat; and how to engage more directly with the local populations they are meant to serve. Informed by a deep knowledge of the political and practical obstacles, this excellent volume invites serious reflection on how peace operations must adapt to an increasingly complex security environment."

—Dr. Ian Johnstone, *Professor of International Law, Fletcher School of Law and Diplomacy, Tufts University*

"*The UN at War* face a range of urgent challenges with no easy answers. John Karlsrud, an author with first-hand experience working in UN Peace Operations, looks over the horizon at these challenges and possible responses. His book is timely, accessible and marshals a convincing argument about how the UN has to change to remain relevant, but how it must withstand calls for it to become a war-fighting organisation. This is a must-read book for those interested in the future of the UN and peacekeeping."

—Roger Mac Ginty, *Professor of Peace and Conflict Studies, University of Manchester*

John Karlsrud

The UN at War

Peace Operations in a New Era

John Karlsrud
NUPI
Oslo, Norway

ISBN 978-3-319-62857-8   ISBN 978-3-319-62858-5   (eBook)
https://doi.org/10.1007/978-3-319-62858-5

Library of Congress Control Number: 2017955020

Cover illustration: © proxy minder / Getty Images

Cover design by Samantha Johnson

This Palgrave Macmillan imprint is published by Springer Nature
The registered company is Springer International Publishing AG
The registered company address is: Gewerbestrasse 11, 6330 Cham, Switzerland

In memory of Anne Marie, Frode, and Maria

PREFACE AND ACKNOWLEDGMENTS

In a world where peace is becoming more and more elusive, it is of utmost importance that we uphold the values on which the UN was founded. After a period of guarded optimism in the first decade of the 2000s, there has been an increase in violent conflict during the last few years. Violence seems to be emerging as the only way of expressing anger and frustration at the lack of agency and participation. There is an urgent need to reflect on what role UN peacekeeping, and more generally UN peace operations, should be given in this context.

"Theory is always for someone and some purpose," asserted Robert Cox, a former UN employee and professor of international relations (1981: 128). Thus, the aim of this book is to provide critical reflections on UN peace operations, and constructive suggestions as to how the UN and the international system can evolve to remain relevant and tackle the peace and security challenges of the twenty-first century, without abandoning the principles that the UN was founded upon, and on which the legitimacy of UN peace operations rests.

This book began with my article "The UN at War: Examining the Consequences of Peace Enforcement Mandates for the UN Peacekeeping Operations in the CAR, the DRC and Mali," published in *Third World Quarterly* in 2015. The changes that occurred in the mandating and implementation of these three missions from 2013 and onward seemed to me to mark the possible start of an unsettling trend where the key principles of UN peacekeeping—and the UN Charter—were no longer heeded. The arguments for moving away from these principles were and are many—and indeed, many of them present the world with difficult dilemmas that require careful reflection as well as action. Questioning the assumption that we are facing an era of radically new threats that require new responses from the international community, I discuss these challenges and threats, and why we need to treat them as analytically distinct from the responses that the international community may agree on. Basically, I take issue with the trend toward using UN peace operations for peace enforcement purposes, whether against armed opposition groups, violent extremists, or terrorists.

The book focuses on UN peacekeeping operations in sub-Saharan Africa, where most UN peacekeeping missions are and have been for the last 15 years. However, it also looks forward, considering the very real possibility that future missions may be deployed to Libya in the Maghreb, and Syria and Yemen in the Middle East. The book does not deal with all the dimensions of modern UN peace operations, such as security sector reform and the rule of law, or developing a fit-for-purpose mission support concept for robust peacekeeping operations.

I am deeply thankful for the support received from the Training for Peace programme at the Norwegian Institute of International Affairs (NUPI) and from the Fulbright Foundation. The latter granted me a visiting scholar fellowship to spend three months at the Center on International Cooperation (CIC) at New York University, from September to December 2015. I am indebted to CIC and the staff there for hosting me. In particular, I would like to thank Richard Gowan, the then Deputy Director of CIC, and Barnett Rubin, the then acting Director, for initially supporting my proposal, and to the Center's leadership Sarah Cliffe and Jim Della-Giacoma for taking me on board and supporting me in every way possible during my stay. I am also grateful for the continued support from colleagues at the Peace and Conflict Research Group (PCRG) at NUPI, without which this book would not have come to fruition. I have benefited from countless discussions and received incisive and very helpful comments on various drafts of the manuscript from my colleagues around the world, including Arthur Boutellis, Camilla Campisi, Cedric de Coning, Ingvild Magnæs Gjelsvik, Richard Gowan, Ian Johnstone, Jim Della-Giacoma, Kiyoshi Matsukawa, Hanny Megally, Kari Osland, Niels Nagelhus Schia, Alexandra Novosseloff, Yf Reykers, Pernille Rieker, Natasja Rupesinghe, Adam Smith, Andrea Ó Súilleabháin, and Maxime de Taisne. I would also like to thank Jim Della-Giacoma and Ryan Rappa at CIC, and Jair van der Lijn and Timo Smit at the Swedish Stockholm International Peace Research Institute (SIPRI), for permission to use figures and help to develop these.

A previous and shorter version of Chapter 3 was published as Karlsrud, John (2016a) "New Tools for Blue Helmets," in Jim Della-Giacoma (ed.), *Global Peace Operations Review: Annual Compilation 2015*. New York: Center on International Cooperation, New York University, pp. 101–107. Reused with permission of *Global Peace Operations Review*. A previous and shorter version of Chapter 4 was published as Karlsrud, John (2016b) "UN peace operations and counter-terrorism—A bridge too far?" in Jim Della-Giacoma (ed.), *Global Peace Operations Review: Annual Compilation 2015*. New York: Center on International Cooperation, New York University, pp. 118–124. Reused with permission of *Global Peace Operations Review*. A previous and shorter version of Chapter 6 was published as Karlsrud, John (2016c) "How can the UN move towards more people-centered peace operations?" in Jim Della-Giacoma (ed.), *Global Peace Operations Review: Annual Compilation 2015*. New York: Center on International Cooperation, New York University, pp. 108–11. Reused with permission of Global Peace Operations Review.

Warm thanks go to André Broome and Shaun Breslin, editors of the *Global Reordering* series for Palgrave Pivot, for initially agreeing to publish this book, as well as to my editors Christina Brian, Ulrike Stricker, Amber Husain, and James Safford at Palgrave, and to Susan Høivik and Natasja Rupesinghe at NUPI, who have helped me immensely in the process of finalizing the book. Finally, I would like to thank Astrid Hornslien for her warm support and companionship.

Oslo, Norway   John Karlsrud
February 2017

Previous publications by the same author:

UN Peacekeeping Doctrine in a New Era: Adapting to Stabilization, Protection and New Threats. Co-edited with Cedric de Coning and Chiyuki Aoi. Abingdon: Routledge (2017).

Norm Change in International Relations: Linked Ecologies in UN Peacekeeping Operations. Abingdon: Routledge (2016).

The Future of African Peace Operations: From the Janjaweed to Boko Haram. Co-edited with Cedric de Coning and Linnéa Gelot. London: Zed Books (2016).

CONTENTS

About the Author

John Karlsrud is Senior Research Fellow at the Norwegian Institute of International Affairs (NUPI), and External Associate at the Centre for the Study of Globalisation and Regionalisation, University of Warwick, where he also earned his PhD. He has been a Visiting Fulbright Fellow at the Center on International Cooperation, New York University, and a Visiting Fellow at the International Peace Institute in New York. Topics of particular interests are peace operations, peacebuilding, and humanitarian action. He has served as Special Assistant to the United Nations Special Representative in Chad and was part of the UN Development Programme's leadership program LEAD. He has published articles in *Disasters, Global Governance, International Review of the Red Cross,* and *Third World Quarterly,* among others. Karlsrud has worked in Bosnia and Hercegovina, Chad, Palestine, Norway, and the USA, and conducted field research and shorter missions to Haiti, Liberia, Mali, Mozambique, Serbia, Sierra Leone, South Sudan, and Ukraine.

Acronyms and Abbreviations

ACIRC	African Immediate Crisis Response Capacity
AFISMA	African-led International Support Mission in Mali
AMISISOM	African Union Mission in Somalia
APSA	African Peace and Security Architecture
AQIM	al-Qaeda in the Islamic Maghreb
ASF	African Standby Force
ASG	Assistant-Secretary-General (UN)
ASIFU	All Sources Information Fusion Unit
AU	African Union
AU PSC	African Union Peace and Security Council
C-34	UN General Assembly Special Committee on Peacekeeping Operations
CANs	Community Alert Networks
CAR	Central African Republic
CASEVAC	Casualty Evacuation
CCC	Civilian Contributing Country
CIC	Center on International Cooperation
CODs	Common Operational Datasets
CTITF	Counter-Terrorism Implementation Task Force
CVE	Countering Violent Extremism
CVR	Community Violence Reduction
DDR	Disarmament, Demobilization, and Reintegration
DDVE	Demobilization and Disengagement of Violent Extremists
DFS	Department of Field Support (UN)
DPA	Department of Political Affairs (UN)

DPKO	Department of Peacekeeping Operations (UN)
DRC	Democratic Republic of the Congo
ECCAS	Economic Community of Central African States
ECOWAS	Economic Community of West African States
FARDC	*Forces armées de la République démocratique du Congo*
FDLR	*Forces démocratiques de libération du Rwanda*
FGS	Federal Government of Somalia
FIB	Force Intervention Brigade
FOBs	Forward Operating Bases
FOC	Full Operational Capability
G-5 Sahel	Group of Five Sahel
G-77	Group of 77
HIPPO	High-level Independent Panel on Peace Operations (UN)
IASC	Inter-agency Standing Committee
ICC	International Criminal Court
ICTs	Information Communication Technologies
IED	Improvised Explosive Device
IS	Islamic State
ISSSS	International Security and Stabilization Support Strategy
ITU	International Telecommunications Union
LCBC	Lake Chad Basin Commission
LRA	Lord's Resistance Army
MEDEVAC	Medical evacuation
MINURCAT	United Nations Mission in the Central African Republic and Chad
MINUSCA	United Nations Multidimensional Integrated Stabilization Mission in the Central African Republic
MINUSMA	United Nations Multidimensional Integrated Stabilization Mission in Mali
MINUSTAH	United Nations Stabilization Mission in Haiti
MISCA	African-led International Support Mission to the Central African Republic
MNJTF	Multinational Joint Task Force
MNLA	Movement for the National Liberation of Azawad
MONUC	United Nations Organization Mission in the Democratic Republic of the Congo
MONUSCO	United Nations Organization Stabilization Mission in the Democratic Republic of the Congo
MUJAO	Movement for Unity and Jihad in West Africa

OAU	Organisation of African Unity
OCHA	Office for the Coordination of Humanitarian Affairs
ONUC	*Organisation des Nations Unies au Congo*
ONUCI	United Nations Operation in Côte d'Ivoire
OROLSI	Office of Rule of Law and Security Institutions
OSCE	Organization for Security and Co-operation in Europe
P5	Permanent Five members of the UNSC
PBPS	Policy and Best Practices Service
PCCs	Police Contributing Countries
PoC	Protection of Civilians
PVE	Preventing Violent Extremism
R2P	Responsibility to Protect
RECs	Regional Economic Communities
RMs	Regional Mechanisms for Conflict Prevention, Management and Resolution
SADC	Southern African Development Community
SDGs	Sustainable Development Goals
SFOR	Stabilization Force
SG	Secretary-General (UN)
SIPRI	Stockholm International Peace Research Institute
SNA	Somalia National Army
SRCC	Special Representative of the Chairperson
SRSG	Special Representative of the Secretary-General
STCDSS	Specialized Technical Committee on Defence, Safety and Security
TCCs	Troop Contributing Countries
TechCCs	Technological expertise Contributing Countries
UAS	Unmanned Aerial Systems
UNAMA	United Nations Assistance Mission in Afghanistan
UNAMID	African Union–United Nations Mission in Darfur
UNAMSIL	United Nations Mission in Sierra Leone
UNCCT	United Nations Counter-Terrorism Centre
UNCT	United Nations Country Team
UNDP	United Nations Development Programme
UNDSS	United Nations Department of Safety and Security
UNGA	United Nations General Assembly
UNHCR	United Nations High Commissioner for Refugees
UNHQ	United Nations Headquarters

UNISFA	United Nations Interim Security Force for Abyei
UNMISS	United Nations Mission in the Republic of South Sudan
UNOCC	United Nations Operations and Crisis Centre
UNSC	United Nations Security Council
UN SCR	United Nations Security Council Resolution
UNSG	United Nations Secretary-General
UNSOA	United Nations Support Office for AMISOM
UNSOM	United Nations Assistance Mission in Somalia
UNTSO	United Nations Truce Supervision Organization
UNU	United Nations University
USG	Under-Secretary-General
UUAV	Unmanned and Unarmed Aerial Vehicles

LIST OF FIGURES

LIST OF TABLES

Introduction

In 2013, the United Nations (UNSC) mandated the inclusion of a regional force—the Force Intervention Brigade (FIB)—in the UN peacekeeping mission in the Democratic Republic of the Congo (DRC) (MONUSCO) and authorized the mission to "neutralize" identified rebel groups (UN 2013a: 7). The FIB defeated the M23 rebel group in joint operations with the national *Forces armées de la République démocratique du Congo* (FARDC).

Only days after MONUSCO was authorized, the United Nations Multidimensional Integrated Stabilization Mission in Mali (MINUSMA) was instructed to confront rebel, extremist, and terrorist groups in Mali (UN 2013b). The mission has in its short life-span become one of the deadliest UN peace operations on record, with 70 fatalities due to attacks by rebel and terrorist groups since its deployment in 2013 until October 30, 2016 (UN 2016a).

And in 2014, the UN mission in the Central African Republic (MINUSCA) was deployed to help the country move back onto a path to peace, after sectarian violence had reached levels bordering on genocide. Unfortunately, the mission soon gained notoriety for repeated revelations of sexual exploitation and abuse, shared in equal measure with the African-led International Support Mission to the Central African Republic (MISCA) and the French-backed peacekeeping force known as *Opération Sangaris*.

In South Sudan, the UN mission, United Nations Mission in the Republic of South Sudan (UNMISS), has been struggling to protect

J. Karlsrud, *The UN at War*,
https://doi.org/10.1007/978-3-319-62858-5_1

1

civilians after the outbreak of civil war at the end of 2013. During the last three years, the UN camps have been converted to protection of civilians (PoC) sites, and the mission has been hard pressed to protect even those residing within its camps, much less the millions of people living in fear outside its camps. As a result, the UNSC in August 2016 authorized a regional protection force that should deal preventively and robustly with any actor threatening civilians (UN 2016b).

Each of these challenges, changes, and turns would in itself have been a reason to take pause, and several have resulted in reviews and inquiries. But together, they show that there is a fundamental mismatch between the tasks given to UN peacekeeping operations, and what they are able to do on the ground. It is clear that UN peacekeeping operations are struggling with increasing gaps between its foundational principles and the mandates given by the UNSC. The gaps are both principled and practical—should the UN go beyond the core principles of impartiality, consent, and the minimum use of force except in self-defense, and in defense of the mandate to fight actively against strategic actors? Should the UN Secretariat resist deployment to conflicts when there is no peace on the ground and where a mission may face violent extremists and terrorist without sufficient means to defend itself? How should the UN, and the international community at large, deal with conflicts where no peace operation will be able to offer sufficient protection to civilians, as is the case in South Sudan?

The increasing gap between the expectations to UN peace operations and what was happening on the ground was recognized by the then UN Secretary-General (UNSG) Ban Ki-moon in June 2014 when he announced the establishment of a High-level Independent panel on Peace Operations (HIPPO). The same year, the USA took the initiative to organize a Peacekeeping Summit during the UN General Assembly in September, chaired by the then US Vice-President Joseph Biden. The release of the HIPPO Report in 2015, together with releases of the 2015 review of the UN peacebuilding architecture; the global study of the implementation of UN Security Council Resolution 1325 on women, peace, and security; and a second US-led summit on peacekeeping during the 2015 UN General Assembly chaired by the then President Barack Obama—all these brought a sense of urgency and new momentum for dealing with these gaps and challenges. David Cameron and other world leaders cited the threat of terrorism as one of the factors motivating the contributions of troops, equipment, and training (Mason 2015). The picture that is generally presented is that of an organization that should modernize and be updated to deal more effectively with the arguably new threats of the twenty-first century—violent extremism and terrorism—in addition to the core and traditional task of protecting civilians.

In this book, I argue for a more nuanced picture. The gap between expectations and what UN peace operations are able to deliver is not solely created by a lack of performance, poor management, and lack of capabilities, but is also the result of the increasing tendency of the UNSC to not match mandates with means, and to give to UN peace operations tasks they are not, and will not be, suited to accomplish. UN peace operations are deployed to more difficult theaters and given more robust mandates, including stabilization and enforcement tasks, in some instances veering toward counter-terrorism. In this context, the dissonance between what these missions are capable of providing, measured against the complex realities on the ground, is growing painfully clear. To understand the shift toward more robust mandates for UN peacekeeping operations, we have to look at four other important trends.

First, the financial crisis in 2008–2009 was expected to precipitate a drop in UN peacekeeping operations, as cash-strapped governments wanted to cut costs—particularly those bearing the main burden of the UN peacekeeping budget, like the USA. However, the earthquake in Haiti, the new mission in South Sudan, and two missions deployed successively to Mali and the Central African Republic (CAR) instead resulted in an increase in the number of troops deployed. At the same time, calls for the UN to do more with less have been persistent and actually successful. Since 2010, there has been a general increase in the cost effectiveness of UN peace operations, with the HIPPO Report noting a 17 % cost reduction in the period from 2010 to 2015 (UN 2015).[1]

Third, fatalities caused by terrorism have increased rapidly—from 3329 in 2000 to a spike of 32,685 in 2014 (IEP 2015: 2). Much of the recent increase is due to the Islamic State (IS) and Boko Haram (ibid.). In this period, the UN has moved from being seen as an impartial actor to more often being the target of terrorist attacks—from Baghdad, to Algiers, Kabul, Mazar-i-Sharif, Abuja, Mogadishu, and Mali.

Concurrent with the enduring pressure of economic austerity, the increased numbers of UN peacekeepers in the field, and the growing threat of terrorism comes a fourth and equally important trend. Since the 9/11 attacks, counter-terrorism has been high on the international agenda, but in recent years, the rhetoric has moved from the "Global War on Terror," to less ominous-sounding concepts of "countering violent extremism"

(CVE) and "preventing violent extremism" (PVE). However, while "violent extremism" may be a more inclusive term than "terrorism," it is also a notoriously slippery term, and the UN has not agreed on an official definition of either "terrorism" or "violent extremism" (see Glazzard and Zeuthen 2016). Emergent research on violent extremism underscores that there is a wider range of tools than just military means available for tackling the root causes of these challenges. However, the re-conceptualization has also made it more palatable to see the UN as a possible actor and UN peace operations a possible tool to deal with these challenges, increasing the geographic and thematic scope of UN peace operations.

The release of the HIPPO Report was followed by a plan of action announced by the Secretary-General (SG) in September 2015. The momentum was sustained by a May 2016 debate arranged by the President of the General Assembly on the synergies of these reports and how to implement their recommendations; and then a follow-up summit in September 2016 on peacekeeping arranged by the UK in London, convening the largest number of Ministers of Defense ever to discuss UN peacekeeping. When the previous high-level review of UN peacekeeping ("the Brahimi Report") was released in 2000 (UN 2000), 16 working groups worked for more than two years on implementing some of the more broadly accepted recommendations. That Report has continued to generate debate and serve as a reference ever since. Judging from this fact, and the fact that António Guterres, the new SG who took the helm at the UN in 2017, initiated his term with a number of organizational changes, continuous discussions about the form and function of UN peace operations, and efforts to put all the recommendations into action, are likely to continue for years to come. In this book, I identify and discuss the interests of the permanent five members of the UNSC and key stakeholder groups, like the major troop contributing countries (TCCs), and Western and African states.

Part of the reason why we have ended up in this conundrum, in my view, is that the UN has evolved from being primarily an arena where member states meet and discuss issues, to become an increasingly important actor in international relations in its own right. In the area of peace and security, there was not a single reference to "peacekeeping" in the UN Charter. The tool has been developed from deploying observer missions in its first four decades of existence (with the notable exception of the UN mission to Congo), to a rapid increase and decrease with the deployments to and failures in former Yugoslavia, Rwanda, and Somalia in the early and mid-1990s, and another boom with a concurrent conceptual development during the 2000s until today. What emerges is a potential tension between the role of the UN as an arena and its role as an actor. For cash-strapped governments still under the pressure of economic austerity measures, it might seem like a good idea to offload some conflicts on the lower end of the conflict intensity and/or interest spectrums to the UN.

Related to this, one of the many improvements in UN peace operations since the Cold War has been the development of multidimensional peace-keeping operations, to support peace- and statebuilding efforts while the military and the police are working to help establish a modicum of secu-rity. But this multidimensionality in peacekeeping has developed in tan-dem with the gradual weakening of another central principle—that the deployment of troops, police, and civilians must take place within the framework of a longer-term political strategy, rather than replacing it.

Similarly, UN peace operations have developed in terms of the capabili-ties and equipment they possess, although considerable gaps remain. The calls for updating UN peace operations to the twenty-first century with modern capabilities and equipment are well-founded—but, as discussed in this book, it might be that these calls sometimes want to equip UN peace operations with the right tools, but for the wrong reasons. Technological advances in data collection should serve to provide better protection for civilians, and the implementation of these reforms should not fuel allegations of intelligence-gathering that could be used by actors with vested interests.

With this book I issue a challenge to UN member states and peace operations practitioners to make sure that the calls for reform are anchored in the desire to improve the lives of people suffering in conflicts on the ground—not spurred by intra-organizational turf battles or solely the nar-row self-interests of member states. How can the UN adapt its practices to become more field- and people-centered, in line with its core, primary commitments of protecting and serving local people? What is needed is a move from mandating missions to "extend state authority" to "enhance state–society relations," making UN peace operations a tool to support more inclusive, participatory, and stable states.

OUTLINE OF THE BOOK

I begin by assessing the role and purpose of UN peace operations in the context of rapidly evolving and increasingly complex conflict dynamics. After mapping out some persistent institutional dilemmas facing the UN,

I examine one of the most politically charged trends: the gradual slide toward more robust mandates and peace enforcement. Chapter 1 highlights the necessity of crafting tailored responses and maintaining relevance, always aware of the limits of what the UN can and cannot be expected to do when faced with the widening gap between expectations, principles, and capabilities.

Chapter 2 examines the evolving politics of UN peace operations and presents the interests and motivations of key actors who seek to influence the future of UN peace operations, including the permanent members of the Security Council, Western countries, major TCCs, and emerging economies. It highlights the growing consensus among Western countries to adapt UN peace operations to become a central tool for countering violent extremism and terrorism, while also illustrating the position of countries opposed to this move, including Russia and major traditional peacekeeping TCCs. Here I also note the emerging consensus among many African and Western member states on moving UN peace operations in a more robust direction. The division of responsibilities between member states, regional actors, and the UN must take into consideration the respective capabilities of these actors, and, in the case of the UN, the role that the organization is playing in not only keeping the peace, but also making, mediating, and facilitating peace, humanitarian action, and development.

Chapter 3 explores the opportunities and potential challenges presented by technology and new capabilities available to UN peace operations. On the one hand, the use of intelligence cells, unmanned aerial vehicles (UAVs,) satellite imagery, and geo-tag software can massively improve the UN's situational awareness to protect and serve local populations and the mission itself. On the other, these tools may also be exploited to serve national interests and can infringe upon the right to personal privacy. The All Sources Information Fusion Unit (ASIFU) in MINUSMA, the first explicit intelligence cell in a UN mission, illustrates the promises and pitfalls of these current reforms. If the UN is to add these types of tools to its regular toolkit, both internal and external explanations for how these capabilities will benefit mission objectives and the people they are deployed will need to be articulated, coupled with clear guidelines for their operational use, and protocols and tools for protecting the information and analysis developed.

Proceeding to one of the more contentious debates on reform, Chapter 4 analyzes the ongoing doctrinal discussions on stabilization and counter-terrorism in the context of UN peace operations. It traces the growing prevalence of the concept "stabilization" in UN peace operations and argues that the increase reflects the roots of the concept and imbues UN peace operations with a more militarized understanding of conflict resolution. This is followed by an assessment of what stabilization looks like in practice, drawing on the experience of MINUSMA. The arguably changing conflict environment has given rise to debate on whether UN peace operations should take a more active role in countering and preventing violent extremism and terrorism—with UN itself divided as to how to move forward. Here I warn of the possibility for supply-driven solutions, given that increased funding is being poured into counter-terrorism and "preventing and countering violent extremism" (PCVE), potentially relabeling existing peacebuilding and development efforts and limiting the space for crafting political solutions. Finally, I explore the possible advantages and repercussions associated with the UN developing its own "stabilization" doctrine to guide more robust UN stabilization and peace enforcement missions.

Chapter 5 provides a discussion of evolving partnerships between the UN, the African Union (AU), and sub-regional organizations and how improved sequencing and burden-sharing arrangements should be sought to respond to the demands presented by asymmetric threats. While the AU has gained significant institutional capacity for responding to peace and security challenges on the continent, challenges remain. Here I examine the AU-UN experience in Somalia, issues related to sequencing of operations in the Sahel and Mali in particular, and the opportunities and challenges presented in hybrid solutions that use robust, regional intervention brigades, such as the FIB in MONUSCO. The chapter ends with a discussion of how these partnerships might incite competition between the UN and African regional solutions but are first and foremost constructive—representing a division of labor whereby the AU and regional organizations respond to "harder" security threats where doctrinal as well as capability challenges make UN deployment inadvisable.

Chapter 6 underlines the importance of committing to people-centered peacekeeping, one of the central recommendations to emerge from the review processes of the UN peace and security architecture in 2015. While committing to protecting and serving local people is paramount to the success of UN peace operations, achieving this in practice is much more challenging. I begin with the UNMISS, highlighting persistent shortcomings related to protecting civilians, and then look at the gap between the mandate of MINUSCA and contextual realities which have hindered peacebuilding efforts. I conclude the chapter by detailing current UN best practices that seek to make operations more responsive to local people, while providing suggestions for the way ahead.

In conclusion, my general argument is that, while the threats posed by transnational violent extremists and terrorist networks may in many ways be new, the UN and member states should tread carefully when deciding whether to should use UN peace operations to counter these threats, and need to consider the long-term consequences of such a development. The UN must ensure that it continues to carve out space for political, prevention-orientated responses in a climate where the supply of counter-terror solutions is expanding. The UN should withstand the move toward Chapter 7½ solutions which entail a marriage of regional enforcement forces under the banner of UN missions, and instead strengthen its part-nerships with regional organizations, such as the AU and sub-regional entities like the Economic Community of West Africa (ECOWAS) that are more prepared and willing to commit to using robust force in extraordi-nary circumstances. The organization should resist pressures to compro-mise on its foundational principles to preserve its unique legitimacy as an influential arbiter of conflict resolution. To remain relevant, however, the UN must also consider how it can do more with less, taking on board new technology to make peacekeeping missions better prepared to operate in challenging environments. These steps should be guided by a renewed commitment to "we the peoples," by further developing institutionalized strategies for bottom–up and people-centered peacekeeping, enhancing state–society relations rather than extending state authority, and support-ing the emergence of lasting, inclusive, and sustainable peace.

NOTES

1. When measured against troops and police deployed and adjusted for inflation.

REFERENCES

IEP (2015) *Global Terrorism Index 2015.* Sydney: Institute of Economics and Peace.
Glazzard, Andrew and Marthine Zeuthen (2016) *Violent extremism.* GSDRC Professional Development Reading Pack no. 34. Birmingham, UK: University

of Birmingham. Available at: http://www.gsdrc.org/wp-content/uploads/2016/02/Violent-extremism_RP.pdf. Accessed September 13, 2016.

Mason, Rowena (2015) "UK to deploy troops to help keep peace in Somalia and South Sudan," *The Guardian*, September 27, 2015. Available at: http://www.theguardian.com/politics/2015/sep/27/uk-to-deploy-troops-to-help-keep-peace-in-somalia-and-south-sudan. Accessed January 11, 2016.

UN (2000) *Report of the Panel on United Nations Peace Operations* [Brahimi Report]. New York: United Nations.

UN (2013a) *S/RES/2098*, March 28, 2013. New York: United Nations.

UN (2013b) *S/RES/2100*, April 25, 2013. New York: United Nations.

UN (2015) *A/70/95-S/2015/446. Report of the High-level Independent Panel on Peace Operations on Uniting our Strengths for Peace: Politics, Partnership and People* ("HIPPO Report"). New York: United Nations.

UN (2016a) "(4a) Fatalities by Mission, Year and Incident Type," *United Nations Peacekeeping*, October 30, 2016. Available at: http://www.un.org/en/peacekeeping/fatalities/documents/stats_4a.pdf. Accessed February 7, 2017.

UN (2016b) *S/RES/2304*, August 12, 2016. New York: United Nations.

CHAPTER 1

UN Peace Operations in a Changing World

> *The world is changing, and United Nations peace operations must change with it if they are to remain an indispensable and effective tool in promoting international peace and security—former UN Secretary-General Ban Ki-moon, 31 October 2014, announcing the establishment of the High-level Independent Panel on Peace Operations (HIPPO)*

A record 65.3 million people were forcibly displaced in 2015 (UNHCR 2016). While the number of conflicts had been steadily declining for more than a decade, the last few years have witnessed a wave of new conflicts in the CAR, Mali, Libya, Syria, and Yemen. Old conflicts have reignited and new ones have erupted in Nigeria, South Sudan, Syria, and Ukraine, among others. The UN is struggling with a formidable range of threats— from more "traditional" protection threats in for example the CAR and in South Sudan, to violent extremism and terrorism in Mali.

The first decade of the new millennium was marked by a decrease in the number of state and non-state conflicts in the world, from 51 and 21 (respectively) in 1991, to 31 and 28 in 2010 (UCDP 2016), and evidence of UN peacekeeping contributing to lasting peace and development (Howard 2008; Fortna 2008). In recent years, the number of state and non-state conflicts has been on the increase again: in 2015 the Uppsala Conflict Data Program counted 71 state-based conflicts and 51 non-state conflicts in the world. These data suggest that force is increasingly perceived as the best tool to achieve policy goals and solve disputes, but the

© The Author(s) 2018
J. Karlsrud, *The UN at War*,
https://doi.org/10.1007/978-3-319-62858-5_2

track record is poor. From Afghanistan, to Iraq, Libya, Mali, Nigeria, Somalia, Sudan, Syria, and Yemen, force has contributed to greater suffering, lasting and spreading instability, and refugee flows. With Syria and Ukraine, we may have returned to the proxy wars and zero-sum games of the Cold War, at least in some regions of the world.

In many fragile countries, the elite maintain power by buying allegiance from the potential opposition with the relatively few economic and military resources available. Kleptocratic leadership—in the case of South Sudan characterized as a "militarized, corrupt neo-patrimonial system of governance" (de Waal 2014: 347)—is the very source of fragility, leaving few if any resources for security, education, infrastructure, or social services. The "youth bulge" facing the Southern Hemisphere, and Africa in particular, compounds these challenges. Over the next 15 years, 435 million young people will be searching for jobs in Africa, representing two-thirds of the global growth in the workforce worldwide (African Economic Outlook 2015: xii). Without future prospects, these young people may become involved in crime and violent politics, and be vulnerable to radicalization. Youth also form the bulk of migrants and refugees from Africa in Europe and elsewhere in Africa, fleeing conflict and seeking to support their families. Global remittance flows reached USD 440 billion in 2015 (World Bank 2015).

Youth also formed the core of the "Arab Spring," which started in Tunisia and spread across the Arab world in 2011. However, this Arab Spring was short-lived—for a short while, the use of modern technologies and social media was hailed for leveling the playing field, but it did not take long before these technologies were turned into modern swords of Damocles against those who used them (Karlsrud 2014: 151). The use of modern technologies as a tool for intelligence-gathering on behalf of oppressive regimes was a key trend during the Arab Spring, often with the support of Western companies (ibid.; Elgin and Silver 2012; Wagner 2012). Terrorist groups have also showed their prowess in using the same tools for nefarious purposes. Today, many of the countries of the Arab Spring are embroiled in conflict and may tomorrow be hosting new peace operations deployed by the UN or by coalitions of the willing, regional or sub-regional organizations. Libya, Syria, and Yemen seem likely candidates here.

The challenges of violent extremism and terrorism figure prominently in discussions on the form and shape such future peace operations should take. Although political violence is an age-old phenomenon, and terrorism has long been high on the agenda, particularly since the 9/11 attacks in 2001, violent extremism and terrorism are now portrayed as "new" challenges, central to the ongoing debate on how UN peace operations can be reformed so as to be relevant to the challenges of the world today. The number of fatalities caused by terrorism globally has been rising steadily since 2000, from 3329 in 2000 to 32,685 in 2014 (IEP 2015: 2). A particularly dramatic increase came in 2014, up by 80% compared to 2013, largely because of the so-called IS and Boko Haram (ibid.). Not only have the numbers of victims increased exponentially over the last decade or so, the acts committed by terrorist groups are increasingly aimed at shocking the conscience of humanity. Many constitute war crimes and crimes against humanity (see, e.g., UNHRC 2015). Key groups behind terrorist attacks include al-Qaeda (e.g., Afghanistan, Iraq, and Syria), IS (e.g., Syria and Iraq), Boko Haram (Nigeria, Cameroon, Niger, and Chad), al-Shabaab (Somalia), Ansar Dine (Mali), al-Mourabitoun (Mali), and al-Qaeda in the Islamic Maghreb (AQIM) (Mali).

The shockingly violent acts—largely against civilians and often deliberately targeting women—committed by groups like IS and Boko Haram, with rape, sexual slavery, and forced marriage used as terror tactics (UN 2015b), have made it more urgent to deal with these rapidly growing threats. Violent extremism, and the militarization of societies that follows security-oriented approaches to fighting violent extremism and terrorism, has "an adverse effect on women's security" (Stamnes and Osland 2016: 17), placing women "between this rising tide of violent extremism in their societies and the constraints placed on their work by counter-terrorism policies that restrict their access to critical funds and resources" (UN 2015c: 224). Violent extremism, terrorism, and counter-terrorism put vulnerable groups between a rock and a hard place, narrowing the space for engagement by women peacebuilders and limiting the funding for basic services and peacebuilding activities.

Since 9/11, also the UN has increasingly become the target of terrorist attacks. The attacks in Baghdad in 2003, Algiers in 2007, Kabul in 2009, Mazar-i-Sharif in 2011, Abuja in 2011, Mogadishu in 2013, and several attacks in Mali from 2013 to today, in addition to a great many smaller attacks, have all made it increasingly clear that in many places the UN is not seen as an impartial actor, but rather a participant in the global war on terror. In turn, the UN has adjusted its risk posture by taking precautions on movement and deployment of staff in high-risk zones and bunkerizing itself behind high walls and red-tape risk procedures, increasing the distance with the local populations that the organization is meant to serve (see, e.g., Duffield 2012).

On the other hand, the impression that the UN is increasingly being targeted and is losing more people to hostile attacks now than before deserves further scrutiny. In 2014, UN peace operations suffered 126 fatalities, 39 of which due to hostile acts, most of them in Mali (UN 2016b). A study by the Stockholm International Peace Research Institute (SIPRI) found that while this was a high number, fatality ratios—as measured against the total number of troops, police, and civilians deployed in the field—have remained fairly steady at about 1 per 1000 since 2008 (van der Lijn and Smit 2015). In comparison, the fatality ratio between 1990 and 2005 was more than 1.5 (peaking at 3.3 in 1993), then showing a significant decrease from about 1.7 to less than 1 between 2005 and 2007 (ibid.; see also Henke 2017). In recent years, MINUSMA has added the toll—it has become the deadliest of current UN peacekeeping operations accounting for 40 out of a total of 60 fatalities caused by malicious acts in 2014–2015 alone (ibid.; UN 2016a), with a fatality rate of 2.38 (van der Lijn and Smit 2015: 7).[1] But Mali, as discussed later, is not an ordinary peacekeeping mission, and if Mali is subtracted from the overall fatality count, "2014 actually had the fewest hostile deaths per 1000 since 1990 (0.08 per 1000)" (ibid.: 3) (Fig. 1.1).

The UN is currently in a state of flux when it comes to developing policy on counter-terrorism and countering and preventing violent extremism, with increasing pressure from some member states for the UN to take on a greater share of these challenges. Member states and multilateral organizations have developed various doctrines and guidelines for countering and preventing violent extremism, from military-oriented counter-insurgency to counter-terrorism guidance, such as the US *Counterinsurgency Field Manual* and *NATO's Military Concept for Defence Against Terrorism* (United States Dept. of the Army and United States Marine Corps 2007; NATO 2011). In December 2015, the SG presented a new *Plan of Action to Prevent Violent Extremism,* emphasizing the need to focus on the preventive aspect (2015d).

The heightened attention to the threat of violent extremism and terrorism has come in an environment of economic austerity and fatigue of Western troops after 15 years of warfare in Afghanistan and Iraq. It has been followed by promptings from the USA and other Western powers for the UN to take greater responsibility for the challenges facing the international community. With the increasing pressure on the UN to reform UN

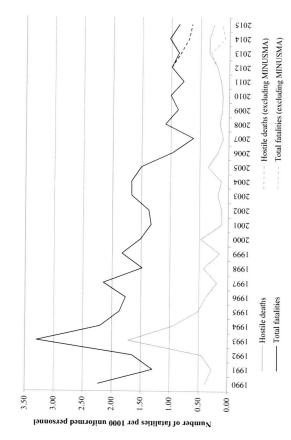

Fig. 1.1 Fatalities per 1000 uniformed personnel in UN peace operations, 1990–2015 (this figure is reprinted, with permission, from van der Lijn and Smit (2015). The values for 2015 were projections based on the fatalities in the first half of the year (up until 2 July) and do not represent the number of deaths in 2015 overall. For further data, see please the SIPRI Multilateral Peace Operations Database)

peace operations to be relevant to these tasks, it is pertinent to ask: should the UN update its principles and practices to a new context—or are existing principles and practices still valid?

This chapter assesses the role of UN peace operations in the context of changing conflict dynamics and introduces some of the core tensions that will be discussed in this book.[2] It gives an overview of some of most pressing challenges facing the UN, questioning the assumptions surrounding "new threats" of violent extremism. It discusses the internal and institutional constraints faced by the organization, such as the rift between headquarter policies and local implementation, and "state-centrism" which has too often resulted in uncritically supporting governments instead of local people. It charts the slide toward peace enforcement and discusses the implications of using contingents that are motivated by national self-interest to intervene in neighboring conflict-affected countries. The push to maintain relevance whereby powerful states use UN peacekeeping operations for intervening to enforce peace ultimately risks undermining UN legitimacy in the long run and has come at a high price. Greater clarity is required on the limits to what the UN can and cannot do in increasingly hostile environments, with its limited capabilities and resources.

UN Peacekeeping: Development and Perennial Dilemmas

UN peacekeeping operations are a relatively new tool for maintaining international peace and security, as is the UN itself. Even so, UN peacekeeping operations have undergone rapid and radical changes from their inception until today. Although not mentioned in the UN Charter, UN peacekeeping quickly evolved from observer missions in UN Truce Supervision Organization (UNTSO) in the Middle East and India/Pakistan (Kashmir) to the UN mission in the Congo (ONUC, 1960–1964), the first to be mandated to use force. However, ONUC remained the exception rather than the rule for a long time. Toward the end of the Cold War, a string of new missions was mandated to Angola, Mozambique, Namibia, El Salvador, Guatemala, and Cambodia—generally in order to help implement a peace agreement, including arranging elections and building institutions (see, e.g., Howard 2008). These operations led to increased optimism as to what UN peacekeeping missions could be used for. There was a sharp increase in the number of peacekeepers on the ground, with new missions deployed to Somalia, Bosnia, and Rwanda in the early 1990s.

However, the failures of the UN to protect civilians in these countries soon made clear the hubris of deploying troops without the requisite mandate or capabilities. The main distinction between these and previous operations was that there was no peace to keep, and the UN found itself operating without the necessary guidance, resources or capabilities. In 1993, John Ruggie warned that the UN had entered "…a vaguely defined no-man's land lying somewhere between traditional peacekeeping and enforcement—for which it lacks any traditional guiding operational concept" (Ruggie 1993: 26), a statement that is eerily recognizable also today. The failures led to a sharp decrease in the number of UN peacekeeping operations and the troops deployed from 1995 to 1999.

Nevertheless, the hiatus in UN peacekeeping after Bosnia and Rwanda did not last long. From the late 1990s, UN peacekeeping operations experienced strong growth, with large multidimensional peacekeeping missions deployed to the DRC, Liberia, Sierra Leone, and Timor-Leste, among others. These missions were mandated to protect civilians: over time their peacebuilding tasks were also expanded, to avoid relapse into conflict (Boutros-Ghali 1992: 3). After the turn of the century came further expansion from 2003 and onward, with missions deployed to, for example, Burundi, Côte d'Ivoire, and Darfur. Then there followed another period of growth, from 2011 and onward, with missions deployed to South Sudan (2011), Mali (2013), and the CAR (2014), after a slight decrease of personnel in the field after the financial crisis. In April 2015, the total number of personnel in the field reached an all-time high, with 126,247 military, police, and civilian peacekeepers deployed to 16 peacekeeping operations (UN 2015e). In addition, another 3700 personnel were serving in 11 UN special political and peacebuilding missions (UN 2015a), bringing the overall total to 130,000 (Fig. 1.2).

This has not been unproblematic, however. One set of dilemmas pertains to the relationship between the UNSC and the Secretariat, in particular the Department of Peacekeeping Operations (DPKO). Reviewing missions until 2000, the *Report of the Panel on United Nations Peace Operations* (known as the "Brahimi Report" after the Panel chair, UN Under-Secretary-General (USG) Lakhdar Brahimi) advised on the "pivotal importance of clear, credible and adequately resourced Security Council mandates" (UN 2000: 1). The findings of the Brahimi Report ring true also today, and the gap between increasingly complex mandates and limited capabilities and resources has arguably increased the risk of a repeat of the failures of the 1990s.

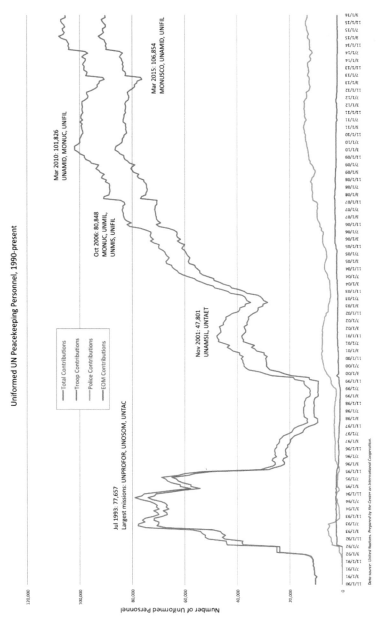

Fig. 1.2 Surge in uniformed personnel 1990—present (the figure was developed by the Global Peace Operations Review at the Center on International Cooperation, New York University. Republished with permission)

Another dilemma is the discrepancy between policies agreed upon at New York headquarters, such as the PoC and the lack of implementation in the field. In 2014, a report by the UN Office of Internal Oversight Services found that "the use-of-force […] appears to have been routinely avoided as an option by peacekeeping operations" to protect civilians (UNGA 2014: 1). Among the reasons cited for persistent inaction on the ground were "a lack of willingness on the part of troop-contributing countries to put troops in danger" and "no unanimity among troop-contributing countries on the definition of what constitutes 'imminent threat of physical violence'" (ibid.: 13–14). Most recently, the continued inability of the UN mission in South Sudan to provide sufficient protection to civilians after civil war broke out in 2013 has been a main motivating factor for US calls to reform UN peacekeeping (Power 2015).

Third, perennial dilemmas arise from the UN being a state-centric organization that charges its peacekeeping missions to protect civilians regardless of who the perpetrator is. Considerable progress has been made in freeing the UN from its state-centric shackles, and most multidimensional missions since the United Nations mission in Sierra Leone (UNAMSIL) have been equipped with a PoC mandate. However, a parallel tendency has been to mandate missions to "extend state authority," without sufficient resources allocated to support the quality, content, and direction of such an authority. The Sustainable Development Goals (SDGs, September 2015) include Goal 16 on the promotion of just, peaceful, and inclusive societies; and all recent reviews in the area of peace and security—the report of the High-level Panel on Peace Operations ("HIPPO Report," UN 2015a), the 2015 review of the UN peacebuilding architecture (UN 2015f), and the global study of the implementation of UN Security Council Resolution 1325 on women, peace, and security (UN 2015c)—have taken a bottom–up approach, emphasizing the need to put *people* at the center of sustaining peace. To take these pronouncements of the international community seriously and put them into practice will require reflection on how the UN is to help build and extend state authority in ways that can respond to people's needs and strengthen state–society relations (de Coning et al. 2015; Karlsrud 2016).

And fourth, the recurring scandals involving peacekeepers who exploit and abuse those whom they are entrusted to protect, including women and children, remain a serious dilemma that leaves deep scars (Deschamps et al. 2015; UN 2016c). I return to these central issues in Chapter 6.

FROM PEACEKEEPING TO PEACE ENFORCEMENT

In 2013, the UN peacekeeping mission in the Democratic Republic of Congo (MONUSCO; DRC) was given a peace enforcement mandate by the UNSC, pitting it against identified rebel groups that it was tasked to "neutralize" (UN 2013: 7).[3] This was in clear violation of the principles guiding UN peacekeeping operations, which are to be impartial, conducted with the consent of the main parties, and employing force only in self-defense or in defense of the mission mandate (Karlsrud 2015). Similarly, the missions in Mali and the CAR have mandates that make them the main force to "stabilize" and "extend state authority," effectively fighting against rebel and extremist groups in Mali and sectarian groups in CAR. The increase in attacks on UN peacekeepers in Darfur, DRC, and Mali is further evidence that more and more UN peacekeeping operations are no longer seen as impartial.

There is a sense among many member states—especially, but not only, Western ones—that the world has become a more dangerous place, and the UN needs to face up to "twenty-first century challenges" and "asymmetrical threats"—euphemisms for the growing prevalence of terrorist groups with regional and global ambitions, often entangled with international organized crime and kleptocratic elites of fragile countries. In recent years, the UNSC has chosen to give increasingly robust mandates to UN peace operations. This is part of a tendency that started with the global war on terror, where the space for maneuver available to the UN has increasingly been limited, hampering its ability to broker peace and prevent conflict. This tendency has been paralleled by the growing belief among Western and African governments in the efficacy of using force to solve conflicts, despite the limited or negative results, as seen in post-intervention Iraq, Afghanistan, and Libya. Arguably, military thinking and terms such as "counter-insurgency" and "counter-terrorism" have replaced more political approaches that seek to understand and deal with the root causes of conflict (Arnault 2015). Parallel ad-hoc coalitions of the willing and national missions are often not linked to a political longer-term strategy (Berdal and Ucko 2014). The UN is increasingly being asked to deploy troops to situations where there is no peace to keep—in contradiction to the recommendations of the Brahimi Panel (UN 2000). Howard (2015) argues that with peacekeepers increasingly deployed where there is no peace to keep, the principal goal of a peace accord and ending the conflict has been replaced with the more limited goal of protecting civilians. As a result, "[i]n current practice, the principles, purposes, and means of peacekeeping and peace enforcement have been conflated" (ibid.: 10).

Wary of the trend toward peace enforcement (see, e.g., Karlsrud 2015), many TCCs have shown great reluctance to use force. Indeed, "some troop-contributing countries [have] imposed written and unwritten 'national caveats' on their contingents, effectively ruling out the use of force" (UNGA 2014: 14). African member states are generally more positive to the use of force when national interests and mission objectives are aligned (Curran and Holtom 2015; Gowan 2015: 18), as affirmed by the Kigali principles adopted in 2015 (International Conference on Protection of Civilians 2015). However, the missions expected to be on the cards for the next years—Libya, Syria, Yemen—are likely to have significantly fewer troops from Africa. All principled discussions aside, it will be difficult for the UN to put together enough troops to man more than one of these missions, and even such a mission will be more of a coalition of the willing under a UN mandate than a UN peacekeeping mission per se. I return to this question in Chapter 4 on UN stabilization operations, violent extremism, and counter-terrorism.

One consequence of the greater willingness to use force—and indeed one of the most significant changes of the past five years—has been the growing ability of African states to use UN peace operations to serve their own self-interests, mirroring their increased participation with troops on the ground (Fig. 1.3).

Previously, it was considered against the principle of impartiality to include TCCs from neighboring countries, as these were expected to be more likely to pursue national objectives and not be impartial in the execution of their duties on the ground (see, e.g., Boulden 2005). With Malawi, Tanzania, and South Africa forming the FIB in MONUSCO in the DRC, with basically only Ethiopian troops staffing the UNISFA mission in the enclave of Abyei in South Sudan on the border to Sudan, and with Chadian troops as part of MINUSCA in the CAR and deployed with troops from neighboring states Guinea and Niger to MINUSMA in Mali, this principle seems to have been shelved for good. While missions deployed by regional organizations would be less constrained as they would not need to be considered impartial, they would have to consider the possible negative effects ensuing from a partial approach, and the possible impact on the overall chances of mission success.

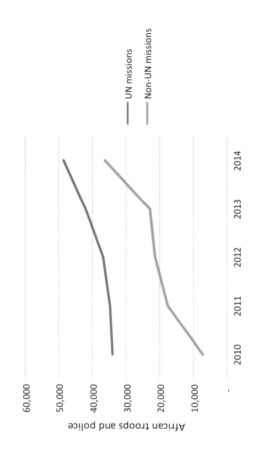

Fig. 1.3 African troops and police in peace operations (figure reprinted with permission of the Center on International Cooperation from "Ten Trends in UN peacekeeping" (Gowan 2015: 19).)

The Future of UN Peace Operations

Faced with the increasing will of the Security Council to mandate the deployment of UN peace operations in the midst of conflict and use force against one or more of the parties to the conflict—taking UN peace operations across the Rubicon of impartiality and stretching the limited capabilities of the organization beyond the breaking point—and given the failure of the missions in Darfur and South Sudan to protect civilians, the SG appointed a high-level independent panel to review UN peace operations in 2014, led by Nobel laureate and former President of Timor-Leste, José Ramos-Horta. The panel was charged to

> ...make a comprehensive assessment of the state of UN peace operations today, and the emerging needs of the future. It will consider a broad range of issues facing peace operations, including the changing nature of conflict, evolving mandates, good offices and peacebuilding challenges, managerial and administrative arrangements, planning, partnerships, human rights and protection of civilians, uniformed capabilities for peacekeeping operations and performance. (UN 2014)

The panel delivered its report to the SG in June 2015 (UN 2015a). Titled *Uniting our Strengths for Peace: Politics, Partnership and People*, the report made a strong case for the primacy of the political dimension in seeking lasting solutions to conflicts, more field- and people-centered peace operations, and stronger partnerships with regional organizations—the AU in particular.

Starting ahead of and running in parallel with the HIPPO review process, the USA spearheaded an initiative aimed at improving the effectiveness of UN peacekeeping operations, modernizing their capabilities and doctrines, and widening the circle of member states contributing troops and capabilities, Western states in particular. The process culminated in a high-level summit on peace operations during the UN General Assembly in 2015, with the then US President Barack Obama leading the meeting, which was co-hosted by Bangladesh, the USA, Japan, Pakistan, Rwanda, Indonesia, the Netherlands, Ethiopia, and the UN. During the summit, 49 member states and three regional organizations—the AU, the EU, and NATO—pledged 8000 standby troops, 26 infantry battalions, 12 hospitals, 12 utility and 5 attack helicopters, as well as a range of other capabilities (Global Peace Operations Review 2015). The summit was generally considered a success, and the US initiative has drawn greater attention to the current and possible role of UN peace operations in dealing with current and emerging challenges around the world.

Future UN peace operations (including special political and peace-building missions) will have to be tailored to the needs and circumstances of the situations to which they will be deployed, and equipped with the necessary capabilities to operate in challenging circumstances. However, the HIPPO Report maintained that there were certain limits to the challenges that UN peace operations could be expected to resolve. It warned against the tendency to deploy missions to "situations of violent conflict and in the absence of a viable peace process or where the peace process has effectively broken down," and referred to such missions as "conflict management" missions (UN 2015a: 43). It advised that wider civilian tasks should be "curtailed until the political conditions become more conducive to success" and that such missions should be set up with sufficient military and medical capabilities, and with contingents willing and able to use force to protect civilians (ibid.: 30). It also argued that such operations should be deployed for limited durations, be premised on the UN being in the lead in the political process, and, that if a viable process would not be forthcoming, the viability of the mission should be reviewed (ibid. 30–31). The report further stated that UN peacekeeping missions "are not suited to engage in military counter-terrorism operations" and that "such operations should be undertaken by the host government or by a capable regional force or an *ad hoc* coalition authorized by the Security Council" (ibid.: 31). The continued attacks on MINUSMA have made clear the dangers of being partial, or considered partial, to the government of the day, when the government enjoys very weak or no legitimacy in large parts of the country. To help countries to sustain peace, difficult questions around representation, participation, and inclusiveness will have to be tackled. I discuss this further in Chapter 6 on people-centered peace operations.

The HIPPO Report also noted that the term "stabilization" has a wide range of interpretations inside and outside the UN, and that the term should be further clarified (ibid.: 44). In *The Future of African Peace Operations,* "stabilization operations" are defined as

> ...operations aimed at helping states in crisis to restore order and stability in the absence of a peace agreement, by using force and other means to help local authorities to contain aggressors (as identified in the relevant UNSC

resolution), enforce law and order and protect civilians, in the context of a larger process that seeks a lasting political solution to the crisis. (de Coning et al. 2016: 10)

This would largely follow the description of "conflict management" missions in the HIPPO Report.

SPECTRUM OF UN PEACE OPERATIONS

The authors of the HIPPO Report deliberately chose to use the term *peace operations*, signaling that they were reviewing not only the challenges and future of UN peacekeeping operations, but also the wider spectrum from light mediation and peacebuilding teams, to observer missions, multidimensional peace operations, security sector reform oriented missions, and UN Country Teams strengthened with peace and development advisers. Fluid and shifting conflicts on the ground may be in need of some or all of these tools at one time or another. However, tailored and sequenced approaches are difficult to develop and sustain, as they criss-cross traditional departmental divides at UN headquarters between the UN DPKO, the Department of Political Affairs (DPA), UN Development Programme (UNDP), and other development agencies, funds, and programs (see, e.g., Stamnes and Osland 2016; Johnstone 2016).

Funding sources vary widely, from assessed contributions negotiated specifically by the General Assembly for UN peacekeeping operations, to special political missions (SPMs) being funded by the regular budget of the UN Secretariat. The result is much less financial resources available for SPMs compared to those accorded to UN peacekeeping operations—although DPKO has been able to do more with less during the last few years, with the HIPPO Report noting a 17% cost reduction in the period from 2010 to 2015 (UN 2015a: 86, see also Selway 2013). The HIPPO Report thus argued for a merger of DPKO and DPA, to enable a "continuum of responses and smoother transitions between different phases of missions" (UN 2015a: 10), echoing HIPPO member Ian Martin, who has argued that *All Peace Operations are Political* (2010).

A full-spectrum approach to peace operations would necessitate a reform of current funding modalities and the bureaucratic setup of the UN Secretariat, and the coordination and funding of the wider UN family. Ideally, the UN should be able to plan and deploy flexible, sequential, and tailored solutions. The HIPPO Report recommended a two-step process, so as to avoid frontloading all mission staff with little regard to when or whether these capacities are needed on the ground when, for example, Forward Operating Bases (FOBs) yet are to be constructed, or possible DDR activities are still being negotiated between the host government and rebel groups. The first six months of a multidimensional peacekeeping operation should be used for properly assessing and mapping the situation, and starting to plan what capacities and capabilities would be needed to deal with short-, mid-, and long-term challenges. Regional and sub-regional organizations may already have deployed a peace operation, and assessed contributions should also be used to cover the bulk of their financial costs. In the first six months, using the open window of a host government in strong need of support, the UN should draw up a compact with the government. This compact should be coined as "National Compacts," implying more active involvement of the various segments and parties of the host population, and not only the host government and national elites. I return to some of these issues in Chap. 6 on people-centered peace operations.

LEADERSHIP AND MAINTAINING RELEVANCE

The SG initiated the HIPPO Report with the aim of updating UN peace operations and making them relevant to the challenges facing the world today. The ambition to remain relevant to today's challenges is laudable, but—as noted in the Report—member states and the Secretariat should also be aware of the limits to what UN peace operations can be used for. In their analysis of the inaction of the UN prior to the genocide in Rwanda, Barnett and Finnemore (2004) argued that the bureaucratic culture of the UN may at times lead to pathologies—with the organization acting in contradiction to the principles on which it was founded and the objectives it was meant to serve.

There is a similar risk facing the UN today, with senior officials calling for UN peace operations to be "relevant" to the threats of violent extremism and terrorism. This would not be a reform of UN peace operations, but rather a fundamental shift of direction. By actively pushing the UN in this direction, these officials are giving the go-ahead to member states keen to move the UN forward on this path, indicating that these are tasks that the UN is willing and able to assume. The result so far has been the very high number of fatalities and casualties in Mali—and the trend is likely to continue if the UN is requested to deploy further missions to

Libya, Syria, and Yemen before there is any peace to keep. Instead, the UN and its staff need to speak truth to power, clearly spelling out what the UN is able to do, in principle and operationally. Certainly, the UN should strengthen its tools for peace and security to enable its peace operations to protect the populations they are serving, as well as themselves—but the organization should not become an instrument for big powers and host states to enforce a peace that cannot be sustained. This will undermine the legitimacy of the tool in the longer term: "by establishing partial mandates within an overarching approach that claims to be impartial creates a fundamental contradiction whose consequences may undermine the Security Council's credibility and moral weight in all situations, not just the conflict at hand" (Boulden 2005: 157, see also Boulden 2001).

António Guterres took up the post as UNSG in January 2017, and a reshuffle of key leadership posts will follow. No matter what the nationality, the new SG and the next USG for DPKO should continue to implement the recommendations of the HIPPO Report and maintain the relevance of UN peace operations by ensuring that they are not used to pursue the interests of key powers on the Security Council.

The HIPPO Report concluded: "[t]here is a clear sense of a widening gap between what is being asked of UN peace operations today and what they are able to deliver. This gap can be—must be—narrowed…" (UN 2015a: vii). However, as I intend to show, expectations as to what UN peace operations should be able to tackle are on the increase—and unfortunately not matched with the requisite resources or capabilities, nor with the outer limits as to what kinds of operations the UN can take on while maintaining its credibility and legitimacy as an impartial arbiter of conflicts.

NOTES

1. MINUSMA had suffered a total of 70 fatalities due to malicious acts, from its inception until October 30, 2016 (UN 2016a).
2. The term "peace operations" is used here to denote the whole spectrum of peace operations, including but not limited to peace enforcement operations, peacekeeping operations, observer missions, and special political missions. However, the focus will be on UN peacekeeping operations.
3. Here I define *peace enforcement* as the application of a range of coercive measures, including the use of force at the strategic level, following the UN peacekeeping Capstone Doctrine (UN 2008).

REFERENCES

African Economic Outlook (2015) *Measuring the pulse of Africa.* Available at: http://www.africaneconomicoutlook.org/fileadmin/uploads/aeo/2015/PDF_Chapters/Overview_AEO2015_EN-web.pdf. Accessed January 7, 2015.

Arnault, Jean (2015) "A background to the report of the high-level panel on peace operations," *Global Peace Operations Review.* Available at: http://peaceoperationsreview.org/thematic-essays/a-background-to-the-report-of-the-high-level-panel-on-peace-operations/. Accessed January 8, 2016.

Barnett, Michael N. and Martha Finnemore (2004) *Rules for the World: International Organizations in Global Politics.* Ithaca, NY: Cornell University Press.

Berdal, Mats and David H. Ucko (2014) "The United Nations and the use of force: between promise and peril," Journal of Strategic Studies, 37(5): pp. 665–673. doi: https://doi.org/10.1080/01402390.2014.937803.

Boulden, Jane (2001) *Peace Enforcement: The United Nations Experience in Congo, Somalia, and Bosnia.* Westport, CT: Praeger.

Boulden, Jane (2005) 'Mandates Matter: An Exploration of Impartiality in United Nations Operations', *Global Governance* 11 (2): pp. 147–160.

Boutros-Ghali, Boutros (1992) *An agenda for peace: preventive diplomacy, peace-making, and peace-keeping: report of the Secretary-General pursuant to the statement adopted by the summit meeting of the Security Council on 31 January 1992.* New York: United Nations.

de Coning, Cedric, John Karlsrud, and Paul Troost (2015) "Towards More People-Centric Peace Operations: From 'Extension of State Authority' to 'Strengthening Inclusive State-Society Relations,'" *Stability: International Journal of Security & Development,* 4 (1): pp. 1–13.

de Coning, Cedric, Linnea Gelot, and John Karlsrud (eds.) (2016) *The future of African peace operations: From the Janjaweed to Boko Haram.* London: Zed Books.

Curran, David and Paul Holtom (2015) "Resonating, Rejecting, Reinterpreting: Mapping the Stabilization Discourse in the United Nations Security Council, 2000–14," *Stability: International Journal of Security & Development,* 4(1): pp. 1–18. doi: 10.5334/sta.gm.

Deschamps, Marie, Hassan B. Jallow, and Yasmin Sooka (2015) *Taking Action on Sexual Exploitation and Abuse by Peacekeepers: Report of an Independent Review on Sexual Exploitation and Abuse by International Peacekeeping Forces in the Central African Republic.* New York: United Nations. Available at: http://www.un.org/News/dh/infocus/centafricrepub/Independent-Review-Report.pdf. Accessed August 17, 2016.

Duffield, Mark (2012) "Challenging environments: Danger, resilience and the aid industry," *Security Dialogue* 43 (5): pp. 475–492.

Elgin, Ben and Vernon Silver (2012) "Syria crackdown gets Italy firm's aid with U.S.-Europe spy gear," *Bloomberg News.* http://www.bloomberg.com/news/2011-11-03/syria-crackdown-gets-italy-firm-s-aid-with-u-s-europe-spy-gear.html. Accessed February 25, 2016.

Fortna, Page (2008) Does Peacekeeping Work? Shaping Belligerents' Choices after Civil War. Princeton, NJ: Princeton University Press.

Global Peace Operations Review (2015) "Leaders' Summit on Peacekeeping," *Global Peace Operations Review.* Available at: http://peaceoperationsreview.org/wp-content/uploads/2015/10/un_2015_peakeeping_summit_pledges.jpg. Accessed January 11, 2016.

Gowan, Richard (2015) "Ten Trends in UN Peacekeeping," in Jim Della-Giacoma (ed.), *Global Peace Operations Review: Annual Compilation 2015.* New York: Center on International Cooperation, New York University, pp. 17–26.

Henke, Marina E. (2017) "UN fatalities 1948–2015: A new dataset," *Conflict Management and Peace Science*: pp. 1–17.

Howard, Lise M. (2008) *UN Peacekeeping in Civil Wars.* Cambridge: Cambridge University Press.

Howard, Lise M. (2015) "Peacekeeping, Peace Enforcement, and UN Reform," *Georgetown Journal of International Affairs* 16 (2): pp. 6–13.

IEP (2015) *Global Terrorism Index 2015.* Sydney: Institute of Economics and Peace.

International Conference on Protection of Civilians (2015) *The Kigali Principles on the Protection of Civilians.* Kigali: International Conference on Protection of Civilians.

Johnstone, Ian (2016) "Between Bureaucracy and Adhocracy: Crafting a Spectrum of Peace Operations," *Global Peace Operations Review,* March 31, 2016. Available at: http://peaceoperationsreview.org/thematic-essays/from-bureaucracy-to-adhocracy-crafting-a-spectrum-of-un-peace-operations/. Accessed April 27, 2016.

Karlsrud, John (2014) "Peacekeeping 4.0: Harnessing the Potential of Big Data, Social Media and Cyber Technology," in J.F. Kremer and B. Müller (eds.) *Cyber Space and International Relations. Theory, Prospects and Challenges.* Berlin: Springer, pp. 141–160.

Karlsrud, John (2015) "The UN at War: Examining the Consequences of Peace Enforcement Mandates for the UN Peacekeeping Operations in the CAR, the DRC and Mali," *Third World Quarterly* 36 (1): pp. 40–54.

Karlsrud, John (2016) "How can the UN move towards more people-centered peace operations?" in Jim Della-Giacoma (ed.), *Global Peace Operations Review: Annual Compilation 2015.* New York: Center on International Cooperation, New York University, pp. 108–11.

van der Lijn, Jaïr and Timo Smit (2015) *Peacekeepers under Threat? Fatality Trends in UN Peace Operations.* Stockholm: Stockholm International Peace Research Institute.

Martin, Ian (2010) "All Peace Operations Are Political: a case for Designer Missions and the Next UN Reform," in Richard Gowan (ed.), *Review of Political Missions 2010*. New York: Center on International Cooperation, New York University. Available at: http://peaceoperationsreview.org/wp-content/uploads/2015/04/political_missions_20101.pdf. Accessed August 20, 2016.

NATO (2011) "NATO's military concept for defence against terrorism," NATO, January 2, 2011. Available at: http://www.nato.int/cps/en/natohq/topics_69482.htm. Accessed January 27, 2016.

Power, Samantha (2015) "Remarks on Peacekeeping in Brussels," *United States Mission to the United Nations,* March 9, 2015. Available at: http://usun.state.gov/remarks/6399. Accessed January 8, 2016.

Ruggie, John G. (1993) "Wandering in the void: Charting the UN's new strategic role," *Foreign Affairs,* 72, pp. 26–31.

Selway, Bianca (2013) "Who Pays for Peace?" *IPI Global Observatory,* November 4, 2013. Available at: https://theglobalobservatory.org/2013/11/who-pays-for-peace/. Accessed August 22, 2016.

Stamnes, Eli and Kari M. Osland (2016) *Synthesis Report: Reviewing UN Peace Operations, the UN Peacebuilding Architecture and the Implementation of UNSCR 1325.* Oslo: Norwegian Institute of International Affairs (NUPI).

UCDP (2016) "Uppsala Conflict Data Program." Available at: http://ucdp.uu.se/. Accessed August 22, 2016.

UN (2000) *Report of the Panel on United Nations Peace Operations* [Brahimi Report]. New York: United Nations.

UN (2008) *United Nations Peacekeeping Operations: Principles and Guidelines.* New York: United Nations Department of Peacekeeping Operations and Department of Field Support.

UN (2013) *S/RES/2098,* March 28, 2013. New York: United Nations.

UN (2014) "Secretary-General's statement on appointment of High-Level Independent Panel on Peace Operations," October 31, 2014. Available at: http://www.un.org/sg/statements/index.asp?nid=8151. Accessed February 25, 2016.

UN (2015a) *A/70/95-S/2015/446. Report of the High-level Independent Panel on Peace Operations on Uniting our Strengths for Peace: Politics, Partnership and People* ("HIPPO Report"). New York: United Nations.

UN (2015b) "Conflict-related sexual violence. Report of the Secretary-General," March 23, 2015. Available at: http://www.un.org/en/ga/search/view_doc.asp?symbol=S/2015/203. Accessed January 29, 2016.

UN (2015c) *Global Study: Preventing Conflict, Transforming Justice, Securing the Peace,* October 14, 2015. New York: United Nations. Available at: http://wps.unwomen.org/~/media/files/un%20women/wps/highlights/unw-global-study-1325-2015.pdf. Accessed June 14, 2016.

UN (2015d) *A/70/674. Plan of Action to Prevent Violent Extremism.* New York: United Nations.

UN (2015e) "UN Peacekeeping Operations Fact Sheet," April 30, 2015. Available at: http://www.un.org/en/peacekeeping/archive/2015/bnote0415.pdf. Accessed February 18, February.

UN (2015f) *The Challenge of Sustaining Peace: Report of the Advisory Group of Experts for the 2015 Review of the United Nations Peacebuilding Architecture.* New York: United Nations.

UN (2016a) "(4a) Fatalities by Mission, Year and Incident Type," *United Nations Peacekeeping,* October 30, 2016. Available at: http://www.un.org/en/peacekeeping/fatalities/documents/stats_4a.pdf. Accessed February 7, 2017.

UN (2016b) "(5) Fatalities by Year and Incident Type up to 31 Jan 2016." Available at: http://www.un.org/en/peacekeeping/fatalities/documents/stats_5.pdf. Accessed February 18, 2016.

UN (2016c) "Fresh allegations of sexual abuse made against UN peacekeepers in Central African Republic," January 5, 2016. Available at: http://www.un.org/apps/news/story.asp?NewsID=52941#.VtAZyG1qhM0. Accessed February 26, 2016.

UNGA (2014) *A/68/787. Evaluation of the Implementation and Results of Protection of Civilians Mandates in United Nations Peacekeeping Operations. Report of the Office of Internal Oversight Services.* New York: United Nations General Assembly.

UNHRC (2015) *A/70/53. Report of the Human Rights Council,* September 9, 2015. New York: United Nations.

UNHCR (2016) *Global Trends: Forced Displacement in 2015.* Geneva: United Nations High Commissioner for Human Rights. Available at: http://www.unhcr.org/576408cd7. Accessed June 21, 2016.

United States Dept. of the Army and United States Marine Corps (2007) *The U.S. Army/Marine Corps Counterinsurgency Field Manual: U.S. Army Field Manual no. 3–24: Marine Corps warfighting publication no. 3–33.5.* Chicago, IL: University of Chicago Press.

de Waal, Alex (2014) "When kleptocracy becomes insolvent: brute causes of the civil war in South Sudan," *African Affairs,* 113 (452): 347–369. doi:10.1093/afraf/adu028.

Wagner, Ben (2012) *After the Arab Spring: New Paths for Human Rights and the Internet in European Foreign Policy.* Brussels: European Union.

World Bank (2015) *Migration and Remittances: Recent Developments and Outlook.* Available at: http://siteresources.worldbank.org/INTPROSPECTS/Resources/334934-1288990760745/MigrationandDevelopmentBrief24.pdf. Accessed January 6, 2016.

CHAPTER 2

The Evolving Politics of UN Peace Operations

The year 2015 marked a turning point for UN peacekeeping operations, as the topic became elevated to the realm of high politics. During the UN General Assembly that year, the then US President Barack Obama personally chaired a summit on peace operations, where heads of state and government pledged troops, capabilities, training, and funding to UN peace operations. It was also a year of reviews of peace operations, the peacebuilding architecture, and the implementation of Security Council Resolution 1325 on women, peace, and security. Moreover, in 2015, member states adopted 17 SDGs, one of which concerns peace and security: Goal 16, on promoting peaceful and inclusive societies, including access to justice for all and building effective, accountable, and inclusive institutions (UN 2015a).

This chapter examines the evolving politics with regard to UN peace operations among the permanent members of the Security Council, Western countries, major TCCs, and emerging economies. The P5 members of the Security Council share an interest in maintaining the status quo of the international system—accompanied by an interest in also maintaining UN peacekeeping and peace operations as a central element in the international peace and security toolbox. Although views diverge as to what kinds of conflicts and threats UN peace operations can be tasked to deal with, one of the perhaps most challenging trends is the apparently emerging consensus among Western countries, and possibly the P5, on giving the UN and its peace operations a greater role in countering violent extremism and tackling terrorism. Major traditional peacekeeping TCCs

© The Author(s) 2018
J. Karlsrud, *The UN at War*,
https://doi.org/10.1007/978-3-319-62858-5_3

33

like Bangladesh, India, and Pakistan have long been skeptical to this. Now, with the relative balance of troop contributions tipping, African states are gaining more influence—and they are generally more open toward such a development.

US Support to UN and African Peace Operations

The most significant calls for reform have come from the USA. Currently, the USA is the largest financial contributor to UN peacekeeping, covering 28.6 % of the peacekeeping budget (see Table 2.1), but had only 72 uniformed personnel deployed as of December 31, 2016 (UN 2016a). In recent years, it has urged a strengthening of UN peace operations and has been encouraging more member states to contribute troops and capabilities. Washington has invested political prestige in the matter, with former Vice President Joseph Biden chairing a meeting on peacekeeping during the General Assembly in 2014, followed by regional meetings and culminating with the summit chaired by the then President Obama on UN peace operations during the General Assembly in 2015. In 2017, President Donald Trump ascended to power, and the new US ambassador to the UN, Nikki Haley, quickly signaled a review of existing peacekeeping missions, with missions in, for example, Haiti and Liberia being eyed as ripe for closure, and an ambition to bring down the contribution to the peacekeeping budget from 28.6 % to 25 % (Landry 2017). The USA has made it clear that it expects its partner countries around the world to increase their contributions to UN peace operations. The success of the Obama summit, resulting in pledges from 49 countries, testified to the significant political pressure exerted by Washington in the run-up to the summit, but also to expectations from countries that their contributions would be noted and could serve to strengthen their relationship with the USA in security and other matters.

Table 2.1 Top ten financial contributors to UN peacekeeping (Data from Global Peace Operations Review (2016) "Those who pay, do not play…")

1. USA	28.6 %
2. China	10.3 %
3. Japan	9.7 %
4. Germany	6.4 %
5. France	6.3 %
6. UK	5.8 %
7. Russian Federation	4 %
8. Italy	3.7 %
9. Canada	2.9 %
10. Australia	2.3 %

"'To be honest, it's much more difficult to turn the U.S. down when asking for something than turning the U.N. down,' said one Western European country's military adviser" (quoted in Anna and Hadjicostis 2015).

Why did the USA under President Obama refocus its attention to UN peace operations? Here, we need to take several factors into account. Part of the picture was the UN's failure to stop the violence in South Sudan from 2013 and onward (Power 2015). The USA was involved in the troika (with Norway and the UK) that brokered the deal with Sudan, giving birth to the new country, and had invested political prestige in the matter. Although sheltering more than 100,000 of internally displaced within their camps, UNMISS could provide only passive protection to civilians, and some of the troops were not keen to leave their camps to protect civilians in danger (interview, former UN official). In the words of Samantha Power, the former US Permanent Representative to the UN, "[t]housands of civilians likely lost their lives as a result. This is unacceptable" (Power 2014). The UN has a long track record of poor performance in other missions as well—particularly in the DRC, where a 2014 UN Office of Internal Oversight (OIOS) report found that, in 507 attacks between 2010 and 2013, peacekeepers rarely used force to protect civilians under attack (UNGA 2014). Deeply disappointed with the UN's poor performance in these countries, the USA wanted the UN to be better equipped and member states to stand by promises made when they commit troops and capabilities to UN missions.

Besides the altruistic will to help the UN do better, the new US attention to UN peace operations is also grounded in more strategic considerations. The same day as Obama chaired the UN peace operations summit at the UN, the White House released a presidential memorandum on "United States Support to United Nations Peace Operations," the first of its kind since 1994 (White House 1994, 2015). The memorandum sketched out a broad support agenda for UN peace operations as a necessary part of US policymaking. Detailing the increasing global risks and threats and the growing number of fragile countries that might serve as safe havens for terrorists and violent extremists, and the potential for large flows of internally displaced and refugees, it argued for strengthening "international response mechanisms that enable the burden to be shared globally" (2015: 1). In early February 2016, James Clapper, the then US Director of National Intelligence, asserted:

> unpredictable instability has become the "new normal," and this trend will continue for the foreseeable future. Violent extremists are operationally active in about 40 countries. Seven countries are experiencing a collapse of

central government authority, 14 others face regime-threatening, or violent, instability or both. Another 59 countries face a significant risk of instability through 2016. (Clapper 2016)

Washington sees UN peace operations as part of a range of tools for dealing with threats beyond its borders in cases where there is not enough national interest to put US troops on the ground but where there is a need to intervene to prevent instability and chaos: "The White House increasingly regards UN peacekeeping as a US national security issue, in large part because Islamist insurgencies from Mali to the Central African Republic, and entrenched conflicts in Nigeria and Somalia, threaten even wider instability" (McGreal 2015a). Under the heading "Guarding the perimeter," Bruce Jones, a Director at the Brookings Institution and initial HIPPO member (he withdrew at an early stage), argued that "U.N. peacekeeping is the only mechanism that allows the United States to combine forces from every region in the world to tackle crises wherever they occur" (Jones 2015).

Several frequent commentators on UN peace operations have held that, with the withdrawal of Western troops from Afghanistan, their experience can be put to use in UN peace operations, helping the organization to update its tools, capabilities, and doctrines. For instance, Paul D. Williams asserts that "the Obama administration was likely correct in assuming that strengthening the UN peacekeeping system will hinge on persuading former members of the International Security Assistance Force (ISAF) in Afghanistan to contribute to UN peace operations in a major way" (2015). As noted above, however, Western troop contributors come with their own baggage, and will seek to influence the conduct of UN peace operations according to their experience with stabilization missions in Afghanistan and Iraq.

Asked whether the renewed focus on UN peace operations is a way of offloading some of the tasks in the global war on terror, US officials have been keen to emphasize that they see the UN as dealing with the lighter part of the spectrum. However, they do not exclude the possibility of delegating more tasks in this area to the UN: "'I wouldn't use the word "outsourcing,"' the official said when asked whether the US was taking that approach to part of the war on terror. 'I'd use the word "burden-sharing"'" (anonymous US official cited in Anna and Hadjicostis 2015). Regional actors like the AU, sub-regional actors like the ECOWAS, and ad hoc coalitions like the Multinational Joint Task Force (MNJTF) formed by Benin, Cameroon, Chad, Niger, and Nigeria to counter Boko Haram are other important parts in the global network of security actors for dealing with terrorist and violent extremist threats.

The USA is engaged in a range of programs to strengthen the capacity of these actors, training and equipping troops on the ground through, for instance, its African Contingency Operations Training and Assistance (ACOTA) and Global Peace Operations Initiative (GPOI) programs (U.S. Department of State 2013, 2016a), the African Peacekeeping Rapid Response Partnership (The White House 2014), and the Global Coalition to Counter ISIL (U.S. Department of State 2016b; DefenceWeb 2015), but also through the provision of special operations forces on the ground. In 2015, the USA had some 1000 special forces on the ground in various theaters in Africa, "executing Obama's relatively low-risk strategy of countering Islamic extremists by finding local partners willing to fight rather than deploying combat troops by the thousands" (Strobel 2015).

Although some US officials are on record as advocating a more robust UN that can deal with terrorist threats, other high-level officials have taken a more cautious approach: "DRC and Mali were outliers. Mali is not a trend" (interview with Victoria K. Holt, former Deputy Assistant Secretary, U.S. Department of State). Future policies of the USA are difficult to predict. On the one hand, the USA has expressed a strong willingness to cut funding to peacekeeping, but it may also be willing to continue to fund missions as long as they align with a narrower set of self-interests.

RUSSIA: RETAINING ITS PLACE AT THE TABLE

Russia needs to maintain its role as a veto power in the UN Security Council and will make sure to balance reluctance toward change with constructive engagement to uphold the relevance of the Council as the main arena for deciding matters of peace and security. As for direct engagement, Russia had 105 police, military experts, and troops deployed in UN peacekeeping missions as of December 31, 2016 (UN 2016a). Although Russia contributes only 4 % of the UN peacekeeping budget (see Table 2.1), Russian companies provide a significant part of contracted services and capabilities. "In 2011, Russian companies held contracts from the UN worth $382 million, which composed 14 % of UN peacekeeping services. Almost all of this is comprised of aviation transportation services provided by Russian aviation and cargo companies" (Nikitin 2013: 163).

Russia is a "status-quo power … and insists on preserving the Yalta-Potsdam international system in its original incarnation" (Bratersky and Lukin 2017: 3). Russia notes with concern that the other Western P5 members are intent on using UN peacekeeping as a foreign policy tool, "increasingly moving beyond its traditional role as a tool for impartial resolution of conflicts" (ibid.: 2). The Kremlin has been skeptical to the push for new technologies and tools for UN peace operations, including unmanned aerial vehicles and a dedicated intelligence capability (to which I return in the next chapter), concerned about infringements on host-country sovereignty. However, Russia has not vetoed the deployment of these tools, which now have been included in the missions in the DRC and Mali. Russia has also been deeply concerned about the expansion of mandates toward a more robust role for UN peacekeeping operations. In the mandate authorizing the FIB in MONUSCO, Russia successfully argued for the inclusion of wording that the FIB was established "on an exceptional basis and without creating a precedent or any prejudice to the agreed principles of peacekeeping" (UN 2013a: 6). When the mandate for MINUSMA was negotiated only days later, and also gave a robust mandate to this mission, the Russian representative stated that "what was once the exception now threatens to become unacknowledged standard practice" (Security Council Report 2014). When the mandate for MINUSMA was renegotiated in June 2016, the mandate was made even more robust, asking the mission to "take robust and active steps to counter asymmetric attacks [and] engaging in direct operations pursuant only to serious and credible threats" (UN 2016b: 9), Russia broke its silence on the agreed text to include the word "only" in the above sentence, "in an effort to further delimit when the mission could use force" (What's in Blue 2016).

On the other hand, it is important for Russia to maintain the international system and the role of the Security Council (see, e.g., Reykers and Smeets 2015). Russia is thus also keen to show that UN peacekeeping is a tool that works and will remain relevant in the future as well:

> The United Nations should remain the center of international relations and coordination in world politics in the twenty-first century, as it has proven to have no alternative and also possesses unique legitimacy. Russia supports the efforts aimed at strengthening the UN's central and coordinating role. (Ministry of Foreign Affairs of the Russian Federation 2013)

The Kremlin seems set to be a cautious supporter of reform efforts, carefully weighing these against other interests. Given its stance toward UN peacekeeping, Russia will consider its options and deal with each mission separately. Missions deemed particularly important by the Permanent Three (France, the UK, and the USA) may be subject to bargaining and horse-trading tactics—as seen with the negotiations over the mandate for UNMISS in South Sudan in the wake of the disputes over the fallout in Libya,[1] and the continuing great power struggle over Syria. Other missions, such as MINUSMA in Mali, are seen as less important, and mandate renewals are negotiated with perhaps surprising ease.

CHINA: FROM PASSIVE RESISTANCE TO ACTIVE SUPPORTER?

In the course of the past few decades, China has gone from being neutral or outright hostile toward UN peacekeeping to becoming a firm supporter (Yin 2017; Hirono and Lanteigne 2012; Lanteigne 2016), and the largest contributor of troops among the Security Council P5 (Global Peace Operations Review 2016). China has also significantly increased its financial contributions in recent years, climbing from being the sixth largest contributor to the second largest contributor from 2015 to 2016 (see Table 2.1).

Former president Hu Jintao introduced the concept of "peaceful rise," later modified to "peaceful development" when he took office in 2002–2003, starting an era of greater engagement in multilateral organizations and balancing the country's growing economic and military powers with soft-power rhetoric (Lanteigne 2014). China's increasing engagement in UN peacekeeping is part of this trend (Yin 2017). Although China provided engineering troops to the UN Transitional Authority in Cambodia (UNTAC) 1992–1993, the real shift came later, when China gradually expanded its participation, sending police officers to Haiti, and engineers to Sudan and the DRC. By 2009, it had surpassed France as the largest contributor among the P5 (ibid.: 117). In the following years, China moved from providing support and logistics capabilities to providing a force protection company of 170 troops to MINUSMA in Mali at the end of 2013 (van der Putten 2015). By December 31, 2016, China contributed 2448 troops and military experts, and 151 police to UN peacekeeping missions (UN 2016a), and was covering 10.3 % of the peacekeeping budget, up from 6.64 % in 2015 and moving from fifth to second place among the ten largest contributors (see Table 2.1 and UN 2016c).

The force protection company in Mali not only is deployed to protect the 70 medical staff and 155 engineers that China has also provided, but is attached to the mission's regional headquarters in Gao. MINUSMA has been mandated to "to stabilize the key population centres, especially in the north of Mali and, in this context, to deter threats and take active steps to prevent the return of armed elements to those areas," if necessary by force (UN 2013b: 7). However, the impression so far is that the Chinese troops may be reluctant to end up in situations where the use of force is necessary. Assessing this particular deployment, Frans P. van der Putten has stated, "the Chinese protection unit in Mali initially appears to have been taking a cautious—rather than a proactive—approach" and the performance of the troops "did not meet Dutch expectations [also the Dutch have troops deployed in Gao], as certain guard duties were performed by Chinese troops during only parts of the day rather than around the clock" (2015: 11). Demonstrations against UN Headquarters in Gao turned violent in 2015, and formed police units opened fire and used excessive force, according to a UN investigation, but Chinese troops were not reported to be directly involved (UN 2015b). The cautious approach may be evidence of concerns about a possible backlash in local sentiment toward China if it is seen as willing to use force against local populations. However, reluctance to use force in accordance with the mandate also risks tarnishing China's reputation as a troop contributor.

When the mandate for MINUSMA was renewed in June 2016, explicitly instructing the mission to "take robust and active steps to counter asymmetric attacks" (UN 2016b: 9), China was among the member states that seemed concerned about whether the new mandate "may expand the mission's posture in a way that could ultimately be used to engage preemptively in counter-terrorism activities" (What's in Blue 2016). The reluctance toward a more robust posture of the mission reflects the longer lines in China's policy on UN peace operations, as well as the fact that it may well be Chinese troops on the ground that will be asked to implement the new mandate.

Nevertheless, China is increasingly supportive toward UN peacekeeping, something which is also reflected in its stance on doctrines for UN peacekeeping. Long a staunch supporter of sovereignty and non-interventionism, China has gradually started to differentiate between "bad" and "good" interventions—with UN peacekeeping in the latter category, and with emphasis on the need to back the host government when supporting more robust peacekeeping. An example of this was the support given to the inclusion of an FIB in the MONUSCO mission in the DRC in 2013. Grounded in humanitarian concerns emanating from the repeated attacks by M23 on civilians, China supported the inclusion of the FIB (Lanteigne 2014: 129). The provision of the force protection company to MINUSMA can be seen as another step in this direction. But China's growing willingness to mandate, and possibly use, force in UN peace operations also increases the risk of its being perceived as a more interventionist state. The French *Opération Serval* in Mali (later replaced by *Opération Barkhane*), a counter-terrorism mission operating alongside MINUSMA, was initially viewed with skepticism (Avezov and Smit 2014), but now seems to be considered to be a "welcome development," as it is countering the increasing threats of violent extremists and terrorists (van der Putten 2015: 18). In this instance, the wish for stability apparently trumps concerns over the former colonial power of France "playing the role of a regional 'policeman'" (ibid.). China has also increasingly welcomed peacekeeping troops in Sudan and South Sudan, countries that export most of their oil to China. In 2013, 86 % of the combined oil production of Sudan and South Sudan went to China, and Chinese national oil companies were among the largest oil producers in these countries (EIA 2014).

During 2016, China experienced the loss of several peacekeepers due to hostile acts. On May 31, one peacekeeper was killed and five were wounded in a mortar attack on the UN peacekeeping base in Gao. Responsibility for the terrorist attack was claimed by the "al-Murabitoun battalion" of the AQIM (AFP 2016). The peacekeeper was the 11th to be killed in the history of UN peacekeeping missions (China Military Online 2016). Only a few weeks later, another two Chinese peacekeepers were killed and another five wounded in South Sudan in an attack on a protection site (Zhuang 2016). The fatalities reflect China's increasing engagement in UN peacekeeping, as well as the greater risks for supplying troops that are expected to take a more active role in the protection of civilians on the ground. The fact that one of the Chinese peacekeepers died after bleeding for 16 hours, due to the lack of medical evacuation (MEDEVAC) in the middle of Juba, the capital of South Sudan, is likely to increase Chinese engagement for improving the force protection and casualty evacuation (CASEVAC)/MEDEVAC routines for UN peacekeepers (Wells 2016).

At the peacekeeping summit arranged by the USA during the UN General Assembly in 2015, Chinese President Xi Jinping surprised everyone by making a pledge of a standby force of 8000 troops (Global Peace Operations Review 2015). This has further raised the expectations that China will need to meet. Crises erupt at frequent intervals, and it is a question of when—not if—the Chinese standby force will be called upon. If the standby force is deployed, China will rise from being the 12th largest troop contributor in December 2016 (Global Peace Operations Review 2016) to become the largest by far. At the same summit in 2015, China announced it was contributing USD 100 million to the AU to strengthen AU peace support operations. China has already constructed the new AU headquarters in Addis Ababa and prefers regional organizations such as the AU to deal with the more robust end of the conflict spectrum. Its stepped-up engagement with both UN and AU peace operations makes China an increasingly important actor, but will also bring higher expectations as to action on the ground, as well as the depth and nuance and not least internal coherence of its policy stances on UN peace operations.

FRANCE: FRIEND OR FOE?

France has staffed the post of Head of UN Department of Peacekeeping Operations for almost two decades; it is a former colonial power of many of the countries hosting peacekeeping operations, a penholder on some of the largest peacekeeping operations (CAR, Côte d'Ivoire, DRC, Lebanon), and has sponsored or co-sponsored "an average of almost two-thirds of the draft resolutions dealing with peacekeeping subsequently adopted by the Security Council" (Tardy 2016: 10). But although France is one of the most strategic and closest supporters of UN peacekeeping, and the fifth largest contributor to the UN peacekeeping budget (6.3 %, see Table 2.1), the French Army has not been keen on providing troops to UN missions. As of December 31, 2016, France had contributed 872 uniformed personnel to UN peacekeeping operations (Global Peace Operations 2016). As of July 31, 786 of these were deployed to the United Nations Interim Force in Lebanon (UNIFIL) mission in Lebanon (UN 2016a). The reasons for this apparent dissonance in the position taken by France come from the diverse sources of its engagement with UN peace operations. One the one hand, France maintains a very active profile in the UN Security Council and on the ground, to legitimize its continued role as a veto power (see, e.g., Tardy and Zaum 2016; Vilmer and Schmitt 2015), and continues to emphasize the central role of the Security Council in dealing with matters of international peace and security. On the other hand, even though "France has been significantly involved in peace operations since the end of the Cold War, the military has never felt comfortable with the peacekeeping concept, seen as a dilution of what they should be trained for" (Tardy 2014: 789), and France is generally "sceptical about the added-value of the UN for its own operations" (2016: 24).

Part of the explanation is that the French military places the use of force at the center of its strategy (ibid.). By contrast, in UN peace operations the use of force is limited to the protection of civilians, not to be employed against strategic-level actors:

> Robust peacekeeping involves the use of force at the tactical level with the authorization of the Security Council and consent of the host nation and/ or the main parties to the conflict. By contrast, peace enforcement does not require the consent of the main parties and may involve the use of military force at the strategic or international level, which is normally prohibited for Member States under Article 2(4) of the Charter, unless authorized by the Security Council. (UN 2008: 34–35)

On the other hand, French doctrine explicitly stresses that when French forces are deployed, they should be able to resort to coercive action—which makes the option of deploying troops to UN peace operations less attractive than deploying troops in national operations, or through the EU and NATO (Tardy 2014, 2016). The use of force in French military strategy is likely to remain central in its stance on UN peace operations.

For France, the UN is a useful actor to follow up on its engagements, after the transition from an enforcement or coercive phase to a stabilization phase, or in parallel deployments (as with *Barkhane*/MINUSMA in Mali). Other examples include *Licorne*/ONUCI in Côte d'Ivoire; EUFOR/MINURCAT in Chad and the Central African Republic (2008–2010); *Serval*/MINUSMA in Mali; and EUFOR and *Sangaris*/ MINUSCA in the Central African Republic. With Mali, the French deployment of *Serval* was made conditional on a UN follow-up mission, much to the irritation of ECOWAS and the AU (AU 2013; Lotze 2015, see also Chapter 5). UN operations are "part of the French exit strategy from these countries, as these missions are supposed to provide for a level of stability that can then allow for the withdrawal of the French parallel forces" (Tardy: 14–15; see also Tardy and Zaum 2016). By maintaining a narrow focus on coercive action, France risks "being simply absent from long-term crisis management operations, as well as from the development of a comprehensive approach" (Novosseloff and Tardy 2017: 15).

The focus on coercive action is also reflected in France's efforts to push UN peacekeeping to engage in more robust operations, using new technologies and protecting civilians in a proactive manner (ibid.: 17). France is the penholder on the mandates for both MONUSCO and MINUSMA, and has been one of the strongest supporters for more robust and even peace enforcement mandates for these missions. Given the environment into which MINUSMA is deployed, these are doctrinal developments that may seem necessary to enable the mission to deal with the threats facing it. France wants to drive innovation and make the UN a partner in the fight against violent extremism, and does not want to close off the option of using UN peace operations in counter-terrorism efforts. This will make the UN a relevant partner for dealing with the challenges that France is facing in its former colonies, challenges that impact directly on French national interests—here we may recall the terrorist attacks in Paris during the latter part of 2015.

Dörrie (2015) argues that France, driven by threats of terrorists and violent extremists, more than any other power, is "investing the most military and political resources to combat terrorist groups in West Africa and the wider Sahel." Former president Nicolas Sarkozy announced in 2009 that France did not want to be "Africa's gendarme" (cited in Dörrie 2015), but with the collapse of Mali in 2012, France feared an implosion of the entire region and made an about-turn, deploying 4000 troops to the country. As mentioned, the parallel deployment of the UN (and the EU) was an integral part of the French exit strategy for Mali. However, the UN has not been prepared for the kind of challenges that Mali has brought. From the point of view of France, and also many other member states, the UN must adapt and update its tools and capabilities rapidly to be able to deal with the threats in the north of Mali. The deployment of Western troops has helped the UN to make some small steps toward achieving such a goal, in terms of adding surveillance drones and an intelligence fusion and analysis unit—but, as the fatality statistics show, these additions have not made the mission sufficiently able to protect itself or counter the threats it is facing. The willingness of France to use UN peace operations to serve its own national interests, with little regard for the short- or longer-term impact on UN peace operations in terms of risks, legitimacy, and buy-in from other countries, is worrisome.

France has long been engaged in longer-term efforts to train and equip national armies, and facilitate and support sub-regional military cooperation. The Group of Five Sahel (G-5 Sahel) countries (Burkina Faso, Chad,

Mali, Mauritania, and Niger) was set up in 2014 with French support, to fight terrorist organizations in the Sahel, and should serve as an accompanying force to the French *Opération Barkhane*, although implementation has been slow (AFP 2017). It is becoming increasingly evident that France will not be able to deal on its own with the terrorist and violent extremist threats in the region. This is also recognized by France, which promotes cooperation with actors in the region but also with multilateral institutions like the UN and the EU (Rieker 2017).

THE UK

Like France, the UK needs to remain active on the UN Security Council to legitimize its role as a veto power (see, e.g., Tardy and Zaum 2016). It too is a former colonial power and penholder on many of the countries hosting UN peace operations, and has been active in promoting new policies to enhance the effectiveness and efficiency of peacekeeping. For instance, France and the UK launched a reform initiative in the form of a non-paper presented to the Security Council in January 2009 titled "Improving the preparation, planning, monitoring and evaluation of peacekeeping operations" (UN 2009). This eventually led to the "New Horizon" process, a reform process launched by the DPKO and DFS to improve the effectiveness and efficiency of UN peacekeeping and to achieve buy-in for reform proposals through improved consultation mechanisms with TCCs and PCCs (UN 2016d).

The UK is the sixth largest contributor to the UN peacekeeping budget (5.8 %, see Table 2.1), and had 345 uniformed personnel deployed as of December 31, 2016 (UN 2016a, including seconded staff officers, military, and police). Most of these troops have been deployed to the UN peacekeeping mission in Cyprus, but at the summit on peacekeeping during the UN General Assembly in 2015, the UK pledged to double its military contributions by sending personnel to the UN Support Office in Somalia and a larger contingent to UNMISS in South Sudan (UK 2015a). The pledge was followed up with a heightened focus on UN peacekeeping in the UK's strategic defense and security review released in November 2015, which established a UN Peacekeeping Unit, hosted by the Foreign and Commonwealth Office, "consolidating existing MOD and FCO expertise to formulate UK policy on UN peacekeeping missions" (UK 2015b: 84). In 2017, the UK planned to deploy about 400 troops, mainly engineers, to South Sudan (Ray 2017). In September 2016, the UK hosted the follow-up summit to the Obama summit in London. During the summit, UK Defence Secretary Michael Fallon announced an expansion of the pledge to UNMISS from 300 to 400 troops, with the inclusion of a field hospital in addition to the engineering companies pledged in 2015 (United Kingdom 2016). This shows that Britain is willing to invest further political capital in its commitment to UN peacekeeping.

Interestingly, the then Prime Minster Cameron cited the need to combat terrorism and migration when announcing the UK's pledge at the Obama summit, offering "help in training and logistics for UN and African Union peacekeepers in attempt to foster 'less terrorism and migration'" (Mason 2015). The reasoning was repeated in 2016, when Defence Secretary Fallon said that the increased contributions to UNMISS were "part of our effort to tackle the instability that leads to mass migration and terrorism" (MacAskill 2016). However, UK officials working on the UN peacekeeping portfolio are concerned about the expansion of the stabilization rhetoric with regard to UN peacekeeping—they see it as carrying too many doctrinal lessons from Afghanistan and Iraq that are not necessarily applicable to UN peacekeeping operations (interviews with UK officials, February 18, 2015; March 17, 2016).

Like France, the UK uses UN peace operations to achieve policy goals, but would prefer to limit the contribution of troops, also to those operations for which it devises mandates. These policy goals are first and foremost to prevent and counter violent extremism and terrorism, and slow down migration from Europe's southern and eastern borders. UN peace operations can be an increasingly important piece of the puzzle in this regard. Together with France, Italy, and the USA, the UK has been pushing for a military operation in Libya to counter the IS and stabilize the country (in theory) (see, e.g., Ryan and Raghavan 2016). It is highly likely that such a mission will eventually be handed over to the UN, bringing similar or greater challenges and threats than those currently facing the UN in Mali.

Curran and Williams argue that "Britain has always taken a pragmatic approach to engaging in crisis management through the UN" (2016a: 5). They identify several challenges to a British return to UN peacekeeping operations. First, there are misaligned strategic priorities—the UN is primarily deployed to sub-Saharan Africa, an area not of "primary strategic concern for the UK" (2016b: 17). This could change if UN peacekeeping operations are deployed to countries like Libya. Second, the perception is that there are significant risks involved in participation in UN peacekeeping operations, because of "shortfalls in contingency planning, health and safety, and logistical support" (ibid.: 19). These risks have been accentuated by the experiences of MINUSMA, the deadliest UN peacekeeping operation on record. Co-deployment with other Western countries, enhancing the capabilities of that particular mission, may help to assuage these concerns, but not fully. Finally, UN peacekeeping operations are simply not "considered a major opportunity to gain promotion" (ibid.: 20). To change this culture, it will be necessary to reflect the renewed engagement at policy levels by recognizing and rewarding UK troops for service in UN peacekeeping operations.

WESTERN POWERS AND UN PEACE OPERATIONS

Together, Western countries contribute about half of the UN peacekeeping budget (see Table 2.1). They want more value for money, in terms of efficiency, but also as regards the types of tasks that UN peace operations can be entrusted to deal with. Following up on the HIPPO Report, these countries are intent on reforming UN peace operations to respond better to current needs, as perceived by them. Many had expected a drop in UN peacekeeping operations and personnel on the ground following the financial crisis of 2008–2009. Instead there came an increase, with new missions being deployed to the Central African Republic, Mali, and South Sudan. Combined with the cost of deploying troops to Afghanistan and Iraq, the austerity measures employed in the wake of the financial crisis, and recent refugee flows from the "arc of instability" surrounding Europe, this has created considerable momentum for making UN peace operations more cost-effective, and more relevant to the needs of Western and African countries.

During the C-34 discussions in March 2016, the Western group of countries, led by the EU, pushed for language on counter-terrorism, declaring that UN peace operations may not be suited to take on counter-terrorism tasks today, but that this option should be retained as a future possibility. However, the entire paragraph on counter-terrorism was eventually removed from the final document, as it proved impossible to achieve consensus on this point. Western member states like Norway are keen to keep this option open. In connection with the Obama summit, the Norwegian Prime Minister stated that Norway wanted "a more aggressive UN" (cited in Bjørgås and Tjørhom 2015).

If considered en bloc, there is a considerable gap between the policy engagement and the deployment of troops from Western countries. This commitment gap also leads to a legitimacy gap when Western states promote reform and change. Furthermore, some commentators on UN peace-keeping, like Richard Gowan at the European Council on Foreign Relations (ECFR), have questioned whether the UN will be able to deal with violent extremists and terrorists, seeing that Western nations have so far struggled greatly: "I think that we may be stumbling into an enormous strategic trap because if we have learned over the last decade that very highly capable Nato forces, US forces, actually can't suppress Islamic extremist groups, why on earth do we think slightly strengthening UN missions is going to give us a tool that allows us to fight terrorists?" (cited in McGreal 2015b).

Major TCCs

Major traditional TCCs have generally been reluctant to any expansion of the mandates of UN peace operations to counter violent extremism and counter-terrorism tasks, as this will increase the risks troops are faced with in countries where there is little national interest. India has been one of the more vocal opponents to forceful peacekeeping, with Asoke Kumar Mukerji, the then Indian Ambassador to the UN, saying that "if peace-keeping is to be seen as peace enforcement, then unfortunately we can't see the UN charter allowing such a radical departure of the use of peace-keeping" (McGreal 2015b). India has held that a move toward peace enforcement would be in conflict with the UN Charter; like the HIPPO Report, it has stressed the primacy of a political approach to conflicts (ibid.). For example, India has not contributed troops to MINUSMA. However, there is increasing acceptance for a more capability-oriented approach and for including new technology to improve the situational awareness of UN missions (see, e.g., Abiola et al. 2017). Several large TCCs that have traditionally been major contributors agree that there is a need to undertake a timely reform to strengthen and update peace operations; however, the aim of the reform should not be to enable the UN to conduct peace enforcement or counter-terrorism.

Today, Asian countries no longer dominate the list of the top ten countries contributing uniformed personnel, and that is changing the dynamics of the group. During the first decade of this century, African countries supplied only about 10 % of the troops in UN peacekeeping operations,

Table 2.2 Top ten contributing countries of military and police contributions to UN peacekeeping as of July 31, 2016 (Data from "Ranking of Military and Police Contributions to UN Operations" (UN 2016e))

1. Ethiopia	8295
2. India	7710
3. Pakistan	7156
4. Bangladesh	6862
5. Rwanda	6152
6. Nepal	5184
7. Senegal	3600
8. Burkina Faso	3040
9. Ghana	2935
10. Egypt	2869

but they now deploy about 50 % of the troops, 60 % of international civilian peacekeepers, and 80 % of national peacekeeping staff (AU 2015). With stronger representation, and the fact that most UN peace operations are deployed to African countries, African proposals for policy shifts carry greater weight. Key features here are a willingness to use troops from neighboring countries that are more likely to have a national interest in the conflict; a turn toward more robust, even peace enforcement mandates; and increased cooperation with the AU and sub-regional organizations, including accessing contributions to fund African peace support operations (see, e.g., de Coning et al. 2016). I return to these points in Chapter 5 (Table 2.2).

Pragmatic Partnerships

In this chapter I have examined some of the key individual and member state groups that influence UN peace operations. The P5 members—the USA, Russia, China, France, and the UK—all have strategic interests involved in the reform of UN peace operations, with discussions coalescing around the need for adaptation on the one hand, and the necessity of recognizing the limits of UN peace operations in responding to new challenges, on the other. The USA will continue to invest in UN peacekeeping as a "burden-sharing" tool for addressing its own national security interests where it is not willing to put troops on the ground. Supporting regional forces like the AU is crucial to this delegation-style approach, in line with the HIPPO argument that building stronger partnerships will be vital in the future, to face peace and security challenges. We have seen that, as regards maintaining the role of the UN Security Council, Russia is also a pragmatic player in international politics, supporting UN involvement and the deployment of peace operations when these are not at odds with great power politics. While Russia remains skeptical to the use of technology, expanded mandates, and the use of force, China is becoming more supportive of robust mandates, in parallel to strengthened engagement with more troops on the ground, and taking its place as the second largest financial contributor to UN peacekeeping. Both the UK and France actively use UN peace operations as a tool to achieve their policy goals, with France viewing the UN as a potential partner in its regional counter-terror efforts in the Sahel particularly. Both countries are, however, reluctant to deploy troops—which entails a legitimacy deficit when these states seek to influence reform.

The growing imbalance between the membership of the UN Security Council and the importance and interests of large economies such as India, Japan, Nigeria, South Africa, Germany, and Brazil to become permanent or semi-permanent members of the UN Security Council has an impact on the politics of UN peace operations. Again and again, policy reform in the area of UN peace operations falls victim for the politics of UN reform in general. This is sometimes reflected in complaints about imposition of Western norms, as the responsibility to protect norm was accused of in the aftermath of the Libya intervention, even if similar norms have been adopted by the very same states: for instance, Article 4(h) of the Constitutive Act of the AU asserts "the right of the Union to intervene in a Member State pursuant to a decision of the Assembly in respect of grave circumstances, namely: war crimes, genocide and crimes against humanity" (AU 2000: 7).

One of the most contentious areas of disagreement between Western countries and major traditional TCCs like India oscillates around whether the UN and its peace operations should play a greater role in countering violent extremism and countering terrorism. Among the P5, as well as a large part of the membership of the General Assembly, there are growing worries about the threat of violent extremism and terrorism. In an environment of economic austerity, the mantra is that the UN should be able to do more with less. To give UN peace operations a larger responsibility in the war on terror and violent extremism may be one of the areas where an emerging consensus is developing among the P5, irrespective of whether this is actually a task that UN peace operations are ready for, or will be. The answer must be greater clarity on the limits of what UN peacekeeping, and UN peace operations at large, are capable of tackling, now and in the future. The division of responsibilities between member states, regional actors, and the UN must be adjusted to the respective capabilities of these actors—but in the case of the UN, it is also essential to heed the role that the organization is playing in not only keeping the peace, but also making, mediating, and facilitating peace, humanitarian action, and development.

Increasingly, the world is facing conflicts that are regional and transnational in scope, requiring complex and sequenced responses, and what Brosig refers to as "cooperative peacekeeping" between lead nations on regional and global levels, regional and interregional institutions like the AU, EU, and NATO, and international organizations like the Brosig (2015). In the words of Ban Ki-moon, we have "entered an era of 'partnership peacekeeping,' where close cooperation among multiple multilateral actors throughout every phase of a crisis is becoming the norm—and an essential component of each organization" (UN 2015c: 17). I will return to this topic in Chapter 5.

NOTES

1. Reykers and Smeets argue that the liberal interpretation by NATO of UNSC Res. 1973 on Libya in 2011, where Russia abstained, has made Russia regain "awareness of its veto power, and particularly the risks of not using it" (2015: 383).

REFERENCES

Abiola, Seun, Cedric de Coning, Eduarda Hamann, and Chander Prakash (2017) "The large contributors and UN peacekeeping doctrine," in Cedric de Coning, Chiyuki Aoi, and John Karlsrud (eds.), *UN Peacekeeping Doctrine in a New Era Adapting to Stabilisation, Protection and New Threats*. Abingdon: Routledge, pp. 152–185.

AFP (2016) "Chinese peacekeeper killed in Mali attack," June 2, 2016. Available at: http://m.news24.com/news24/Africa/News/chinese-peacekeeper-killed-in-mali-attack-20160602. Accessed September 5, 2016.

AFP (2017) "African leaders agree to new joint counter-terrorism force," February 6, 2017. Available at: http://m.france24.com/en/20170206-african-leaders-agree-new-joint-counter-terrorism-force?ns_campaign=reseaux_sociaux&ns_source=twitter&ns_mchannel=social&ns_linkname=editorial&aef_campaign_ref=partage_user&aef_campaign_date=2017-02-06. Accessed February 8, 2017.

Anna, Cara and Menelaos Hadjicostis (2015) "As UN peacekeeping veers toward counterterror, US steps in," Yahoo! News, September 26, 2015. Available at: https://www.yahoo.com/news/un-peacekeeping-veers-toward-counterterror-us-steps-145304737.html?ref=gs. Accessed September 6, 2016.

AU (2000) Constitutive Act of the African Union. Addis Ababa: African Union.

AU (2013a) Communiqué (PSC/PR/COMM. (CCCLXXI), April 25, 2013). Addis Ababa: African Union.

AU (2015a) Report of the Chairperson of the Commission on follow-up steps on the Common African Position on the Review of United Nations Peace Operations, PSC/AHG/3.(DXLVII), 26 September 2015. Addis Ababa: African Union.

Avezov, Xenia and Timo Smit (2014) "The consensus on Mali and international conflict management in a multipolar world," SIPRI Policy Brief, September 2014. Available at: http://books.sipri.org/files/misc/SIPRIPB1403.pdf. Accessed April 21, 2016.

Bjørgås, Tove and Vegard Tjørhom (2015) "Vil ha eit meir aggressivt FN i krigsfelten," NRK, September 28, 2015. Available at: http://www.nrk.no/urix/vil-ha-eit-meir-aggressivt-fn-i-krigsfelten-1.12574869. Accessed January 11, 2016.

Bratersky, Maxim and Alexander Lukin (2017) "The Russian perspective on UN peacekeeping: today and tomorrow," in Cedric de Coning, Chiyuki Aoi and John Karlsrud (eds.), UN Peacekeeping Doctrine in a New Era Adapting to Stabilisation, Protection and New Threats. Abingdon: Routledge, pp. 132–151.

Brosig, Malte (2015) Cooperative Peacekeeping in Africa: Exploring regime complexity, Abingdon: Routledge.

China Military Online (2016) "Hundreds honor Chinese soldier killed in Mali," China Military Online, June 11, 2016. Available at: http://english.chinamil.com.cn/news-channels/china-military-news/2016-06/11/content_7095122.htm. Accessed September 5, 2016.

Clapper, James (2016) "Remarks as delivered by The Honorable James R. Clapper, Director of National Intelligence. Senate Armed Services Committee Hearing: IC's Worldwide Threat Assessment Opening Statement," February 9, 2016. Available at: https://fas.org/irp/congress/2016_hr/020916-sasc-ad.pdf. Accessed April 14, 2016.

de Coning, Cedric, Linnea Gelot, and John Karlsrud (eds.) (2016) The future of African peace operations: From the Janjaweed to Boko Haram. London: Zed Books.

Curran, David and Paul D. Williams (2016a) "The UK and UN Peace Operations: A Case for Greater Engagement." London: Oxford Research Group. Available at: http://www.oxfordresearchgroup.org.uk/publications/briefing_papers_and_reports/uk_and_un_peace_operations_case_greater_engagement. Accessed 6 September 2016a.

Curran, David and Paul D. Williams (2016b) "The United Kingdom and United Nations peace operations," International Peacekeeping 23 (5): pp. 1–22. DOI: 10.1080/13533312.2016.1235098.

defenceWeb (2015) "Eastern Africa Standby Force, U.S. forge new partnership," *defenceWeb*, November 3, 2015. Available at: http://www.defenceweb.co.za/index.php?option=com_content&view=article&id=41262:eastern-africa-standby-force-us-forge-new-partnership&catid=56:Diplomacy%20&%20Peace&Itemid=111. Accessed January 11, 2016.

Dörrie, Peter (2015) "France's Overstretched Military Not Enough to Stabilize the Sahel," *World Politics Review*, December 15, 2015. Available at: http://www.worldpoliticsreview.com/articles/17460/france-s-overstretched-military-not-enough-to-stabilize-the-sahel. Accessed January 11, 2016.

EIA (2014) "Country Analysis Brief: Sudan and South Sudan," September 3, 2014. Washington DC: U.S. Energy Information Administration. Available at: https://www.eia.gov/beta/international/analysis_includes/countries_long/Sudan_and_South_Sudan/sudan.pdf. Accessed June 20, 2016.

Global Peace Operations Review (2015) "Leaders' Summit on Peacekeeping," *Global Peace Operations Review*. Available at: http://peaceoperationsreview.org/wp-content/uploads/2015/10/un_2015_peakeeping_summit_pledges.jpg. Accessed January 11, 2016.

Global Peace Operations Review (2016) "Those who pay, do not play…" *Global Peace Operations Review*. Available at: http://peaceoperationsreview.org/infographic/top-10-financial-contributors-to-un-peacekeeping-budget-aug-2016/. Accessed September 5, 2016.

Hirono, Miwa and Marc Lanteigne (2012) "Introduction: China and UN Peacekeeping," in Miwa Hirono and Marc Lanteigne (eds.) *China's Evolving Approach to UN Peacekeeping*. Abingdon: Routledge.

Jones, Bruce (2015) "Why the U.S. needs U.N. peacekeeping," *Brookings*, December 10, 2015. Available at: http://www.brookings.edu/blogs/order-from-chaos/posts/2015/12/10-un-peacekeeping-serves-us-strategic-interests-jones. Accessed January 11, 2015.

Landry, Carole (2017) "US envoy eyes cuts to UN peacekeeping," *Yahoo! News*, February 5, 2017. Available at: https://www.yahoo.com/news/us-envoy-eyes-cuts-un-peacekeeping-075524323.html?soc_src=social-sh&soc_trk=tw. Accessed February 8, 2017.

Lanteigne, Marc (2014) "Red and Blue: China's Evolving United Nations Peacekeeping Policies and Soft Power Development," in Chiyuki Aoi and Yee-Kuang Heng (eds.) *Asia-Pacific Nations in International Peace Support and Stability Operations*. New York: Palgrave Macmillan.

Lanteigne, Marc (2016) *Chinese Foreign Policy: An Introduction* (3rd ed.). Abingdon: Routledge.

Lotze, Walter (2015) "United Nations Multidimensional Integrated Stabilization Mission in Mali (MINUSMA)," in J. A. Koops, N. Macqueen, T. Tardy, and P. D. Williams. (eds.), *The Oxford Handbook of United Nations Peacekeeping Operations*. Oxford: Oxford University Press, pp. 854–864.

MacAskill, Ewen (2016) "UK to send more troops to South Sudan," *The Guardian*, September 8, 2016. Available at: https://www.theguardian.com/uk-news/2016/sep/08/uk-to-send-more-troops-to-south-sudan. Accessed September 19, 2016.

Mason, Rowena (2015) "UK to deploy troops to help keep peace in Somalia and South Sudan," *The Guardian*, September 27, 2015. Available at: http://www.theguardian.com/politics/2015/sep/27/uk-to-deploy-troops-to-help-keep-peace-in-somalia-and-south-sudan. Accessed January 11, 2016.

McGreal, Chris (2015a) "Countries to pledge troops to bolster UN peacekeepers after intense US pressure," *The Guardian*, September 27, 2015. Available at: http://www.theguardian.com/world/2015/sep/27/un-peacekeeping-obama-countries-pledge-troops-counterterror. Accessed January 11, 2015a.

McGreal, Chris (2015b) "What's the point of peacekeepers when they don't keep the peace?" *The Guardian*, September 17, 2015b. Available at: http://www.theguardian.com/world/2015/sep/17/un-united-nations-peacekeepers-rwanda-bosnia. Accessed January 11, 2016.

Ministry of Foreign Affairs of the Russian Federation (2013) "Concept of the Foreign Policy of the Russian Federation. Approved by President of the Russian Federation V. Putin on 12 February 2013." Available at: http://www.mid.ru/brp_4.nsf/0/76389FEC168189ED44257B2E0039B16D. Accessed April 20, 2016.

Nikitin, Alexander (2013) "The Russian Federation," in Alex Bellamy and Paul Williams (eds.) *Providing Peacekeepers. The Politics, Challenges, and Future of United Nations Peacekeeping Contributions*. Oxford: Oxford University Press.

Novosseloff, Alexandra and Thierry Tardy (2017) "France and the evolution of the UN peacekeeping doctrine," in Cedric de Coning, Chiyuki Aoi, and John Karlsrud (eds.), *UN Peacekeeping Doctrine in a New Era Adapting to Stabilisation, Protection and New Threats*. Abingdon: Routledge, pp. 90-108.

Power, Samantha (2014) "Remarks by Ambassador Samantha Power: Reforming peacekeeping in a time of conflict," *American Enterprise Institute*, November 7, 2014. Available at: https://www.aei.org/publication/remarks-ambassador-samantha-power-reforming-peacekeeping-time-conflict/. Accessed April 18, 2016.

Power, Samantha (2015) "Remarks on Peacekeeping in Brussels," *United States Mission to the United Nations*, March 9, 2015. Available at: http://usun.state.gov/remarks/6399. Accessed January 8, 2016.

van der Putten, Frans P. (2015) *China's Evolving Role in Peacekeeping and African Security*. The Hague: Clingendael Institute.

Ray, John (2017) "Britain's contributing 400 troops to South Sudan peacekeeping mission," ITV, February 7, 2017. Available at: http://www.itv.com/news/2017-02-07/britains-contribution-to-un-peacekeeping-in-south-sudan/. Accessed February 8, 2017.

Reykers, Yf and Niels Smeets (2015) "Losing control: a principal-agent analysis of Russia in the United Nations Security Council's decision-making towards the Libya crisis," *East European Politics*, 31 (4): pp. 369–387. DOI: 10.1080/21599165.2015.1070729.

Rieker, Pernille (2017) *French Foreign Policy Practices in the Age of Globalization and Regional Integration. Challenging Grandeur.* New York: Palgrave Macmillan.

Ryan, Missy and Sudarsan Raghavan (2016) "Another Western intervention in Libya looms," April 3, 2016, *Washington Post*. Available at: https://www.washingtonpost.com/world/national-security/another-western-intervention-in-libya-looms/2016/04/03/90386fde-f76e-11e5-9804-537defcc3cf6_story.html. Accessed July 8, 2016.

Security Council Report (2014) "In Hindsight: Changes to UN Peacekeeping in 2013," January 31, 2014. Available at: http://www.securitycouncilreport.org/monthly-forecast/2014-02/in_hindsight_changes_to_un_peacekeeping_in_2013.php. Accessed July 8, 2016.

Strobel, Warren (2015) "Exclusive: In Niger, U.S. soldiers quietly help build wall against Boko Haram," *Reuters*, September 18, 2015. Available at: http://www.reuters.com/article/us-usa-niger-boko-haram-idUSKCN0RI0C020150918. Accessed January 11, 2016.

Tardy, Thierry (2014) "The Reluctant Peacekeeper: France and the Use of Force in Peace Operations," *Journal of Strategic Studies* 37 (5): pp. 770–792. doi: 10.1080/01402390.2014.905472.

Tardy, Thierry (2016) "France: The unlikely return to UN peacekeeping," *InternationalPeacekeeping*23(5):1–20.DOI:10.1080/13533312.2016.1235091.

Tardy, Thierry and Dominik Zaum (2016) "France and the United Kingdom in the Security Council," in Sebastian von Einsiedel, David M. Malone, and Bruno S. Ugarte (eds.) *The UN Security Council in the 21ˢᵗCentury.* Boulder, CO: Lynne Rienner, pp. 121–138.

UK (2015a) "PM pledges UK troops to support stability in Somalia and South Sudan," September 28, 2015a. Available at: https://www.gov.uk/government/news/pm-pledges-uk-troops-to-support-stability-in-somalia-and-south-sudan. Accessed April 26, 2016.

UK (2015b) *A Secure and Prosperous United Kingdom: National Security Strategy and Strategic Defence and Security Review 2015b.* London: HM Government of the United Kingdom.

UN (2008) *United Nations Peacekeeping Operations: Principles and Guidelines.* New York: United Nations Department of Peacekeeping Operations and Department of Field Support.

UN (2009) *Peacebuilding in the Immediate Aftermath of Conflict.* New York: United Nations.

UN (2013a) *S/RES/2098*, March 28, 2013a. New York: United Nations.

UN (2013b) *S/RES/2100*, April 25, 2013b. New York: United Nations.

UN (2015a) *Transforming Our World: The 2030 Agenda for Sustainable Development*. New York: United Nations. Available at: https://sustainablede-velopment.un.org/post2015/transformingourworld. Accessed June 14, 2016.

UN (2015b) "Daily Press Briefing by the Office of the Spokesperson for the Secretary-General," *United Nations,* April 2, 2015. Available at: http://www.un.org/press/en/2015/db150402.doc.htm. Accessed April 21, 2016.

UN (2015c) *S/2015/229. Partnering for peace: moving towards partnership peace-keeping, April 1, 2015*. New York: United Nations.

UN (2016a) "Contributors to United Nations peacekeeping operations (Police, UN Military Experts on Mission and Troops," December 31, 2016. Available at: http://www.un.org/en/peacekeeping/contributors/documents/Yearly_Summary.pdf . Accessed February 8, 2017.

UN (2016b) *S/RES/2295*, June 29, 2016. New York: United Nations.

UN (2016c) "Financing peacekeeping" Available at: http://www.un.org/en/peacekeeping/operations/financing.shtml. Accessed April 26, 2016.

UN (2016d) "The 'New Horizon' process." Available at: http://www.un.org/en/peacekeeping/operations/newhorizon.shtml. Accessed April 25, 2016.

UN (2016e) "Ranking of Military and Police Contributions to UN Operations." Available at: http://www.un.org/en/peacekeeping/contributors/2016/jul16_2.pdf. Accessed August 22, 2016.

UNGA (2014) *A/68/787. Evaluation of the Implementation and Results of Protection of Civilians Mandates in United Nations Peacekeeping Operations. Report of the Office of Internal Oversight Services*. New York: United Nations General Assembly.

United Kingdom (2016) "LIVE WEBCAST - UN Peacekeeping Defence Ministerial: London 2016," September 8, 2016. Available at: https://www.gov.uk/government/news/live-webcast-un-peacekeeping-defence-ministe-rial-london-2016. Accessed September 8, 2016.

U.S. Department of State (2013) "African Contingency Operations Training and Assistance (ACOTA) Program," *U.S. Department of State*, February 6, 2013. Available at: http://www.state.gov/r/pa/prs/ps/2013/02/203841.htm. Accessed April 19, 2016.

U.S. Department of State (2016a) "Global Peace Operations Initiative (GPOI)," *U.S. Department of State*. Available at: http://www.state.gov/t/pm/ppa/gpoi/. Accessed April 19, 2016.

U.S. Department of State (2016b) "The Global Coalition to Counter ISIL," *U.S. Department of State*. Available at: http://www.state.gov/s/seci/. Accessed January 11, 2016.

Vilmer, Jean-Baptiste Jeangène and Olivier Schmitt (2015) "Frogs of War: Explaining the New French Interventionism," *War on the Rocks*, October 14, 2015.Availableat:http://warontherocks.com/2015/10/frogs-of-war-explaining-the-new-french-military-interventionism/. Accessed January 11, 2016.

Wells, Matt (2016) "The UN has failed its peacekeepers in S Sudan," *al-Jazeera,* September 10, 2016. Available at: http://www.aljazeera.com/indepth/opinion/2016/09/failed-peacekeepers-sudan-160908091206526.html. Accessed September 16, 2016.

What's in Blue (2016) "Renewal of UN Mission in Mali's Mandate," June 28, 2016. Available at: http://www.whatsinblue.org/2016/06/renewal-of-minusmas-mandate.php. Accessed July 8, 2016.

The White House (1994) *U.S. Policy on Reforming Multilateral Peace Operations.* Washington, DC: The White House. Available at: http://nsarchive.gwu.edu/NSAEBB/NSAEBB53/rw050394.pdf. Accessed June 13, 2016.

The White House (2014) "FACT SHEET: Summit on Peacekeeping," September 26, 2014. Available at: https://www.whitehouse.gov/the-press-office/2014/09/26/fact-sheet-summit-un-peacekeeping. Accessed January 8, 2016.

The White House (2015) *United States Support to United Nations Peace Operations.* Washington, DC: The White House. Available at: http://www.defense.gov/Portals/1/Documents/pubs/2015peaceoperations.pdf. Accessed June 13, 2016.

Williams, Paul D. (2015) "Keeping a Piece of Peacekeeping," *Foreign Affairs,* October 6, 2015. Available at: https://www.foreignaffairs.com/articles/2015-10-06/keeping-piece-peacekeeping. Accessed April 19, 2016.

Yin, He (2017) "China's Doctrine on UN Peacekeeping," in Cedric de Coning, Chiyuki Aoi, and John Karlsrud (eds.), *UN Peacekeeping Doctrine Towards the Post-Brahimi Era? Adapting to Stabilization, Protection and New Threats.* Abingdon: Routledge, pp. 109–131.

Zhuang, Pinghui (2016) "Two Chinese UN peacekeepers killed, two seriously injured in attack in South Sudan," *South China Morning Post,* July 11, 2016. Available at: http://www.scmp.com/news/china/diplomacy-defence/article/1988348/two-chinese-un-peacekeepers-killed-two-seriously. Accessed September 5, 2016.

CHAPTER 3

New Capabilities, Tools, and Technologies

Entering the Twenty-First Century

"The United Nations has entered the twenty-first century," the then USG for Peacekeeping Hervé Ladsous told the troops at the ceremony for the first deployment of UAVs in the DRC in 2013 (UN Office of the Spokesperson 2013). In 2014, the peacekeeping mission in Mali (MINUSMA) established a new type of military intelligence capability in a UN context, the All Sources Information Fusion Unit (ASIFU), composed of European troops and including human intelligence operators, surveillance drones, and Apache attack helicopters. Also in 2014, the then SG Ban Ki-moon launched an expert panel review of technology and innovation in peacekeeping, led by Jane Holl Lute, a former US and UN peace operations official. When the panel delivered its report in February 2015, it noted that "the gap between what the average peacekeeping mission does have and what it should have is so pronounced, that some of the countries with the world's most capable military and police forces have been reluctant to participate in many of the more difficult and challenging peacekeeping operations" (UN 2015b: 3). The momentum in giving peacekeeping new tools and capabilities continued with the June 2015 release of the HIPPO Report of the UN high-level independent panel, which also recommended that the UN should "ensure effective uptake of field appropriate technology in support of its peace operations" (UN 2015a: 14).

Information communication technologies (ICTs) have rapidly developed over the last two decades, with exponential growth in affordable

© The Author(s) 2018
J. Karlsrud, *The UN at War*,
https://doi.org/10.1007/978-3-319-62858-5_4

mobile technology, also in developing countries. In 2015, more smartphones than non-smartphones were sold in developing countries (Internet Society 2015: 17), and the UN International Telecommunications Union (ITU) has reported that 43.4% of the world's population now has Internet access, with 35.3% living in the developing world (ITU 2015), and the figure is rising rapidly. Although often in zones of low or no mobile connection and with very few means available to buy smartphones, affected populations in conflict zones are increasingly able to engage through mobile services and mobile internet, potentially leveling the playing field. This development opens up the possibility for more two-way communication with those suffering during conflict, and for better understanding their needs. UN peace operations must seize this opportunity to become more connected with the people they are to serve.

New capabilities and better use of technology can improve peacekeeping at every level of operations. Peace operations, including MONUSCO in the DRC, have experienced armed groups committing atrocities near their compounds. UN contingents need to know what is going on around them and should be able to share their information with field commanders and headquarters officials. New capabilities and technologies may help protect civilians and deter threats, while also contributing to peace and stability in the longer term. However, in the complex political environment of peace operations, these new tools are potential double-edged swords that can exacerbate tensions between various parts of the UN membership over the direction of UN peacekeeping. There are fears that intelligence operators and surveillance drones will involve spying on host and neighboring countries. Understandably, local populations are often mistrustful of the UN gathering data and information on their daily activities, especially if they do not know how it will be used, or who will have access to the information later on.

This chapter details some of the ongoing and proposed reforms and how these impact on UN peace operations in political, economic, and social terms. It is mainly Western countries that have been seeking to promote change in terms of including new capabilities, tools, and technologies in UN peace operations. This has been driven by the experiences gained in stabilization operations over the past two decades, through NATO and in coalitions of the willing. During the past decade, a few Western states have re-engaged with UN peace operations, albeit only in selected missions. In Lebanon and later Mali, Western countries have infused UN missions with logistic, intelligence, aviation, medical, and other capabilities that have proven very helpful. However, these local reforms have also had some consequences that were perhaps unforeseen.

If the UN is to strengthen the intelligence capability of UN peace operations, and add surveillance drones and other tools to its regular toolkit, there will have to be more compelling internal and external explanations for how new capabilities and technologies benefit mission objectives. There must also be clear guidelines for their operational use, along with protocols for protecting the information they gather. The political aspects of their adoption will need to be addressed as much as the tactical side of their deployment. However, the rationale remains clear: UN peace operations need to be enabled to have sufficient situational awareness to provide adequate force protection and implement their mandate—and for this objective to be reached, reform is needed.

From Afghanistan to Mali

Experiences from a decade of network-centric warfare in Iraq and Afghanistan are slowly permeating into UN peacekeeping. In the network-centric paradigm, information flows rapidly between sensors, commanders, and front actors on the battlefield, flattening the hierarchy and increasing the speed of command and precision (Alberts et al. 2000). Western countries with experience from these interventions rotate staff with battlefield experience from Afghanistan and Iraq through permanent missions and UN headquarters in New York, and increasingly to the UN peace operations in Lebanon, Mali, and South Sudan. They are keen to draw upon their experience to update the planning and execution of UN peace operations, with the aim of enabling the right troops to be deployed at the right place, at the right time, and with the right information.

The UN peace operations in the DRC, Lebanon, and Mali have been the prime laboratories for testing these new tools.[1] In 2015, European member states contributed about 1000 peacekeeping troops to MINUSMA, mostly as a function of the ASIFU (Karlsrud and Smith 2015). The most sizeable contributions have come from the Netherlands with about 300 troops (The Netherlands Ministry of Defence 2016) and Sweden with about 250 troops (Swedish Armed Forces 2016). In January 2017, the German government decided to increase its contribution to 1000 troops, including helicopters (German Federal Government 2017).

From 2013 to 2017, the ASIFU consisted solely of European troops. Supported by special forces, it analyzed information obtained from various sources (or "sensors" in NATO parlance). Apache helicopters were deployed to gather image intelligence and provide force protection for the special forces; and Chinook helicopters were provided to ensure the availability of CASEVAC/MEDEVAC capabilities according to NATO standards. The ASIFU was then planned to provide analyses of this information to the Force Commander. Sources or sensors have included intelligence, surveillance and reconnaissance (ISR) companies, but as of September 2016 there was no ISR company in northern Mali where the need may have been the greatest. The two ISR companies provided by the Netherlands and Sweden to Gao and Timbuktu have used local interpreters when interacting with the local population. They have collected intelligence to try to understand local political dynamics better and uncover the networks behind and locations of possible threats. The ASIFU has also received visual information from the Apache helicopters and short-range UAVs (the mission also received mid-range UAVs from a private contractor in 2015). The ASIFU has also been equipped with an open source section that has been monitoring local and regional newspapers, local and regional TV, web-based news, and social media where many of the armed groups and their members are active. In addition, the ASIFU could draw upon reporting from the military troops, police, and civilian officers that MINUSMA has deployed across the country.

Most Western contributions should be seen in conjunction with aspirations to become non-permanent members of the UNSC. Both the Netherlands and Sweden campaigned for several years to be appointed non-permanent members of the UNSC from 2017 to 2019. Both countries were elected in June 2016, although the Netherlands eventually had to split its two-year term with Italy after receiving an equal number of votes (Lederer 2016). Also in June 2016, Germany launched a bid to become a non-permanent member from 2019 to 2020. Norway, which has had a smaller contribution to the ASIFU from the beginning, and decided to contribute a C-130 in 2016, aims for a non-permanent seat from 2020 to 2021 (Norway Mission to the UN 2015).

The Future Is Here

Technology can help to improve situational awareness and better protect risk-exposed civilians and peacekeeping forces alike (Dorn 2016). Real-time tracking of the movements of personnel and capabilities on all levels can provide the precise location of each soldier, vehicle, and unit (Dorn and Semken 2015), but this remains an aspiration in UN peace operations. Although tracking individual soldiers may still be impractical, MINUSMA in Mali has experimented with Ushahidi software to map and geo-tag security incidents in real time.[2] Visual organization of information can be more intuitive and provide a better tool for decision-makers at tactical, operational, and strategic levels, rather than written reports where patterns and emerging developments may be missed. Information can be layered according to type and classification, with access to sensitive layers protected by passwords. UN peace operations have potential access to a wide range of sources, including personnel on the ground, local partners, and open source material.

Commercial satellite imagery can provide up-to-date images at low cost, enabling missions to monitor evolving situations on the ground. In Darfur, for example, the Satellite Sentinel Project, a cooperation between the Enough Project, "a project of the Center for American Progress to end genocide and crimes against humanity" (Satellite Sentinel Project 2016a), and DigitalGlobe, a satellite imagery company, used satellite images to monitor developments on the ground and warn about impending attacks or document atrocities (Satellite Sentinel Project 2016b). However, the images, openly accessible on the Internet, were also possible tools for perpetrators to identify new targets—which highlights the need for caution when deciding on access and how information collected for humanitarian or human rights purposes can be vulnerable to misuse by hostile third parties (Raymond et al. 2012). The UN mission in South Sudan (UNMISS) used geospatial imagery and analysis to detect an imminent threat against civilians in Bor in 2014 and enabled the mission to "improve the situational awareness of peacekeepers, giving them the option to take preventive action such as taking up strategic positions and protecting pockets of civilians" (Convergne and Snyder 2015: 572).

UN peace operations could also engage with the volunteer technologists who normally support NGOs during disasters and in conflict situations such as Libya. Since 2010, thousands of these volunteers have responded to earthquakes in Haiti and Chile, and to flooding in Pakistan. They have processed large volumes of data and created valuable information by plotting it on maps. As volunteer labor, networks such as Crisismappers can add human processing power to solve complex tasks during crises (Crisismappers 2016). During the Haiti earthquake in 2010, these networks were able to turn a disaster area into one of the most accurately mapped areas in the world, scanning satellite pictures from remote locations and populating a common map—all in a matter of hours (Harvard Humanitarian Initiative 2011: 30). As volunteers, they can act much faster than multilateral organizations. But despite good intentions, they do not always adhere to or are aware of accepted standards for humanitarian action, such as do no harm, humanity, neutrality, impartiality, and independence (OCHA 2012). The result can be that volunteers end up harming those they seek to aid (see, e.g., Iacucci 2013). For this reason, the umbrella groups coordinating them are seeking to professionalize their activities by establishing codes of conduct and guidelines to avoid unintended negative consequences of volunteers' involvement (see, e.g., Gilman and Baker 2014; Karlsrud and Mühlen-Schulte 2017).

The UN mission in the DRC, MONUSCO, established Community Alert Networks (CANs) and distributed mobile phones to key individuals in local communities, who were to alert MONUSCO when under threat. The CANs were part of a larger effort to improve responsiveness to local populations' needs and better protect them. The networks could also be used for simple perception surveys, helping the mission to capture, understand, and integrate local observations into daily decision-making. However, MONUSCO changed its approach when it realized that those who had received the mobile phones were potential targets for retaliation, and instead provided phone numbers that local populations could use for voicing their concerns.

The UN has a long history of using radio for communicating strategic objectives and engaging with local communities. However, there is still room for improvement when it comes to using social media and other tools for engaging in two-way conversations with local populations to understand needs, fears, and aspirations (see also Gordon and Loge 2015). Social media can improve engagement with local populations, especially if they are used as a tool for discussion and not solely the provision of information. Social media outlets can be invaluable for communicating mission objectives, receiving feedback on performance, answering queries, and dealing with misinformation.

POLITICAL, PRINCIPLED, AND PRACTICAL HURDLES

Developing and adapting new tools and technologies to the UN context is not without challenges, and the example of the ASIFU in MINUSMA is instructive in this regard. The ASIFU is the first explicit ISR capability in a UN mission. Also, other UN missions have collected and analyzed intelligence, but under various euphemisms—to gain "situational awareness," for "force protection," and to have "informed information." At the UN, the word "intelligence" has long been anathema, but now more and more member states are accepting the need for the UN to gather information in order to achieve its objectives. The ASIFU and the considerable presence of European officers and staff in the mission have also led to increased attention to UN peacekeeping among the contributing countries. Of course, the ASIFU was bound to face some hurdles, internally and with member states long skeptical to the UN acquiring intelligence capabilities (Dorn 2011). There has been widespread concern that the introduction of the term "intelligence" in the UN system may jeopardize the legitimacy of ongoing efforts to generate data, information, and knowledge through overt channels; in fact, the high-level independent panel on peace operations reviewing peace operations in 2015 did not use the word in their report (UN 2015a). In a lessons-learned exercise on the ASIFU, it was emphasized that the UN should not be in the business of doing covert intelligence gathering or paying for intelligence—both regular methods in traditional intelligence gathering when carried out by member states (UN 2016a).

Alongside MINUSMA, the French *Opération Serval* and subsequently *Opération Barkhane* have conducted offensive operations under the same UNSC mandate. *Opération Barkhane* was launched on August 2014 to fight Islamist fighters in the Sahel (Barluet 2014). *Opération Barkhane* covers Burkina Faso, Chad, Mali, Mauritania, and Niger; it is led from Chad, but maintains a sizeable presence in Mali and also includes two Reaper drones that became operational on January 16, 2014, and have since conducted more than 15,000 flight hours in the Sahel (ibid.; defence-Web 2016). Concerns have been voiced about information being shared with *Opération Barkhane* and subsequently used for targeting and killing selected individuals—in violation of UN rules and regulations, and international humanitarian law (interview with former UN official, September 15, 2015). *Opération Barkhane* also embedded liaison teams with the African TCCs during the African-led International Support Mission in Mali (AFISMA) that stayed on through the re-hatting and are still embedded (interview with French MOD official, January 15, 2015, New York), and there is reason to believe that this also could give *Opération Barkhane* access to privileged information available to these troops. The Military Concept of Operations for MINUSMA sketches out a very close relationship: "MINUSMA military forces will coordinate their activities closely with Operation Barkhane forces that are targeting the terrorist threat directly" (cited in UN 2016a: 14). The French have been happy with the information shared: "Apparently we were happy with what the Dutch are providing to us. There are some exchanges, but very informal ones" (interview with French MOD official, January 15, 2015, New York). However, these practices have raised eyebrows, internally and externally. An internal review of the ASIFU and the MINUSMA intelligence structure highlighted the political, legal, and ethical risks that information-sharing with a parallel counter-terrorism force entail:

> First, existing guidance does not specify the parameters for decision-making on information sharing, which may expose the mission to political and ethical risk. Given the plausible outcomes of sharing sensitive information with Operation Barkhane, this would seem a critical gap. The UN should clarify its position on whether, in sharing information with a parallel force, the expected outcome of this action should be commensurate with activities permissible under the mission's mandate, or whether information may be shared more liberally.
>
> Second, given that the sharing of information with Operation Barkhane may have political implications, it would seem that decisions on whether or not to share information should be taken at the political level, i.e. by senior mission leadership and informed by UN policy, rather than by the ASIFU Commanders. Legally, MINUSMA may have an obligation to monitor action taken by other forces in regards to information it has shared, and may also have obligations under the Human Rights Due Diligence Policy. Moreover, decisions to share information should be informed by considerations of political impact and risks to the mandate, including the possibility of the mission being perceived as a party to the conflict. Should senior mission leadership elect to delegate that authority to subordinate personnel, this delegation should be accompanied by guidance on principles and parameters for information sharing with partners that take these considerations into account. (UN 2016a: 15)

Practices like these can partially explain the sensitivity of including intelligence in the repertoire of UN peace operations. They also highlight the dilemma of whether it is a good idea at all to use the word "intelligence" in the context of UN peace operations. In their review of current practices as well as the needs of the UN relating to intelligence gathering and analysis, Abilova and Novosseloff recommended that the UN should focus on

...on improving its current structures and on strengthening information analysis and sharing more than information collection. The UN should prioritize developing a comprehensive information-management system rather than new intelligence infrastructure, which most member states are likely to oppose for reasons of funding and politics. (2016: 3)

Their emphasis on the word "information" rather than "intelligence" is telling, and highlights the sensitivities of introducing the word "intelligence," rather than actual practices, in UN peace operations. For anyone vaguely familiar with UN peace operations, it is clear that they are generating information from a range of sources including military, police, and civilian officers on a daily basis. However, these practices do not currently qualify as intelligence gathering and analysis, as the structure and quality of collection, analysis, coordination, sharing, and control of information and analysis vary widely. All these dimensions can and should be improved, while avoiding instrumentalization and monopolization by these processes for military ends, or inadvertently making the mission a party to the conflict.

UN peacekeeping missions have so far mostly relied on daily reports from their military observers and civilian staff in the field, or what could be called "overt" information gathering. With a high number of officers and civilians deployed in most missions, this provides a good tool for gathering data, turning this into contextualized information and generating knowledge over time. However, there is not an institutionalized culture for structurally collected information—or intelligence—in the UN system. Senior civilian management has little or no experience in identifying priority information requirements (PIRs), and few are able to distinguish between intelligence needs on strategic, operational, and tactical levels. For the collection of information, this means that liaison officers on the ground and operators of technical sensors are not given clear enough guidance on what type of information they should collect and with who they are to engage. In MINUSMA, the ASIFU has, for good reasons, been requested to find out who is attacking the troops on the ground—a tactical issue—perhaps to the detriment of focusing on the operational outlook of the mission, in terms of main actors and their intentions and capabilities. Lindboe and Nordlie argue that this weakens the ability of senior management to not only take decisions that respond to day-to-day challenges, but also chart a longer-term course for how to achieve strategic objectives (2017).

There have also been significant challenges in the coordination and sharing of information in MINUSMA: "the intelligence generated by the ASIFU and related assets is limited in its benefit to the mission by issues related to the integration of the unit into the mission structure, information classification, ownership and sharing, levels of focus and analysis and tasking relationships" (UN 2016a: 2). Several steps have been taken to address these issues, like setting up a Joint Coordination Board (JCB)—a "forum for information sharing, coordination, de-confliction and tasking for all mission intelligence and analysis entities" (ibid.: 7). Although the ASIFU is specific to MINUSMA, lessons related to sharing and coordination are very likely to apply to other UN peace operations as well.

Geographically, the ASIFU headquarters are located separate from the rest of MINUSMA headquarters in Bamako, which makes day-to-day coordination and cooperation difficult. The ASIFU was set up explicitly drawing on NATO experiences in Afghanistan: "An All Sources Information Fusion Unit (ASIFU) is a military intelligence concept with its origins in the NATO International Security Assistance Force mission in Afghanistan" (UN 2016a: 3). Due to the considerable lapse in any long-term and close engagement, there is today little institutional capacity and knowledge about UN peacekeeping in European capitals, where energies have focused on participating in NATO missions since the mid-1990s. The European TCCs come from Afghanistan with an organizational culture that has been developed and refined in the more than decade-long NATO-led campaign there.[3] The ASIFU has accentuated the meeting of different organizational cultures. One example is the development of regional stabilization and recovery plans. These were developed by the civilian-led regional offices of MINUSMA, in close cooperation and for joint ownership with the national government, the rest of MINUSMA, UN system, donor agencies, and humanitarian and development partners (UN 2014a). The UN asked the ASIFU to assist with the analysis part for this exercise and found the cooperation positive (interview with UN official, February 5, 2015). However, there were some initial snags—for instance, ASIFU staff viewed "stabilization" through the lens of their Afghanistan experience (ibid.). As will be discussed in the next chapter, in the NATO context, "stabilization" denotes a strategy that is military-centered and aimed at creating conditions conducive to the exit of the (military) mission. By contrast, in the UN context there is less emphasis on the military component, and more on an integrated approach for dealing with the root causes of the conflict in question. As such, the Stabilization and Recovery Strategy of MINUSMA had five main objectives: (1) improve the security situation; (2) strengthen the rule of law; (3) support socio-economic development; (4) strengthen social cohesion; and (5) strengthen delivery of social services (UN 2014a). The presence in the Dutch ISR company in Gao of a Dutch civilian advisor with long development experience in Mali helped the ISR company and the ASIFU to adjust to the new context and provide analyses that not only took military considerations into account, but were also open to a wider understanding of the challenges and possible solutions (interview with UN official, February 5, 2015). This shows that the UN has been able to shift some Europeans from a NATO-focused to a more UN-focused integrated approach and understanding of the situation on the ground—but this effort is context-specific and dependent on individuals rather than an expression of a general shift in approach.

While NATO competence is strong, there is in European capitals scant capacity on UN peace operations in the Ministries of Defense and Ministries of Foreign Affairs (see, e.g., Karlsrud and Osland 2016; Koops and Tercovich 2016), as regard the UN as well as Africa and Mali (except in the UK and in France, because of their colonial past). It will take time to come up to speed with current procedures and practices for force generation, mission planning, and day-to-day engagement with United Nations Headquarters (UNHQ) in New York and how UN peacekeeping missions are conducted out on the ground. There are also many areas of friction, competition, and struggle over what peace operations should do and how they should do it: "The Dutch arrived with NATO standards so they progressively wanted to control what MINUSMA was doing but did not want to share what the ASIFU was doing, so at one point people did not know nor understand what the ASIFU was doing" (interview with French MOD official, January 15, 2015, New York). The gradual acclimatization of European troops—as seen in the story of the development of the regional stabilization and recovery strategies above—shows that over time the UN has been able to sway some Europeans from a NATO to a more UN-focused approach and understanding of the situation on the ground. However, due consideration should be given to the fact that military contingents, and in particular Western contingents, generally only remain on the ground only for short periods of up to a year, while civilian UN staff generally stay for several years. This means it is more difficult to imbue Western contingents with an understanding of the differences between NATO and UN operations, and makes pre-deployment training even more important.

Another example is the surveillance drones—or UAVs—initially deployed in the DRC, and now also included in MINUSMA. The drones in the DRC have received considerable attention since their deployment in December 2013. They have been used in operations of the FIB and the FARDC against the M23 and *Forces démocratiques de libération du Rwanda* (FDLR). They also identified a sinking boat on Lake Kivu and aided the UN mission in rescuing several civilians. In fact, however, the surveillance drones in the DRC are not the first in a UN context: drones were used in the DRC in 2006 and in Chad in 2009, and there has been extensive deployment of helicopter-based reconnaissance in the DRC and Mali. However, the UN did not have guidelines for this capability, and there is an urgent need to develop both country-specific and general guidelines that deal with all dimensions of the deployment of surveillance drones in UN missions (see, e.g., Rosén and Karlsrud 2014; Karlsrud and Rosén 2017).

Such tools can enable the UN to improve its situational awareness radically. Aerial surveillance makes it possible to survey large areas for troop and population movements, also at night and in forested terrain. Conflict-affected areas in the DRC are otherwise inaccessible due to the dense jungle and poor infrastructure. UAVs may also improve the security and safety of UN troops and local civilians by ensuring that forces are correctly deployed in situations of emerging violence. Drones could aid in the pursuit of belligerent groups and in avoidance of ambushes. With the right adaptions, they can scan roads for improvised explosive devices (IEDs).

The UN considers the deployment of drones in the DRC a success. The capability has been sought for missions in the CAR, Mali, and South Sudan. In Mali, the UN aims to include longer-range UAVs, drawing on experience from the DRC. But not every host country wants UN missions to have aerial surveillance capability, particularly not when a government is engaged in an ongoing conflict. South Sudan rejected the proposal outright (Sengupta 2014). UAVs are also vulnerable—after the Organization for Security and Co-operation in Europe (OSCE) deployed two short-range drones to eastern Ukraine, combatants attempted to thwart their use with electronic countermeasures and shoot them down. Obviously, these difficult conditions place severe constraints on their effectiveness (Borger 2015).

The use of drones also gives rise to some difficult questions: how long should data be stored, and who can require access post facto? Can the International Criminal Court (ICC) request the UN to share the data at a later date? The UN will have to deal with these questions and develop an institutional framework not only at the mission level, but at the global level as well (Karlsrud and Rosén 2017).

New tools and technologies like the ASIFU and surveillance drones have thus accentuated the need to update the doctrinal framework guiding UN peace operations, so that it can reflect the changing operational environment. MINUSMA has developed a standard operating procedure (SOP) for management of the intelligence cycle in the mission (UN 2014b), and in 2015–2016 the UN conducted a fact-finding mission to Mali to gather lessons learned and provide recommendations for improving the collection, analysis, and dissemination of military intelligence in UN peacekeeping operations, at tactical, operational, and strategic levels. Their report recommended the "ASIFU HQ and U-2 to be merged into a Military All Sources Information Cell (MASIC)" to "integrate more effectively into the mission structure" (UN 2016a: 9). The conclusion of the report also noted the need for the Western troops and capabilities to be more strongly integrated into the UN system.

CAN TECHNOLOGY HELP THE UN BECOME MORE PEOPLE-CENTRIC?

The UN has recently also developed general guidelines to promote better understanding of local perceptions. These guidelines highlight the critical need for mission leadership to "take full advantage of opportunities to collect systematically and effectively analyse information on local perceptions to enhance missions' situational awareness, inform confidence building, and support inclusive post-conflict governance" (UN 2014c: 1). While this is a good first step, the UN Secretariat will need to ensure that these principles are reflected when developing guidance for intelligence collection through various sensors.

European member states were heavily influenced by their long engagement with NATO in Afghanistan, giving them a particular set of frames for understanding the situation in northern Mali. Northern Mali is indeed beset by many challenges similar to those in Afghanistan—asymmetric threats; organized crime; local, political, and tribal dynamics—but in a UN perspective, the primacy of politics and addressing the root causes of the conflict should still be the main focus. The government of Mali is also very much part of the struggle over the rationale and objectives of MINUSMA. The government, referring to the mandate of MINUSMA to strengthen and extend state authority, would like MINUSMA to be more robust and help it to fight the Islamist and rebel groups. On the other hand, many of the UN staff emphasize the importance of maintaining the impartiality of the mission, and the primary need to reach a political agreement to facilitate further progress and peace. For this reason, relations with the government have at times been difficult. In April 2013, when the mission was authorized, the Security Council instructed MINUSMA, "in support of the transitional authorities of Mali, to stabilise the key population centres, especially in the north of Mali and, in this context, to deter threats and take active steps to prevent the return of armed elements to those areas" (UN 2013). The mandate was moderated in 2014 after the government conducted military operations in Kidal, and the new mandate had less emphasis on supporting the government in fighting armed elements, and more on protection of civilians and facilitating stabilization and recovery (UN 2014d).

Duffield has argued that technology can replace ground truth—through technological innovation, simulation, and visualization premised on an "uncritical technological-determinist vision of modulating the moods, expectations and actions of remote disaster-affected populations" (Duffield 2013: 4, see also Sandvik et al. 2014). The experience from Mali, however, is so far not conclusive. On the one hand, European contributions have involved a combination of human intelligence operators with an explicit mandate to interact with local populations and the use of aerial and image intelligence collected by UAVs and the Apache helicopters. While this gives the impression of willingness to search for ground truth, engaging with local populations, and trying to understand underlying conflict drivers, the reluctance of western troops to deploy to the north of Mali points in another direction. The risk-averse posture undermines the ability of the ASIFU and the mission in general to get to grips with the situation on the ground. The background of Western troops in counter-insurgency and counter-terrorism operations in Afghanistan might also further securitize the operation, unless they can be socialized into the UN organizational culture of an integrated approach ultimately seeking political solutions.

SURF, NOT TURF

Adding these new capabilities to UN peace operations risks creating a data deluge. The challenge will be to sift through rapid data streams, analyze them, and then produce actionable information in real-time. Managing this without overload will require new ways of decision-making at all levels, and the ability to overcome intra-organizational turf wars. New capabilities, tools, and technology will shift the relationship between the field and UNHQ in New York as well as between mission headquarters and staff at the tactical level.

Most UN peace operations rely on satellite links to connect the field and headquarters. Access to high-speed optical fiber networks or using local providers is rarely an option. Increased data flows will require more bandwidth at all levels to enable large amounts of data to flow between FOBs and troops in the field, mission headquarters, and UNHQ in New York. If a host country's telecommunications infrastructure is inadequate, deployment of these tools will require the UN itself to pay for upgraded data transmission capabilities for its own missions.

These new systems also require highly qualified technicians to run them. The Expert Panel on Technology and Innovation in UN Peacekeeping suggested that member states could provide network engineers to set up efficient and secure communication at an early phase of mission deployment (UN 2015b). The panel proposed the establishment of a mechanism to furnish the UN with technological expertise as Civilian-Contributing Countries (CCCs) and Technological expertise contributing countries (TechCCs). This new measure, a practical follow-up to the civilian capacities reform initiative rolled out in 2009 (UN 2009), would parallel existing arrangements for police contributing countries (PCCs) and TCCs. For instance, member states could provide network engineers to set up efficient and secure communications in an early phase of mission deployment. However, so far the recommendations of the expert panel have received little support from member states.

Also inter-organizational cooperation needs further strengthening. The integration of operations and crisis centers at the UN in the UN Operations and Crisis Centre (UNOCC) is matched by similar initiatives at the global level. The EU has taken the initiative by encouraging collaboration between the crisis rooms of, among others, the UN, NATO, and the OSCE, as well as regional organizations like the AU and the League of Arab States (Pawlak and Ricci 2014). But closer cooperation is needed. Organizations must ensure inter-operability and enable real-time exchange of data, if this collaboration is to be useful to decision-makers. However, concerns about sharing sensitive information remain. The UN has a history of severe difficulties with safeguarding confidential data, and there are few measures the organization can take in case confidence is breached.

Increasing convergence between information platforms gives rise to another difficult question: how should UN peace operations cooperate with humanitarian actors? In the humanitarian field, common operational datasets (CODs) were developed by NGOs and the UN agencies under the leadership of the Office for the Coordination of Humanitarian Affairs (OCHA) (IASC 2010). CODs ensure that common standards are followed during the collection and storage of information, and enable easy exchange of information between organizations in the UN system. UN peace operations have access to this information, and increasing convergence between data platforms allows real-time information sharing and swift decision-making. But humanitarians insist on their neutrality and are wary about sharing more sensitive information with peace operations, especially those with robust mandates. Humanitarian partners are also reluctant to use information gathered by surveillance drones and other new technologies (IRIN 2014). The OCHA has developed guidance for humanitarian workers regarding surveillance drones and new technologies (OCHA 2013; Gilman 2014; Gilman and Baker 2014), but UN peace operations still lag behind.

Cooperation with the private sector is on the rise, but more can be done. Leaders in information technology, such as Google and Microsoft, can and do help the UN become more effective in sorting through the vast piles of data it gathers. Military components, Civil Affairs, human rights officers, and other civilians in the field send written reports up the chain of command each day. How can this information be formatted, quantified, presented, and then analyzed for longer-term trends? The UN expert panel recommended equipping military, police, and civilian peacekeepers with smartphones and tablets to enable real-time and geo-tagged reporting (UN 2015b).

Data provided by local populations through social media, twitter messages, and other forms of communication must be cross-checked in real-time with other sources to ensure validity as well as relevance and possible actionability for decision-makers. Digital "exhaust" can be useful for detecting macro-trends. For example, group geo-tagging of mobile phones can detect population movements, while sudden spikes in remittance transfers can help detect geographical locations where tensions are building up (UN Global Pulse 2016). Discussions should take place with banking, telecom, and remittance industries to determine how they might be able to share their data without compromising business secrets or personal details.

BEWARE OF TECHNO-HUBRIS

While new technology opens up many possibilities, there are those who are skeptical to its use. Having more information does not automatically lead to better actions to protect civilians or troops. Surveillance drones and other tools can have a potential deterrent effect on would-be perpetrators by making it clear that they are under surveillance—one hopes, raising the bar for committing atrocities. However, the use of drones in particular must be accompanied by effective public information campaigns. Host populations need to know the rationale for drone deployment and understand the limits of what drones can and cannot do. UN drones are used solely for surveillance: they are not intended to carry offensive weapons. In eastern DRC, the local population has dubbed the drones "loud mosquitos," as if they were an unwanted annoyance, rather seeing them as the eyes of a mission sent to protect them (IRIN 2014).

With collection of personal data and information come concerns about ensuring the right to privacy. For greater accountability and effectiveness of aid, vulnerable and affected populations must often share personal information before they receive any support. In the wrong hands, such data could be used against the very people its collection was intended to help.

Satellites can provide detailed images of private property. Tapping phone calls infringes on private conversations. If such information needs to be gathered, it must be for a clear purpose, done in a regulated and legal way, and stored securely. Management systems need to be developed with checks and balances to ensure that UN peace operations gather this information in a responsible and respectful way. Populations in host countries should not be treated as second-class citizens simply because the legal frameworks protecting their privacy may not be as well developed or respected as in the West.

After data is gathered, new questions arise: where will it be stored, will it be secure, and for how long will it be kept? There are also jurisdictional concerns about control, access, and redistribution of this information. Can it be obtained by member states, the ICC, or NGOs? Is it considered admissible evidence to be used in court? Who pays for the long-term data warehousing, archiving, and management of information collected from a mission of limited duration? Will such information be kept if it reveals UN inaction in the face of blatant violations of international law? Nor is the UN totally safe from offensive cyber-attacks. The more sensitive information it holds, the more likely is it to become the target of such intrusions (see, e.g., BBC 2011; Schia 2016).

A Brave New World

The past two decades have witnessed massive technological shifts, with disruptive potential for restructuring relationships between the governed and those who govern, also in conflict-affected areas. Social media and mobile technology may offer a voice to affected populations. New technologies can also enable a new type of proximity, through surveillance drones, social media, and the harvesting of "big data" such as remittances mapped at national and local levels, and tracking population movement through mobile phone towers. However, these new technologies may also help increasingly risk-averse actors like the UN to distance themselves further from those they are meant to serve, enabling remote observation and control. If this proceeds unchecked, it can speed up the tendency of bunkerization. What is needed is greater granularity of information on all levels, matched by increased mobility and agility of troops, police, and civilians, to serve people in need and under threat.

The exit of Western troops from Afghanistan and the return to UN peacekeeping could be mutually beneficial, creating new sources of capabilities. The UN can offer Western member states theaters where troops can continue to deploy and maintain their capacities. Such peace operations can also serve as arenas for sharing of experiences between major traditional and new TCCs, supporting greater triangular cooperation between TCCs, the Secretariat, and the Security Council (see Novosseloff 2015). But suspicions persist because the term "new technologies" is typically seen as a catchall euphemism for "intelligence gathering." As the first explicit intelligence component of an UN peacekeeping operation, the ASIFU had the potential to bring new insights into local dynamics. However, if the knowledge generated serves the objectives of particular member states rather than the longer-term political objectives of the mission, it would undermine the core principles of UN peacekeeping, and turn the operation into an actor used for counter-insurgency and counter-terrorism purposes (Karlsrud 2017). Suspicions about intelligence also linger on. When a new mandate for MINUSCA in the CAR was negotiated in July 2016, France proposed that the wording "enhancing MINUSCA's intelligence capacities, including surveillance and monitoring capacities" should be included (What's in Blue 2016)—but the final text read "enhancing MINUSCA's personnel, mobility assets and capabilities for gathering timely, reliable and actionable information on threats to civilians and the analytical tools to use it…" (UN 2016b: 8).

UN peacekeeping vitally needs new technology far beyond surveillance drones. UN missions need CANs, partnerships with "crisismappers," and new ways of managing relations between the field and headquarters. It must be made clear that these tools are not so much about making missions more robust, as making them better informed, more efficient, and increasingly connected to the communities with whom they work (Karlsrud 2014). New tools will also require new capacities. Implementing and operating such tools will call for more highly trained experts, analysts, technicians, and decision-makers, rather than the generalists often sent to missions or staffing headquarters. Mission budgets will need to spend more funds on capital-intensive equipment and satellite bandwidth, to get the most out of new systems.

That being said, the push for more technology should do no harm to those populations whom peace operations are sent to serve. There are legitimate concerns about privacy that will have to be addressed. Legal frameworks, management systems, and internal security will need to be reviewed and adjusted to prevent negative and unintended consequences. On the other hand, some of these new tools also offer the promise of building bridges and opening channels of communication with local populations. SMS messaging and social media feedback can give missions a better understanding of what local populations are thinking, as well as allowing them to communicate mission priorities. In this way, new technologies can help missions achieve political, not just military, objectives.

The implementation of new capabilities and technologies needs to be less ad hoc and more firmly anchored in the UN doctrinal framework. These innovative tools can provide opportunities for more informed decision-making in military, police, and civilian components. If used sensibly and sensitively, they offer an opportunity to create people-centered peacekeeping. However, if this is to be achieved, their use and benefits must be strategically communicated to host states and beneficiaries.

Notes

1. Here, I focus on developments in Mali and the DRC.
2. Interview with UN official, August 21, 2014. Ushahidi is a web-based reporting system that utilizes crowdsourced data to formulate visual map information of a crisis on a real-time basis. The data can be provided via text messages, e-mail, twitter, and web-forms. "Ushahidi which means 'testimony' in Swahili, was a website that was initially developed to map reports

of violence in Kenya after the post-election fallout at the beginning of 2008"
Ushahidi (2014).

3. While Sweden is not a NATO member, it has deployed troops as part of the
ISAF operation in Afghanistan and has arguably developed the same organizational culture.

REFERENCES

Abilova, Olga and Alexandra Novosseloff (2016) *Demystifying Intelligence in
UN Peace Operations: Toward an Organizational Doctrine.* New York:
International Peace Institute. Available at: https://www.ipinst.org/wp-content/
uploads/2016/07/1608_Demystifying-Intelligence.pdf. Accessed August
25, 2016.

Alberts, David S., John J. Garstka and Frederick P. Stein (2000) *Network Centric
Warfare: Developing and Leveraging Information Superiority.* Washington DC:
United States Department of Defense.

Barluet, Alain (2014) "Au Sahel, l'opération 'Barkhane' remplace 'Serval'," *Le
Figaro,* July 13, 2014. Available at: http://www.lefigaro.fr/international/
2014/07/13/01003-20140713ARTFIG00097-au-sahel-l-operation-
barkhane-remplace-serval.php. Accessed September 19, 2016.

BBC (2011) "Governments, IOC and UN hit by massive cyber-attack." August 3,
2011. Available at: http://www.bbc.com/news/technology-14387559.
Accessed April 27, 2016.

Borger, Julian (2015) "Arming Ukraine army may escalate conflict, west warned."
The Guardian. February 8, 2015. Available at: http://www.theguardian.com/
world/2015/feb/08/arming-ukraine-army-escalate-conflict-ocse.   Accessed
27 April 2016.

Convergne, Elodie and Michael R. Snyder (2015) "Making maps to make peace:
geospatial technology as a tool for UN peacekeeping," *International
Peacekeeping* 22 (5): pp. 565–586.

Crisismappers (2016) "CrisisMappers: The Humanitarian Technology Network."
Available at: http://crisismappers.net/. Accessed July 8, 2016.

defenceWeb (2016) "French UAVs exceed 15 000 flight hours in the Sahel,"
defenceWeb, March 14, 2016. Available at: http://www.uavexpertnews.com/
french-uavs-exceed-15-000-flight-hours-in-the-sahel/. Accessed September
19, 2016.

Dorn, A. Walter (2011). *Keeping Watch: Monitoring, Technology & Innovation in
UN Peace Operations.* Tokyo: United Nations University Press.

Dorn, A. Walter (2016) *Smart Peacekeeping: Toward Tech-Enabled UN Operations.*
New York: International Peace Institute. Available at: https://www.ipinst.
org/2016/07/smart-peacekeeping-tech-enabled. Accessed July 21, 2016.

Dorn, A. Walter and Christoph Semken (2015) "Blue Mission tracking: real-time location of UN peacekeepers," *International Peacekeeping* 22 (5): pp. 545–564.

Duffield, Mark (2013) *Disaster Resilience in the Network Age: Access-Denial and the Rise of Cyber-Humanitarianism.* Copenhagen: Danish Institute for International Studies.

German Federal Government (2017) "More soldiers for Mali," February 26, 2017. Available at: https://www.bundesregierung.de/Content/EN/Artikel/2017/01_en/2017-01-11-minusma-mali_en.html. Accessed February 7, 2017.

Gilman, Daniel (2014) "Unmanned aerial vehicles in humanitarian response," *OCHA Policy and Studies Series, June 2014, 10.* New York: OCHA.

Gilman, Daniel and Leith Baker (2014) *Humanitarianism in the Age of Cyber-warfare: Towards the Principled and Secure Use of Information in Humanitarian Emergencies.* New York: OCHA.

Gordon, Robert and Peter Loge (2015) "Strategic Communication: A Political and Operational Prerequisite for Successful Peace Operations," *Occasional Papers* No. 7, November 2015. Stockholm: International Forum for the Challenges of Peace Operations. Available at: http://www.challengesforum.org/en/Reports--Publications/CF/Occasional-Paper-No-7/?retUrl=/Templates/Public/Pages/PublicReportList.aspx?id%3D962%26epslanguage%3Den. Accessed July 8, 2016.

Harvard Humanitarian Initiative. *Disaster Relief 2.0: The Future of Information Sharing in Humanitarian Emergencies.* Washington, DC, and Newbury, UK: UN Foundation & Vodafone Foundation Technology Partnership, 2011.

Iacucci, Anahi A. (2013) "The conundrum of digital humanitarianism: when the crowd does harm," November 15, 2013. Available at: https://anahiayala.com/2013/11/15/the-conundrum-of-digital-humanitarianism-when-the-crowd-does-harm/. Accessed July 8, 2016.

IASC (2010) *IASC Guidelines: Common Operational Datasets (CODs) in Disaster Preparedness and Response.* Geneva: Inter-Agency Standing Committee.

Internet Society (2015) *Global Internet Society Report 2015.* Washington DC: Internet Society. Available at: http://www.internetsociety.org/globalinternetreport/assets/download/IS_web.pdf. Accessed June 16, 2016.

IRIN (2014) "NGOs against MONUSCO drones for humanitarian work." July 23, 2014. Available at: http://www.irinnews.org/report/100391/ngos-against-monusco-drones-for-humanitarian-work. Accessed April 27, 2016.

ITU (2015) "Key ICT indicators for developed and developing countries and the world (totals and penetration rates)." Available at: http://www.itu.int/en/ITU-D/Statistics/Pages/stat/default.aspx. Accessed April 27, 2016.

Karlsrud, John (2014) "Peacekeeping 4.0: Harnessing the Potential of Big Data, Social Media and Cyber Technology," in J.F. Kremer and B. Müller (eds.) Cyber Space and International Relations. Theory, Prospects and Challenges. Berlin: Springer, pp. 141–160.

Karlsrud, John (2017) "Towards UN counter-terrorism operations?," Third World Quarterly 38 (6): pp. 1215–1231. doi: https://doi.org/10.1080/014 36597.2016.1268907.

Karlsrud, John and Adam Smith (2015) "Europe's Return to UN Peacekeeping in Africa? Lessons-Learned from Mali," *Providing for Peacekeeping*, No. 10. New York: International Peace Institute.

Karlsrud, John and Arthur Mühlen-Schulte (2017) "Quasi-Professionals in the Organisation of Transnational Crisis Mapping," in L. Seabrooke and L.F. Henriksen (eds.) Professional Networks in Transnational Governance. Cambridge: Cambridge University Press.

Karlsrud, John and Kari M. Osland (2016) "Between self-interest and solidarity: Norway's return to UN peacekeeping?," *International Peacekeeping* 23 (5), pp. 1–20. DOI: 10.1080/13533312.2016.1235096.

Karlsrud, John and Frederik Rosén (2017) "Lifting the Fog of War? Opportunities and Challenges of Drones in UN Peace Operations," in Maria G. Jumbert and Kristin B. Sandvik (eds.), *The Good Drone*. Abingdon: Routledge: pp. 45–64.

Koops, Joachim A. and Giulia Tercovich (2016) "A European return to United Nations peacekeeping? Opportunities, challenges and ways ahead" *International Peacekeeping*, 23 (5), pp. 1–14. DOI: 10.1080/13533312.2016.1236430.

Lederer, Edith M. (2016) "Netherlands and Italy agree to split Security Council term," June 28, 2016. Available at: https://www.washingtonpost.com/world/europe/sweden-wins-seat-on-un-security-council-on-first-ballot/2016/06/28/53a306a0-3d4c-11e6-9e16-4cf01a41decb_story.html. Accessed July 1, 2016.

Lindboe, Morten and David Nordlie (2017) Intelligence in United Nations Peace Operations: A case study of the All Sources Information Fusion Unit in MINUSMA. Oslo: Norwegian Defence Research Establishment (FFI) & Norwegian Defence International Centre (NODEFIC).

The Netherlands Ministry of Defence (2016) "Mali". Available at: https://www.defensie.nl/english/topics/mali. Accessed July 1, 2016.

Norway Mission to the UN (2015) "Norway's priorities for the 70th UN General Assembly," September 21, 2015. Available at: http://www.norway-un.org/NorwayandUN/Norwegian-UN-Politcies/UNGA-Norwegian-priorities/#.V3Z0jeOO5Q4. Accessed July 1, 2016.

Novosseloff, Alexandra (2015) "Triangular Cooperation – Key to All," November 10, 2015. Available at: http://peaceoperationsreview.org/thematic-essays/triangular-cooperation-key-to-all/. Accessed on June 20, 2016.

OCHA (2012) *OCHA on Message: Humanitarian Principles*. Geneva: UN Office for the Coordination of Humanitarian Affairs. Available at: https://docs.unocha.org/sites/dms/Documents/OOM-humanitarianprinciples_eng_June12.pdf. Accessed July 8, 2016.

OCHA (2013) *Humanitarianism in the Network Age*. New York: OCHA.

Pawlak, Patryk and Andrea Ricci (eds.) (2014) *Crisis Rooms: Towards a Global Network?* Paris: EU Institute for Security Studies.

Raymond, Nathaniel, Caitlin Howarth, and Jonathan Hutson (2012) "Crisis Mapping Needs an Ethical Compass," *GlobalBrief*, February 6, 2012. Available at: http://globalbrief.ca/blog/2012/02/06/crisis-mapping-needs-an-ethical-compass/. Accessed 27 April 2016.

Rosén, Frederik and John Karlsrud (2014) "The MONUSCO UAVs: The implications for actions and omissions," *Conflict Trends* 2014 (4): 42–48.

Sandvik, Kristin B., Maria G. Jumbert, John Karlsrud, and Mareile Kaufman (2014) "Humanitarian Technology: A Critical Research Agenda," *International Review of the Red Cross*: pp. 1–24.

Satellite Sentinel Project (2016a) "Partner Organizations." Available at: http://satsentinel.org/our-story/partner-organizations#enough. Accessed July 8, 2016.

Satellite Sentinel Project (2016b) "Documenting the Crisis." Available at: http://www.satsentinel.org/our-story. Accessed July 8, 2016.

Schia, Niels N. (2016) "'Teach a person how to surf': Cyber security as development assistance." *NUPI Report no. 4.* Oslo: Norwegian Institute of International Affairs. Available at: https://brage.bibsys.no/xmlui/bitstream/id/415569/NUPI_Report_4_16_Nagelhus_Schia.pdf. Accessed June 20, 2016.

Sengupta, Somini (2014) "Unarmed Drones Aid U.N. Peacekeeping Missions in Africa." July 2, 2014. Available at: http://www.nytimes.com/2014/07/03/world/africa/unarmed-drones-aid-un-peacekeepers-in-africa.html?_r=1. Accessed April 27, 2016.

Swedish Armed Forces (2016) "Sweden in MINUSMA, Mali and the Sahel – a long-term commitment to peace and progress," June 20, 2016. Available at: http://www.forsvarsmakten.se/en/news/2016/06/sweden-in-minusma-mali-and-the-sahel-a-long-term-commitment-to-peace-and-progress/. Accessed July 1, 2016.

UN (2009) *Peacebuilding in the Immediate Aftermath of Conflict.* New York: United Nations.

UN (2013) *S/RES/2100*, April 25, 2013. New York: United Nations.

UN (2014a) *Plan Régional de Stabilisation de la Région de Gao.* Bamako: United Nations Multidimensional Integrated Stabilisation Mission in Mali. [Draft] On file with the author.

UN (2014b) *Standard Operating Procedure: Intelligence Cycle Management.* Bamako: United Nations Multidimensional Integrated Stabilisation Mission in Mali.

UN (2014c) *Guidelines on Understanding and Integrating Local Perceptions in UN Peacekeeping.* New York: United Nations.

UN (2014d) *S/RES/2164*, June 25, 2014. New York: United Nations.

UN (2015a) *A/70/95-S/2015/446. Report of the High-level Independent Panel on Peace Operations on Uniting our Strengths for Peace: Politics, Partnership and People* ("HIPPO Report"). New York: United Nations.

UN (2015b) *Performance Peacekeeping.* New York: United Nations. Available at: http://www.performancepeacekeeping.org/offline/download.pdf.   Accessed June 14, 2016.

UN (2016a) *Lessons Learned Report. Sources Information Fusion Unit and the MINUSMA Intelligence Architecture: Lessons for the Mission and a UN Policy Framework. Semi-final draft for USG Ladsous' review, 1 March 2016.* New York: United Nations. On file with the author.

UN (2016b) *S/RES/2301,* July 26, 2016. New York: United Nations.

UN Global Pulse (2016) "About." Available at: http://www.unglobalpulse.org/about-new. Accessed April 27, 2016.

UN Office of the Spokesperson (2013) "Highlights of the noon briefing. By Martin Nesirky, Spokesperson for Secretary-General Ban Ki-Moon. Tuesday, 3 December 2013," *United Nations.* Available at: http://www.un.org/sg/spokesperson/highlights/index.asp?HighD=12/3/2013&d_month=12&d_year=2013. Accessed January 8, 2016.

Ushahidi (2014) "About Ushahidi." Available at: https://www.ushahidi.com/about. Accessed April 27, 2016.

What's in Blue (2016) "Mandate Renewal of the UN Mission in the Central African Republic," July 25, 2016. Available at: http://www.whatsinblue.org/2016/07/renewal-of-the-central-african-republic-mission-mandate.php. Accessed August 25, 2016.

CHAPTER 4

UN Stabilization Operations, Violent Extremism, and Counter-Terrorism

Over the last two decades, "stabilization" operations have gradually emerged as a separate type of operations. The concept was first employed by NATO in Bosnia and Herzegovina from 1996 to 2004, and the UNSC introduced the term "stabilization" in the name of the UN mission to Haiti also in 2004. Since 2009, three more missions have had stabilization included in their mission names—MONUSCO in the DRC (2010), MINUSMA in Mali (2013), and MINUSCA in CAR (2014). In the same period, there has been an exponential growth in the use of the concept of "stabilization" in UNSC meetings (Curran and Holtom 2015).

Counter-terrorism has been high on the international agenda since the 9/11 attacks. There is a pervasive sense that terrorist groups have multiplied and changed their modi operandi to become a much greater threat to international peace and security. As noted in Chapter 2, fatalities caused by terrorism have increased rapidly over the last few years, from 3329 in 2000 to 32,685 in 2014 (IEP 2015: 2).

Conceptually, there has been a gradual shift from counter-terrorism to the less threatening-sounding concepts of "countering violent extremism" (CVE) and "preventing violent extremism" (PVE). These two concepts are currently in the process of being merged as "preventing and countering violent extremism" (PCVE). The re-conceptualization is intended to denote that there is a wider range of tools that could and should be used in tackling these threats—from hard security to governance and socio-economic tools dealing with the root causes of radicalization and disenfranchisement. However, the re-conceptualization as PCVE also makes

© The Author(s) 2018
J. Karlsrud, *The UN at War*,
https://doi.org/10.1007/978-3-319-62858-5_5

counter-terrorism more "palatable" in UN circles, easing the move from the margins to center stage.

In December 2015, the then UNSG Ban Ki-moon presented his *Plan of Action to Prevent Violent Extremism* (UN 2015b). In the plan, he outlined a prevention agenda, stressing that the UN needs to better understand the motivations for joining groups like the IS; to avoid using "terrorism" as a label to eliminate political opposition; and to deal with root causes by strengthening governance, respect for human rights, more accountable institutions, service delivery, and political participation (UN News Centre 2015).

Just a few months prior to this, the then US President Barack Obama chaired two summits during the UN General Assembly. The first was on peace operations, on September 28, and the following day on counter-terrorism. This showed the level of commitment of the USA to these topics, and the conviction that the UN is relevant for tackling these challenges. In this chapter, I analyze developments underway in the area of UN peace operations, and the implications of the growing interest in whether and how UN peace operations can take on counter-terrorism and countering and preventing violent extremism tasks.

At the summit on peacekeeping held during the 2015 General Assembly, the then UK Prime Minister David Cameron was among the state leaders citing terrorism (Mason 2015) as a motivating factor for contributing more troops, capabilities, and resources to UN peace operations (for a summary of pledges, see Global Peace Operations Review 2015). The US Mission to the UN cited the "jihadist insurgency" in Mali as an example of a challenge that the UN needed to be better equipped for tackling (Goldberg 2015). However, there is still disagreement on whether UN peace operations should be equipped for dealing with the threat of violent extremism and terrorism and should protect themselves and civilians, or whether operations should be given a stronger, more robust mandate to go in pursuit of these groups in a robust manner. When asked if the increased support to UN peace operations amounted to "outsourcing" the War on Terror to the UN, US officials emphasized that Washington prefers to label its approach as "burden-sharing," not "outsourcing" (anonymous US official cited in Anna and Hadjicostis 2015). On the other hand, the September 28, 2015, Presidential Memorandum on *United States Support to United Nations Peace Operations* stressed that the UN would not be able take on "more forceful military interventions that need to be carried out in non-permissive environments" (White House

2015: 2). However, using peace operations to deal with situations of counter-terrorism is one area where the veto powers of the Security Council may be able to agree (Gowan 2015a).

UN peace operations have traditionally been limited to situations where there is a peace to keep, but in recent years this principle has been balanced against the growing emphasis on the need to deploy peace operations to protect civilians, also when there is no peace to keep. This has meant a greater role for the use of force in UN peace operations, and the acceptance of a revised form of the impartiality principle. UN peacekeeping missions have become increasingly assertive, employing force at the tactical level to protect civilians—exemplified by the attack on rebels in eastern DRC on March 1, 2005, and the attack on gang members during Operation Iron Fist on August 15, 2005 (Rhoads 2016; Lynch 2005). Rhoads argues that a new assertive conception of impartiality has been established, where the use of force is deemed acceptable and presumed apolitical if employed to protect civilians (2016). The Capstone Doctrine for UN peacekeeping defined robust peacekeeping as "the use of force at the tactical level with the authorization of the Security Council and consent of the host nation and/or the main parties to the conflict" (UN 2008: 34). Today, as noted in the HIPPO Report, UN peace operations are often given a conflict management role (UN 2015a)—without sufficient political support for mediating a solution, or capabilities or troops sufficient to protect the mission or civilians under threat. *Opération Barkhane*, including the support given by MINUSMA, is part of a tendency where wars are increasingly fought away from the public view, and there seems to be increasing acceptance of using force to solve what are essentially political problems (Guéhenno 2015; Bode 2016). This tendency is combined with increasing assertiveness of mandates issued to UN peace operations, moving them from robust peacekeeping to peace enforcement.

This chapter examines the ongoing doctrinal discussions on stabilization and counter-terrorism in the context of UN peace operations. The HIPPO Report was quite explicit on both these points. It noted that the term "*stabilization* has been used "for a number of missions that support the extension or restoration of State authority, in at least one case during ongoing armed conflict"; further, that "[t]he term 'stabilization' has a wide range of interpretations, and the Panel believes the usage of that term by the United Nations requires clarification" (ibid.: 44). Concerning counter-terrorism, the report was even clearer: "United Nations troops should not undertake military counter-terrorism operations" and that UN peace operations "are not suited to engage in military counter-terrorism operations. They lack the specific equipment, intelligence, logistics, capabilities and specialized military preparation required, among other aspects" (ibid.: 12, 45). This chapter critically details the evolving understanding of what stabilization entails in UN operations. As part of this, it also examines the efforts of some parts of member states and the UN Secretariat to carve out a space for UN peace operations in counter-terrorism, as well as PCVE. I conclude that the UN neither is nor will be ready to fight terrorist groups—in principle or operationally—and that coalitions of the willing and regional organizations are best positioned to take on these tasks. Furthermore, the increasing focus on PCVE, with the attendant resources brought to the table, limits the space for more politically oriented approaches. That also risks marginalizing, politicizing, and securitizing the agendas of humanitarian action, peacebuilding, local governance, and development, and jeopardizes the preventive work of the UN system.

Stabilization in UN Peacekeeping

"Stabilization" as a concept was introduced to UN peacekeeping with the inclusion of "stabilization" in the name of the UN mission to Haiti in 2004. It continued a trend from NATO operations, starting with the operation in Bosnia in 1995—Stabilization Force (SFOR)—followed by a gradual development of the concept of stabilization during the NATO deployments to Kosovo, Iraq, and Afghanistan. US and NATO understandings of stabilization center on the use of force. Other tasks—such as strengthening the governance framework of a country, and pushing for security sector reform—are undertaken in order to create stability and secure the military and more kinetic parts of the mission spectrum. Under the "clear, hold, and build" credo of the US counter-insurgency strategy, developed under the leadership of General David Petraeus, force must be supported by other means ancillary and supportive to maintaining and sustaining peace once military has established control over an area (United States Dept. of the Army and United States Marine Corps 2007). Building on this, the 2011 US stabilization doctrine stressed the need to establish "a monopoly on the use of force by a single entity [...] normally to support a legitimate HN [Host Nation]" (Joint Chiefs of Staff (USA): xvi). The UK and other Western definitions have put more emphasis on the civilian dimension, but the central element of the use of force remains:

Stabilisation is one of the approaches used in situations of violent conflict which is designed to protect and promote legitimate political authority, using a combination of integrated civilian and military actions to reduce violence, re-establish security and prepare for longer-term recovery by building an enabling environment for structural stability. (UK Stabilisation Unit 2014)

Perhaps paradoxically, the development of the concept of stabilization was inspired by the "success" of UN peacekeeping operations in the late 1990s and early 2000s, under the banner of integrated missions. These missions "in some ways laid the conceptual and institutional groundwork for the next generation of stabilization that emerged following the terrorist attacks of 11 September 2001" (Barakat et al. 2010: 308). However, an important distinction between these two types of missions was the UN's insistence on the need for a peace to keep when deploying a mission, although the Security Council often failed to heed this in practice. NATO and Western countries, on the other hand, developed their concept with ongoing conflicts in mind, most often when confronting significant armed opposition and terrorist groups.

After the UN Stabilization Mission in Haiti (2004), "stabilization" featured in the names of the missions in the DRC (2010), Mali (2013), and CAR (2014). Including "stabilization" in the names of UN missions would appear to indicate a belief that force is a key element in solving conflict. Its inclusion stems particularly from the activism of the UNSC Permanent 3—France, the UK, and the USA (Curran and Holtom 2015), who have "uploaded" "their conceptualisations of stabilization into UN intervention frameworks" by serving as penholders and by including stabilization in the names and tasks of UN missions (ibid.: 1, see also Schia 2016). Although these three countries have slightly different understandings of what stabilization entails in practice—from the USA with its more military-centric understanding, to the UK putting more emphasis on civilian, police, and development tasks—the cumulative effect has been a growing belief in military approaches to solving conflicts in "failed" or fragile states, and the need to combine these military efforts with development and humanitarian action to shore up the military gains made (Fig. 4.1).

As indicated, the development of the stabilization doctrine has followed the trajectory of Western interventions since the end of the Cold War, starting with the SFOR mission in Bosnia and Herzegovina, and gaining

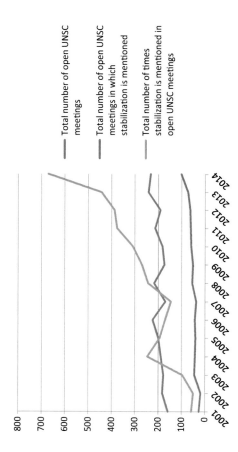

Fig. 4.1 Frequency of the use of the word "stabilization" in UN Security Council open meetings, 2001–2014. (The figure has been developed on the basis of research conducted by Curran and Holtom (2015). The data exclude instances where "stabilization" has referred to the EU "stabilization and association process," and when "stabilization" appears in the title of the meeting.)

strength from the continued efforts to try to produce an effective strategy for winning against Islamist groups in Iraq and the Taliban and al-Qaeda in Afghanistan. With Barack Obama as US President, a massive offensive was started in Afghanistan—to "clear" and "hold"—and the USA and the UK developed large pools of civilian experts who were to "build" in the space created by the security guarantee provided by these troops. Taken together, this formed a "comprehensive approach" to statebuilding or "armed nation building" (Cordesman 2009), accompanied by significant efforts going into the doctrinal development of this approach from NATO, member states, think-tanks, and academia.

Friis (2010: 58) has argued that there are areas of convergence between US counter-insurgency doctrine and UN peacekeeping operations, but with some important differences—for instance, both include protection of civilians as a task, but only the UN sees this as an end in itself. NATO's comprehensive approach can be seen as the equivalent of the UN's integrated approach, but some significant differences remain (for a comparison, see, e.g., de Coning and Friis 2011). NATO is a military organization of member states, and this has led to a military- and state-centric understanding of conflict management and peacebuilding, when transferred to the UN context in the shape of the concept of "stabilization." It has thus contributed to securitizing UN peace operations after the period of Boutros-Ghali's *Agenda for Peace* reports and the doctrinal development for UN peacekeeping operations since the turn of the century, where there was more emphasis on the civilian and peacebuilding dimensions (Boutros-Ghali 1992, 1995; UN 2000, 2008). This is a key point made by the HIPPO Report, which recommends that the UN should avoid using the term "stabilization" until the concept is further clarified (UN 2015a: 30).

Stabilization in Practice

In practice, it is far from clear what stabilization entails in UN missions. In MONUSCO, at least two possible interpretations can be discerned. The first conceptualization of stabilization followed the 2008 Goma Accords, in the International Security and Stabilization Support Strategy (ISSSS). According to Hugo de Vries (2015), this strategy built on the principles of counter-insurgency operations, of "clearing, holding and building" to restore the state and build its capacities for conflict management. MONUC would support military government operations to fight armed groups, and to gain the support of local populations. The military campaign was followed by road construction, to create axes of state authority where the police, judiciary, and civil administration were established. MONUC constructed buildings to house these institutions, provided equipment and training. To achieve a peace dividend, the new presence of state authorities was accompanied by various early recovery and development programs in the fields of socio-economic recovery, health, sanitation, and education. The results of these stabilization efforts were unclear, however. The construction of roads and deployment of state administration and security officials actually added to the drivers of conflict, as these officials often received no salaries and had to make their own income, increasing the formal and informal tax burdens on local populations and competing with traditional authorities and forms of security provision (de Vries 2015).

A second understanding of "stabilization" can also be discerned. "Stabilization" was formally included in the mission name 2010, when the mission was renamed from MONUC to MONUSCO, at a time when the country was enjoying a period of relative stability. The renaming came after government pressure on the mission to scale down its presence and prepare for exit; and, at this particular stage, stabilization was understood as efforts toward peacebuilding and peace consolidation. Conceptually, there was no clear link between the inclusion of "stabilization" in the name of the mission and the ISSSS strategy. These understandings were actually quite far apart on the conflict spectrum—the ISSSS-version being in the "clear, hold, and build" end, while "stabilization" in the mission name was at the other end in the "peacebuilding" part of the spectrum.

The ISSS strategy was revised in the period 2012–2015, reorienting from a top–down supply-driven approach geared toward the extension of state authority, to a more consultative and bottom–up approach geared toward strengthening state–society relations, using community dialogue as a central tool (ibid.). In the process, the mission, acknowledging that there was a wide range of interpretations of what stabilization entailed in practice, provided the following definition:

> Stabilization is an integrated, holistic but targeted process of enabling state and society to build mutual accountability and capacity to address and mitigate existing or emerging drivers of violent conflict, creating the conditions for improved governance and longer term development. (MONUSCO 2013: 19)

The ISSSS has not been the only stabilization-labeled strategy in the mission. Following the failure with the loss of Goma to the M23 in 2012, the mission was reinforced with a peace enforcement mandate and a FIB composed of troops from Malawi, South Africa, and Tanzania in 2013 (UN 2013a). The FIB mainly supported the Congolese troops, but also took active part in combat, using gunship helicopters and sniper fire (News24 2013). However, after the M23 was defeated, at least militarily, FIB member states were reluctant to use the FIB in fighting the FDLR, which was composed of Hutus of the former Interahamwe group in Rwanda, responsible for the genocide against the Tutsis in 1994. This showed the limits of using regional troops for peace enforcement—they took orders only as long as these served the national interests of the sending countries.

Concurrently, the mission came to include a Community Violence Reduction (CVR) program modeled on the experience with youth gangs from Haiti; the construction of buildings for state authority was modeled on a Justice and Security Hubs program from Liberia; and finally, the mission developed an Islands of Stability concept for using quick-impact projects to support the military efforts of the Congolese army, focusing on urban centers (Vogel 2014; Barrera 2015; de Vries 2016).

What does this conceptual confusion say about the status of "stabilization" in UN peace operations today? For the military, stabilization is a doctrine that has been elaborated over the past two decades; in its current iterations, it generally entails counter-insurgency and counter-terrorism operations, complemented with a range of civilian activities for securing military progress on the ground. The ISSSS and Islands of Stability strategies basically conform to this understanding, but with slightly stronger emphasis on deployment of the civilian pillar, including police, judiciary, and other state officials.

In MONUSCO, stabilization seems to have become a catch-all term used for discursively engaging and winning the support of TCCs (the military understanding of stabilization), the host government (providing buildings, equipment, and training), and donors (following their comprehensive understanding of stabilization). The ISSSS, the CVR program, the Justice and Security Hubs, and the Islands of Stability could just as well have been labeled "early peacebuilding" or "early recovery," but this would not have exerted the same pull on donor funding. Seen from this angle, the proliferating use of "stabilization" has been quite successful—the mission has been able to raise significant funding for the various phases of the

ISSSS and other strategies (de Vries 2016). However, most of the key donors—like the Netherlands, the UK, and the USA—bring with them their own understanding from years in Afghanistan, and "stabilization" is a concept they can relate to. This also explains the difficulty of reaching consensus on what "stabilization" entails in UN peace operations—it is not only a concept but also an instrument to attract donor funding for a range of activities that are only loosely connected, and without a unifying theory of change with a set of complementary tasks (see also Barakat et al. 2010). Put simply, the term "stabilization" now denotes military-led state-centric counter-insurgency operations as well as bottom–up peacebuilding—two types of activity almost impossible to combine in doctrine or in practice in UN peace operations. This inherent tension is evident when we turn to MINUSMA. The regional stabilization strategies of MINUSMA focus on the building peace from the bottom and up, while the military part of the mission involves sharing information with the French counter-terrorism operation *Barkhane*, as previously mentioned.

Taken together, these operations show a development of a more robust understanding of what stabilization entails in UN peace operations—particularly with the inclusion of the Force Intervention Brigade in MONUSCO and the deployment of MINUSMA in an ongoing conflict with armed and terrorist groups in Mali. These understandings of stabilization move away from the earlier under robust peacekeeping, toward what was defined as peace enforcement in the 2008 UN peacekeeping Capstone Doctrine: "By contrast, peace enforcement does not require the consent of the main parties and may involve the use of military force at the strategic or international level" (UN 2008: 34).

A Changing Context for UN Peace Operations?

As noted, 2015 was a big year for UN peace operations, with the release of the HIPPO Report, and the US-sponsored summit on peacekeeping during the UN General Assembly. Arguably, the "new" threats of violent extremism and organized crime, combined with record-high numbers of refugees and IDPs and growing instability in several parts of the world, served to propel discussions of change at the UN—particularly regarding its peace operations. Boko Haram, IS, al-Shabaab, and other extremist groups in Libya, Mali, Syria, and Yemen have challenged policy-makers and the multilateral system, which is poorly equipped to respond to these violent and multifaceted challenges. These groups add to the political complexity and strengthen the intractable nature of conflict in these countries. It is possible to talk with some groups, whereas others have no interest in negotiating with the UN.

Since 2013, the UNSC has been giving increasingly expansive and robust mandates to UN peace operations. MONUSCO was in 2013 instructed to "neutralize" armed groups (UN 2013a: 7), making it a party to the conflict, and the missions authorized in 2013 and 2014 in Mali and CAR were given mandates to "stabilize" and "extend state authority," which in effect would entail confronting rebel and extremist groups in Mali as well as sectarian groups in CAR. At UN Headquarters, staff only half-jokingly say that the organization has moved from being in the crossfire into the crosshairs, attacked no longer for where they are, but for who they are. The increasing attacks on blue helmets in Darfur, the DRC, and Mali back up this perception.

Parallel deployment with counter-terrorism operations open up a host of challenges, as the experiences from Mali have shown. It is more than likely that the UN, equipped with a mandate to extend state authority to northern Mali, is seen as partial by local communities. The mission has paid a high price for its deployment so far—70 military peacekeepers have been killed in "malicious acts" since deployment in April 2013 (UN 2016a, as of October 30, 2016). It is difficult to draw the line as to when the pursuit of armed groups that are behind the attacks turns into a counter-terrorism operation, particularly when the Security Council has explicitly asked

> MINUSMA to move to a more proactive and robust posture […] to support the cantonment, disarmament, demobilization and reintegration of armed groups […] and to take robust and active steps to protect civilians, including through active and effective patrolling in areas where civilians are at risk, and to prevent the return of armed elements to those areas, engaging in direct operations pursuant only to serious and credible threats". (UN 2016b: 7–8)

COUNTER-TERRORISM AND PCVE AT THE UN SECRETARIAT

Inside the UN Secretariat, a growing number of bodies deal with counter-terrorism and PCVE, and more are joining the field. The UNSC Counter-Terrorism Committee, established by the Security Council in the immediate aftermath of the 9/11 attacks (UN 2001), provides guidelines, suggestions for codes and standards, and facilitates technical assistance to member states in fighting financial support to terrorism (UN 2016c).

In 2005, the SG established a Counter-Terrorism Implementation Task Force (CTITF) (UN 2016d), endorsed by member states of the UN General Assembly through the Global Counter-Terrorism Strategy adopted in 2006 (UN 2006). Within CTITF, the UN Counter-Terrorism Centre (UNCCT) has been established (UN 2016e). The Centre received a donation from Saudi Arabia of USD 100 million in 2014 to strengthen its "tools, technologies and methods to confront and eliminate the threat of terrorism" (UNCCT 2015). It is also partially funded by Germany, the UK, and the USA. According to one UN official, the CTITF/UNCCT in 2015 accounted for roughly half of the operational budget of the DPA. It has reached out to the UN mission in Mali, UN agencies, and others to develop projects, with more than 30 projects at the beginning of 2016 (UN 2016f).

The Office of Rule of Law and Security Institutions (OROLSI) within the UN DPKO has shown keen interest in expanding its activities to help countries prevent and counter violent extremism, also those not hosting active peace operations. A 2015 report by the United Nations University indicated that the UN may need to adapt its guidelines for DDR in order to take on new tasks such as dealing with foreign terrorist fighters, conducting terrorist rehabilitation, and involuntary detention (Cockayne and O'Neil 2015). It stated that UN peace operations are already moving in such a direction, and acknowledged that this is in contradiction to the aforementioned peacekeeping principles. The report also noted that such contradictions present "a host of safety, legal, ethical, operational, and reputational risks to the UN, its staff, Member States, and donors" (ibid.: 35). Despite this, the report recommended stronger UN engagement in these areas. Overall, the unclear division of labor between the UN Secretariat and other UN departments and agencies, combined with the risk of supply-driven programming, should be recognized as a matter of great concern.

UN Peace Operations, Terrorism, and Violent Extremism

The IS, the al-Shabaab, and several other terrorist groups today are qualitatively different from many earlier terrorist groups because what they are seeking is not necessarily recognition from the international community, or the control of a particular state territory. Instead, the IS wants to establish a new caliphate, irrespective of existing borders, and is willing to use abominable levels of violence to achieve these objectives. A further key characteristic is the use of modern tools of communication and technology for intimidation, communication of the atrocities committed, and recruitment and radicalization of new followers. Furthermore, these groups present clear challenges to their enemies, as they are often able to provide a level of security, jobs, and service provision that local populations have not enjoyed from the central state authority. International interventions may even further deteriorate the situation of local populations, by not being able to provide peace dividends in the wake of their military engagements—as in Afghanistan, Mali, Nigeria, or Somalia, to name but a few.

Terrorism and violent extremism are part of the same spectrum. Both are willing to use violence to pursue political goals, but to different degrees. When the objective is to limit, counter, and prevent violent extremism, it is vital not to further alienate those who may have legitimate governance and development concerns but are not yet fully radicalized. Characterizing all groups and individuals as terrorists, irrespective of where they are located on the spectrum, risks further radicalization and strengthening of the most extreme groups. It also reinforces the trend toward securitization of the issue, looking solely for military solutions, and narrowing the options available.

It is important to nuance the understanding of and strategies for dealing with violent extremism. Violent extremism can stem from a whole range of root causes—from injustice, marginalization, under-development, governance structures undermined by corruption, lack of responsive governments and social cohesion, weak and limited state–society relations, to externally supported religious radicalization (see, e.g., Wolffe and Moorhead 2014; IEP 2015; Glazzard and Zeuthen 2016). Awareness of this multitude of root causes of violent extremism must be reflected in the register of tools and approaches of member states and global and regional institutions seeking to deal with these challenges.

The UN is a state-centric organization. However, in many of the states it seeks to support, the government enjoys weak legitimacy among much of the population. Material and ideational resources are concentrated among the elites, and access to education and other basic services is limited to urban centers, leaving ample room for radicalization and recruitment to violent extremist groups. Adding to this vulnerable starting point, weak governments often pursue militarized solutions to the challenges they face, thereby fueling and perpetuating the problems. Precisely because it is a state-centric organization, the UN risks following the same pattern in supporting member states in the fight against violent extremism and terrorism.

In considering the roles and responsibilities that UN peace operations have and should have in the future, we first need to see where UN peace operations feature among the means available in the UN toolbox, examine the relevant guidance communicated by member states through the General Assembly and the Security Council, and finally how the UN has chosen to operationalize this guidance. The UN Global Counter-Terrorism Strategy, adopted by the General Assembly in 2006, had four pillars:

I. tackling conditions conducive to terrorism;
II. preventing and combating terrorism;
III. building national capacity to combat terrorism and to strengthen the role of the UN system in that regard;
IV. ensuring respect for human rights for all and the rule of law while countering terrorism. (UN 2006)

In the action plan, former SG Ban Ki-moon lamented the fact that so far there has been "a strong emphasis on the implementation of measures under pillar II of the Global Strategy, while pillars I and IV have often been overlooked" (UN 2015b: 3).

In pillar II, we find counter-terrorism operations. Currently, the UN is not in principle or operationally set up to fight terrorist groups by force. The UN should seek to maintain its impartiality also when there is a UN peace operation on the ground. And operationally, the HIPPO Report stated that "UN peacekeeping missions, due to their composition and character, are not suited to engage in military counter-terrorism operations" (UN 2015a: 31). Unfortunately, that statement might be interpreted as indicating that *if* UN peace operations were given other and more robust capabilities and stronger mandates, they might be able to take on such operations.

If the UNSC continues to deploy UN peacekeeping operations to countries like Mali, the UN must be equipped to prevent attacks against itself and the local population, if necessary by preventive action. In practice, that means confronting violent extremists and terrorists—moving UN peace operations across the line drawn by the HIPPO Report. For MINUSMA, this has already become reality. Future missions may be deployed to Libya, Somalia, Syria, and Yemen, where similar environments and threats can be expected.

A House Divided Against Itself?

As noted in the HIPPO Report, "there is a clear sense of a widening gap between what is being asked of [UN] peace operations today and what they are able to deliver" (UN 2015a: 9). Inside UN DPKO, some are arguing that the UN needs to adapt to maintain its "market share" of peace operations, facing increasing competition from regional organizations, coalitions of the willing and bilateral deployments such as the MNJTF fighting Boko Haram. The alternative may be a decline in UN peace operations over the next few years. Some believe that the UN has the greatest competence, has been in the peacekeeping business the longest, and should not be frightened by the challenges and uncertainties on the ground: now it should rather adapt and become relevant to changing challenges on the ground, rather than being limited by what are perceived as outdated principles.

This stands in stark contrast to the conclusions of the HIPPO panel, which drew the line against UN peace operations engaging in counter-terrorism operations. The HIPPO Report argued that UN peace operations were veering from peacekeeping toward conflict management, and that they "lack the specific equipment, intelligence, logistics, capabilities and specialized military preparation required" for dealing with violent extremists (UN 2015a: 45). The report emphasized that when deployed in parallel with a counter-terrorism operation, "[t]he UN must in these situations maintain a strict adherence to its impartial commitment to the respect for human rights. When such non-UN forces depart, the UN should not be called upon to assume residual tasks beyond its capability" (ibid.: 46). Also others have questioned whether UN peace operations are the right tool for counter-terrorism situations, particularly when not supported by a strong political mandate (Atwood 2015; Karlsrud 2016a). Discussions in the Special Committee on Peacekeeping Operations (C-34) in March 2016 ended with the paragraph on counter-terrorism being omitted altogether.

The UN DPKO is today a house divided between those who want UN peace operations to "evolve" and be "relevant" and those who think that such a development may undermine the legitimacy of UN peace operations. Those diverging opinions have created a "massive rift in DPKO" (interview with UN official, September 29, 2015). But the question remains: is the UN in places like Mali mandated to deal with conflicts that go against the principles of the organization, and can the UN's one-sided engagement in these conflicts undermine the long-term support and legitimacy of UN peacekeeping as a tool to help countries emerging from conflict?

Engaging with Terrorists and Violent Extremists

Alvaro de Soto, the former UN Special Envoy to the Middle East, resigned from his post in 2007 because he was not allowed to engage with Hamas, an elected government in Palestine, and with Syria, a member state of the UN. Because of the limitations that were placed on his role as a Special Envoy, he condemned the UN and the SG for limiting the space to engage with everybody, also those considered "beyond the pale" (de Soto 2007). He warned that the UN was giving in to external pressure to not talk to groups labeled as "terrorists", and that this would "seriously weaken our hand as a peacemaking tool" (ibid.: 34). Labeling political actors and rebel groups as terrorists is a well-known strategy for marginalizing and limiting the influence of groups competing with the incumbents for power. The UN has over the course of many years carved out a space for engaging with all actors, also those considered beyond the pale. If the UN is forced to limit its engagement to those that have been accepted by the host state or strong powers like the USA, this will weaken the ability of the UN to broker conflict and maintain peace and security.

In parallel, the period starting with the invasion in Afghanistan following the 9/11 attacks has been marked by a growing belief in the use of military force to solve conflict, limiting the space for dialogue, political engagement, and long-term solutions. The results have been dismal, considering the fall-out from Western engagements in Afghanistan, Iraq, and Libya. In Afghanistan, Kai Eide stepped down from his post as Special Representative of the Secretary-General (SRSG) for the UN operation UNAMA, after admitting to have initiated contacts with the Taliban (Doucet 2010), in accordance with his mandate, but challenging key veto powers like Russia, the UK and the USA on the issue (Karlsrud 2013). The fact that the UNSC had set up a list of persons labeled as terrorists "made it operationally more complicated and sensitive to initiate contacts with Taliban members" (Eide cited in Karlsrud 2016b: 55). This is but one example of how conflicts have been securitized and militarized during the last decade, with terms like "counter-insurgency" and "counter-terrorism" replacing more political approaches to conflict solution (Arnault 2015), and efforts to understand and deal with root causes.

The HIPPO Report emphasized the primacy of politics, and argued for scaling up the engagement of the UN to address root causes, supporting an inclusive political dialogue in countries where there is no peace to keep. However, the line drawn against counter-terrorism by the HIPPO Report seems to be fast fading under the pressure of increased engagement in the areas of PCVE and counter-terrorism. Solutions are often supply-driven, more concerned with what a particular organization can offer, than what the needs are on the ground. UN peace operations may not be the best placed to deal with the complex root causes that fuel recruitment to extremist groups, and should coordinate its actions with other multilateral, bilateral, and NGO development actors who may be better placed and suited to undertake these tasks. However, the increased attention and resources to PCVE and counter-terrorism is creating a momentum of its own, and risks politicizing, securitizing, and marginalizing the humanitarian action, peacebuilding, local governance, and development agendas. A concept note on the role of UN peacekeeping in countering and preventing violent extremism circulated by the UN in 2016 noted that "little empirical evidence exists on the success and failures of past or ongoing programming under the PVE rubric, making the judgment on approaches that would most suit peacekeeping contexts difficult" (UN 2016g: 1). Furthermore, it asserted that engaging in government-driven CVE "would be sending the signal that it [UN peace operation] supports one side in a conflict" (ibid.).

When the then SG Ban Ki-moon presented his *Plan of Action to Prevent Violent Extremism* in late 2015, he emphasized the preventative pillar (UN 2015b). While this is a positive sign, there is still a risk of supply-driven programming and relabeling existing programs, with the result that current development and peacebuilding work on facilitating consultation, addressing root causes, strengthening service delivery, justice and the rule of law may be rebranded as "countering and preventing violent extremism," in order to access new funding streams. The UNDP, for instance, has years of experience in working in this area under banner of "community violence reduction" (UNDP 2016). The above-mentioned concept note on PCVE also highlighted the risk of subsuming and relabeling existing peacebuilding activities under a PCVE rubric, as this would have the "potential to skew the focus of early peacebuilding efforts away from a balanced analysis of the causes of conflict towards actions that could be ticked off as contributing to the defeat of violent extremism" (UN 2016g: 2).

UN STABILIZATION AND COUNTER-TERRORISM MISSIONS?

There are no easy answers to the challenges that some of today's—and most of tomorrow's—peace operation theatres will bring. For instance, how should the burden-sharing among the UN, regional organizations, coalitions of the willing, and national interventions be organized? Part of the solution must be to clearly delineate what UN peace operations can and cannot do. The HIPPO Report and the follow-up report from the SG both drew the line against counter-terrorism operations. The 2015 US presidential memorandum, *United States Support to United Nations Peace Operations,* argued that although UN peace operations in "select and exceptional cases" can be tasked to "conduct offensive military operations against armed groups that act as spoilers outside of a peace process," it added that UN "peace operations cannot substitute for diplomatic solutions to end a war, nor for more forceful military interventions that need to be carried out in non-permissive environments by individual states or coalitions that possess the will and capacity to do so" (White House 2015: 2). The memorandum indicated that UN peace operations could "replace national or coalition military forces in operations once an area has transitioned from an immediate crisis to a more permissive environment" (ibid.). It did not seem to support the kind of co-deployment of a counter-terrorism force and a UN peace operation that we see in Mali.

The HIPPO panel advised that UN peace operations should be able to detect, mitigate, and defend itself against violent extremism and terrorist threats. Theoretically, in some cases it *may* be possible to align impartiality with limited offensive measures against transnational terrorist groups, if these are seen as externally driven and motivated, and not representing the local population. However, terrorist groups are entwined in illicit economic activities and organized crime that tend to involve local and national elites, making the issue more complex as well as political.

The HIPPO panel was opposed to UN involvement in counter-terrorism, but it also requested further clarification on the use of the concept of "stabilization" in UN peace operations. As we have seen, there are divergent understandings of this term among member states and the UN, ranging from peace enforcement to peacebuilding efforts. What future role should the UN have in Iraq, Libya, Syria, and Yemen? If the UNSC is not able or willing to outsource peace enforcement missions in these countries to other organizations, new options and modi operandi could be considered. Several authors have argued that, for this reason, the UN should consider conceptualizing UN stabilization missions, equipped with principles and tools for better dealing with such threats and mission environments (Boutellis 2015; Karlsrud 2016a; de Coning et al. 2017). As there is increasing pressure to move the UN in this direction, it can be useful to sketch out the intended and unintended consequences of such a development.

Stabilization missions would be deployed to support the government in stabilizing a territory, if necessary by force. They would have to be able to conduct offensive operations against armed and terrorist groups. In a previous article (Karlsrud 2015), I noted that the UN was quite literally "going green" in Mali: troop-contributing countries have resisted painting their vehicles and helicopters white, or simply have not cared to do so. In my view, the UN blue helmets and white vehicles should be preserved as tool that signify impartiality, consent, and limited use of force. By contrast, if a stabilization force were to be set up, it should not use blue helmets and white vehicles, so as to demarcate itself from traditional UN peacekeeping missions. Stabilization missions could in theory be mandated with counter-terrorism tasks for limited durations. Such operations would have a very limited programmatic/civilian component, as also the HIPPO Report recommended for UN peace operations in a conflict management situation where there is no peace to keep.

A new category of *UN stabilization operations* would have to be clearly delineated from other UN peace operations. It could be allowed to engage in offensive operations for limited durations, but the focus should be more on long-term stability. Because such operations would be seen as partial to the government of the day, they would not necessarily be mandated to mediate between the parties. In developing a doctrine for UN stabilization operations, care must be taken to consider the implications of an offensive posture for the routine substantive tasks, and limiting these accordingly, in line with the recommendations of the HIPPO Report.

However, while UN stabilization missions are possible to contemplate at least in theory, and may provide a level of legitimacy and funding, several other aspects should also be taken into account. Participants in these missions are likely to be coalitions of the willing, but under a UN banner. There are strings attached to funding provided through the UN, as the AU is increasingly coming to realize (see next chapter). Coalitions of the willing deploying as UN stabilization operations would thus be encumbered with several new sets of UN accountability and human rights reporting mechanisms, as well as management and procurement rules, and it is unlikely that these actors would accept all the layers of accountability and management red tape. Two current missions, the French *Barkhane* mission in Mali (Ministère de la Défense 2016) and the Global Coalition to Counter ISIL (U.S. Department of State 2016), are less burdened by these forms of accountability, or by having to develop and relate to complicated UN rules for contracting and management, or slowing down deployment, construction of new bases and logistics in the field, among a host of other issues. As to the pragmatic challenges, the question for member states will be whether there are sufficient incentives for them to undertake these tasks under a UN heading, or whether they should participate in a coalition of the willing outside the UN framework. Here, it will be difficult to have it both ways—on the one side, UN stabilization missions would give more legitimacy and spread the costs of counter-terrorism interventions, but the accountability and management hurdles are likely to be too high for such missions to become reality.

UN STABILIZATION MISSIONS OR INCREASED BURDEN-SHARING?

How will the UN mission in Mali fare? The mission is already among the deadliest in UN peacekeeping history. Its troops in Tessalit in northern Mali have been isolated, and have had to survive on minimum rations of water and food, poorly protected against IEDs and ambushes. As a result, they and other troops in Mali have been bunkerized to a large degree, and the same goes for most of its civilian staff in these areas. It is telling that the ISR companies feeding the ASIFU with information only have been deployed to Gao and Timbuktu, and not to northern Mali where the need perhaps is the greatest. Western troops are unwilling to be deployed for longer periods in these areas, as they consider the force protection to be insufficient. This raises the question of whether the UN is, or can be, equipped to deal with asymmetric threats in areas such as northern Mali, in the middle of the Sahara. The combination of poorly equipped troops, weak or non-existing tactical intelligence, intermittent logistical support and little to no trust in the local population means that the chances of success are slim without a political dialogue that can be inclusive and decentralize power, improve security, create jobs, and provide services. The UN is seen as a party to the conflict, supporting the government. It is thus more than surprising that Mali seems to be the model for possible future UN peacekeeping operations in Libya, Yemen, and Somalia.

Failure in Mali will mean loss of UN legitimacy as well as loss of a central measure for dealing with issues of global peace and security. The UN is still a relatively young organization, and its tools for managing international peace and security have been developed gradually, based on consensus among the permanent five members of the Security Council, with buy-in from other member states. This fledgling consensus may be shattered if UN peace operations are used to promote the objectives of the USA and other Western member states.

UN peace operations are operating in increasingly difficult theatres, facing the threats of violent extremism and transnational terrorist networks. This is partly because the Security Council has called for deployment of missions long before the conditions were ripe (as in Mali), and partly because of structural developments in technology and communications that have made violent extremists and terrorists far more interconnected and media-savvy. If it is to continue operations in difficult and at times hostile environments, the UN will have to improve at all levels, also in cases when it has not been explicitly requested to undertake counter-terrorism tasks: "The UN may not undertake overt counter-terrorism missions in the near future, but it will almost certainly have to contain and mitigate threats from extremist groups to the communities it defends, as well as its own forces" (Gowan 2015b: 7).

It seems likely that the UN will continue to be deployed in parallel with regional organizations that have a counter-terrorism mandate—and here we should note the security, reputational, and legitimacy risks entailed in such parallel deployments (Karlsrud 2017). The UN will need to mitigate increasing security risks by limiting its engagement in substantive tasks where it is in parallel deployment with a counter-terrorism operation; it must intensify its efforts to establish a functioning and integrated intelligence concept for UN missions; and strengthen its conflict prevention agenda, with particular emphasis on engagement with local marginalized populations at risk of radicalization. As borders are only lines in the sand, inter-mission cooperation must be intensified, with regular sharing of information, analysis, and capabilities. Regional strategies like the UN Integrated Strategy for Sahel should be fully funded by donors (UN 2013b).

As similar ongoing operations have been shouldered by the AU and sub-regional organizations on the African continent, and with likely future operations in Libya, Syria, and Yemen, it may be advisable to mandate such operations to coalitions of the willing. This would give the lead regional organization/group of states the space to decide on a range of issues that might be more constrained in a UN setting. Such missions should be sequenced, so as not to further undermine traditional UN peace operations. Coalitions of the willing, and in some instances regional organizations, will remain the only options with the requisite political will, capabilities, rapid deployment, doctrines, and staying power to conduct counter-terrorism operations, furnished with a UN mandate. However, with a major figure like former CIA Director John Brennan declaring that "a military solution is just impossible" in countries like Libya, Syria, Iraq, and Yemen (*Daily Mail* 2015), it is clear that also counter-terrorism operations will need to be paralleled with a long-term political strategy, if they are to enjoy any chance of success.

The HIPPO panel recommended that the UN should use the full spectrum of its operations more flexibly to respond to changing needs on the ground. In many instances, SPMs combined with strong mediation, inter-community dialogue, rule of law, and governance components addressing state–society relations from the bottom up could effectively address challenges in fragile states before they erupt (see also Johnstone 2016). However, the way SPMs are financed, combined with sensitivities about sovereignty and the wish to be seen as doing something, will keep larger-scale state-centric peacekeeping operations as the preferred choice of the Security Council.

Achieving balance and burden-sharing between the UN and other actors is more important than ever. I have argued that there are principled as well as operational reasons why the UN should not conduct counter-terrorism, and that the UN should carefully consider the implications of bringing significant parts of its core business under a PCVE umbrella. In broad terms, the limits of the UN also converge with the disincentives for member states and regional actors for conducting counter-terrorism operations under a UN banner.

References

Anna, Cara and Menelaos Hadjicostis (2015) "As UN peacekeeping veers toward counterterror, US steps in," Yahoo! News, September 26, 2015. Available at: https://www.yahoo.com/news/un-peacekeeping-veers-toward-counterterror-us-steps-145304737.html?ref=gs. Accessed September 6, 2016.

Arnault, Jean (2015) "A background to the report of the high-level panel on peace operations," *Global Peace Operations Review*. Available at: http://peaceoperationsreview.org/thematic-essays/a-background-to-the-repoi level-panel-on-peace-operations/. Accessed January 8, 2016.

Atwood, Richard (2015) "Violent extremism and crisis International Crisis Group, June 4, 2015. Available at: https: com/news/un-peacekeeping-veers-toward-counterterror-us-steps-145304737.html?ref=gs. Accessed June 30, 2016.

Barakat, Sultan, Seán Deely, and Steven A. Zyck (2010) "'A tradition of forgetting': stabilization and humanitarian action in historical perspective," *Disasters,* 34 (3): pp. 297–319. DOI: 10.1111/j.1467-7717.2010.01207.x.

Barrera, Alberto (2015) "The Congo trap: MONUSCO islands of stability in the sea of instability," *Stability: International Journal of Security & Development,* 4 (1): pp. 1–16. doi: 10.5334/sta.gn.

Bode, Ingvild (2016) "How the world's interventions in Syria have normalised the use of force," *The Conversation,* February 17, 2016. Available at: https://the-conversation.com/how-the-worlds-interventions-in-syria-have-normalised-the-use-of-force-54505. Accessed 27 February 2016.

Boutellis, Arthur (2015) "Can the UN stabilize Mali? Towards a UN stabilization doctrine?," *Stability* 4 (1): pp. 1–16.

Boutros-Ghali, Boutros (1992) *An agenda for peace: preventive diplomacy, peace-making, and peace-keeping: report of the Secretary-General pursuant to the statement adopted by the summit meeting of the Security Council on 31 January 1992.* New York: United Nations.

Boutros-Ghali, Boutros (1995) *A/RES/51/242: Supplement to An Agenda for Peace.* New York: United Nations.

Cockayne, James and Siobhan O'Neil (eds.) (2015) *UN DDR in an Era of Violent Extremism: Is It Fit for Purpose?* Tokyo: United Nations University.

de Coning, Cedric and Karsten Friis (2011) "Coherence and coordination: the limits of the comprehensive approach," *Journal of International Peacekeeping,* 15 (1–2): pp. 43–56.

de Coning, Cedric, Chiyuki Aoi and John Karlsrud (eds.) (2017) *UN Peacekeeping Doctrine in a New Era Adapting to Stabilisation, Protection and New Threats.* Abingdon: Routledge.

Cordesman, Anthony H. (2009) *Shape, Clear, Hold and Build: The Uncertain Lessons of the Afghan and Iraq Wars.* Washington, DC: Center for Strategic and International Studies.

Curran, David and Paul Holtom (2015) "Resonating, Rejecting, Reinterpreting: Mapping the Stabilization Discourse in the United Nations Security Council, 2000–14," *Stability: International Journal of Security & Development,* 4(1): pp. 1–18. doi: 10.5334/sta.gm.

Daily Mail (2015) "Military solution 'impossible' in parts of Middle East: CIA chief," *Daily Mail,* October 28, 2015. Available at: http://www.dailymail.co.

uk/wires/afp/article-3292855/Military-solution-impossible-parts-Middle-East-CIA-chief.html. Accessed January 11, 2016.

Doucet, Lyse (2010) "Afghanistan: A job half done," BBC News, December 4, 2006. Available at: http://news.bbc.co.uk/2/hi/south_asia/6205220.stm. Accessed June 30, 2016.

Friis, Karsten (2010) "Peacekeeping and Counter-insurgency – Two of a Kind?," *International Peacekeeping* 17(1):pp.49–66.DOI:10.1080/1353331100358919.

Glazzard, Andrew and Marthine Zeuthen (2016) *Violent extremism*. GSDRC Professional Development Reading Pack no. 34. Birmingham, UK: University of Birmingham. Available at: http://www.gsdrc.org/wp-content/uploads/2016/02/Violent-extremism_RP.pdf. Accessed September 13, 2016.

Global Peace Operations Review (2015) "Leaders' Summit on Peacekeeping," *Global Peace Operations Review*. Available at: http://peaceoperationsreview.org/wp-content/uploads/2015/10/un_2015_peakeeping_summit_pledges.jpg. Accessed January 11, 2016.

Goldberg, Mark Leon (2015) "Why President Obama is Hosting a Summit on UN Peacekeeping," *UN Dispatch*, September 28, 2015. Available at: http://www.undispatch.com/why-president-obama-is-hosting-a-summit-on-un-peacekeeping/. Accessed January 11, 2016.

Gowan, Richard (2015a) "How the UN Can Help Create Peace in a Divided World," *Huffington Post*, October 7, 2015. Available at: http://www.huffingtonpost.ca/centre-for-international-policy-studies/un-world-powers_b_8248628.html. Accessed January 11, 2016.

Gowan, Richard (2015b) *European Military Contributions to UN Peace Operations in Africa: Maximizing Strategic Impact*. New York: Global Peace Operations Review. Available at: http://peaceoperationsreview.org/wp-content/uploads/2015/12/european_military_contributions_gowan_dec_2015.pdf. Accessed July 23, 2016.

Guéhenno, Jean-Marie (2015) *The Fog of Peace*. Washington, DC: Brookings Institution Press.

IEP (2015) *Global Terrorism Index 2015*. Sydney: Institute of Economics and Peace.

Johnstone, Ian (2016) "Between Bureaucracy and Adhocracy: Crafting a Spectrum of Peace Operations," *Global Peace Operations Review*, March 31, 2016. Available at: http://peaceoperationsreview.org/thematic-essays/from-bureaucracy-to-adhocracy-crafting-a-spectrum-of-un-peace-operations/.   Accessed April 27, 2016.

Karlsrud, John (2013) "SRSGs as Norm Arbitrators? Understanding Bottom–Up Authority in UN Peacekeeping," *Global Governance*, 19 (4), pp. 525–544.

Karlsrud, John (2015) "The UN at War: Examining the Consequences of Peace Enforcement Mandates for the UN Peacekeeping Operations in the CAR, the DRC and Mali," *Third World Quarterly* 36 (1): pp. 40–54.

Karlsrud, John (2016a) "UN peace operations and counter-terrorism—A bridge too far?" in Jim Della-Giacoma (ed.), *Global Peace Operations Review: Annual Compilation 2015*. New York: Center on International Cooperation, New York University, pp. 118–124.

Karlsrud, John (2016b) *Norm Change in International Relations: Linked Ecologies in UN Peacekeeping Operations*. Abingdon: Routledge.

Karlsrud, John (2017) "Towards UN counter-terrorism operations?," *Third World Quarterly*, 38 (6): pp. 1215–1231. doi: http://dx.doi.org/10.1080/01436597.2016.1268907.

Lynch, Colum (2005) "UN Peacekeeping More Assertive, Creating Risk for Civilians," *Washington Post*, August 14, 2005. Available at: http://www.washingtonpost.com/wp-dyn/content/article/2005/08/14/AR2005081400946.html. Accessed September 13, 2016.

Mason, Rowena (2015) "UK to deploy troops to help keep peace in Somalia and South Sudan," *The Guardian*, September 27, 2015. Available at: http://www.theguardian.com/politics/2015/sep/27/uk-to-deploy-troops-to-help-keep-peace-in-somalia-and-south-sudan. Accessed January 11, 2016.

Ministère de la Défense (2016) "Opération Barkhane," November 30, 2016. Available at: http://www.defense.gouv.fr/operations/sahel/dossier-de-presentation-de-l-operation-barkhane/operation-barkhane. Accessed January 8, 2017.

MONUSCO (2013) *International Security and Stabilization Support Strategy*. Kinshasa: MONUSCO. Available at: http://www.unpbf.org/wp-content/uploads/ISSSS-2013-2017-Strategic-Framework-FINAL_EN.pdf. Accessed March 2, 2016.

News24 (2013) "Snipers hit M23 targets 2.2km away," *News24*, August 29, 2013. Available at: http://www.news24.com/Africa/News/Snipers-hit-M23-targets-22km-away-20130829-2. Accessed June 17, 2016.

Rhoads, Emily P. (2016) *Taking Sides in Peacekeeping: Impartiality and the Future of the United Nations*. Oxford: Oxford University Press.

Schia, Niels N. (2016) "Horseshoe and catwalk: Power, complexity and consensus-making in the United Nations Security Council," in Ronald Niezen and Maria Sapignoli (eds.), *The Anthropology of Global Institutions: Palaces of Hope*. Cambridge: Cambridge University Press, pp. 55–77.

de Soto, Alvaro (2007) "End of Mission Report," *The Guardian*. Available at: http://image.guardian.co.uk/sys-files/Guardian/documents/2007/06/12/DeSotoReport.pdf. Accessed January 11, 2016.

UK Stabilisation Unit (2014) The UK Government's Approach to Stabilisation (2014). London: UK Stabilisation Unit. Available at: file:///C:/Users/Karljoh/Downloads/uk-approach-to-stabilisation-2014.pdf. Accessed March 2, 2016.

UN (2000) Report of the Panel on United Nations Peace Operations [Brahimi Report]. New York: United Nations.

UN (2001) *S/RES/1373*, September 28, 2001. New York: United Nations.

UN (2006) *A/RES/60/288*, September 20, 2006. New York: United Nations.

UN (2008) *United Nations Peacekeeping Operations: Principles and Guidelines.* New York: United Nations Department of Peacekeeping Operations and Department of Field Support.

UN (2013a) *S/RES/2098*, March 28, 2013. New York: United Nations.

UN (2013b) *S/2013/354. United Nations Integrated Strategy for the Sahel*, June 14, 2013. New York: United Nations.

UN (2015a) *A/70/95-S/2015a/446. Report of the High-level Independent Panel on Peace Operations on Uniting our Strengths for Peace: Politics, Partnership and People* ("HIPPO Report"). New York: United Nations.

UN (2015b) *A/70/674. Plan of Action to Prevent Violent Extremism.* New York: United Nations.

UN (2016a) "(4a) Fatalities by Mission, Year and Incident Type," *United Nations Peacekeeping*, October 30, 2016a. Available at: http://www.un.org/en/peacekeeping/fatalities/documents/stats_4a.pdf. Accessed February 7, 2017.

UN (2016b) *S/RES/2295*, June 29, 2016. New York: United Nations.

UN (2016c) "Security Council Counter-Terrorism Committee," *United Nations.* Available at: http://www.un.org/en/sc/ctc/practices.html. Accessed January 11, 2016.

UN (2016d) "UN Counter-Terrorism Implementation Task Force," *United Nations.* Available at: http://www.un.org/en/terrorism/ctitf/. Accessed January 11, 2016.

UN (2016e) "UN Counter-Terrorism Centre," *United Nations.* Available at: http://www.un.org/en/terrorism/ctitf/uncct/. Accessed January 11, 2016.

UN (2016f) "Main Projects," *United Nations.* Available at: https://www.un.org/counterterrorism/ctitf/en/uncct/main-projects. Accessed April 27, 2016.

UN (2016g) *Summary of Concept Note: Countering and preventing violent extremism: role of UN peacekeeping. Proposed areas for DPKO/DFS research and policy development.* New York: United Nations. On file with the author.

UNCCT (2015) "Kingdom of Saudi Arabia Donates USD 100 Million for the United Nations Counter-Terrorism Centre," *The Beam*, Winter 2013–Summer 2014. Available at: http://www.un.org/es/terrorism/ctitf/pdfs/The%20Beam%20Vol%208.pdf. Accessed January 11, 2016.

UNDP (2016) "Community security and armed violence reduction," *UNDP.* Available at: http://www.undp.org/content/undp/en/home/ourwork/democratic-governance-and-peacebuilding/rule-of-law--justice-and-security/community-security-and-armed-violence-areduction.html. Accessed January 11, 2016.

UN News Centre (2015) "Preventing violent extremism, promoting human rights go hand-in-hand, Ban tells Washington summit," *UN News Centre*, February

19, 2015. Available at: http://www.un.org/apps/news/story.asp?NewsID=
50123#.VpOdrcmEr9d. Accessed January 11, 2016.

United States Dept. of the Army and United States Marine Corps (2007) *The
U.S. Army/Marine Corps Counterinsurgency Field Manual: U.S. Army Field
Manual no. 3–24: Marine Corps warfighting publication no. 3–33.5.* Chicago,
IL: University of Chicago Press.

U.S. Department of State (2016) "The Global Coalition to Counter ISIL,"
U.S. Department of State. Available at: http://www.state.gov/s/seci/.
Accessed January 11, 2016.

Vogel, C. (2014) *Islands of Stability or Swamps of Insecurity? MONUSCO's
Intervention Brigade and the Danger of Emerging Security Voids in Eastern
Congo.* Brussels: Egmont Institute.

de Vries, Hugo (2015) *Going Around in Circles: The Challenges of Peacekeeping
and Stabilization in the Democratic Republic of Congo.* The Hague: Netherlands
Institute of International Relations Clingendael.

de Vries, Hugo (2016) "The Ebb and Flow of Stabilization in the Congo," *PSRP
Briefing Paper 8.* Nairobi: Rift Valley Institute.

The White House (2015) *United States Support to United Nations Peace Operations.*
Washington, DC: The White House. Available at: http://www.defense.gov/
Portals/1/Documents/pubs/2015peaceoperations.pdf. Accessed June 13,
2016.

Wolffe, John and Gavin Moorhead (2014) *Religion, Security and Global
Uncertainties.* Milton Keynes: The Open University. Available at: http://www.
open.ac.uk/arts/research/religion-martyrdom-global-uncertainties/sites/
www.open.ac.uk.arts.research.religion-martyrdom-global-uncertainties/files/
files/ecms/arts-rmgu-pr/web-content/Religion-Security-Global-
Uncertainties.pdf. Accessed September 13, 2016.

CHAPTER 5

Competition or Burden-Sharing? UN and Regional Peace Operations in Africa

The AU has become an essential UN partner in the area of peace and security. However, although progress has been made in developing the institutional capacity of the AU and other sub-regional organizations in planning and fielding peace operations, much work still remains. This chapter discusses the increasing partnerships between the UN, the AU, and sub-regional organizations as a means of responding to the twenty-first-century challenges. With growing institutional capacity, particularly of the African Peace and Security Architecture (APSA) and more troop contributions, the AU, regional economic communities (RECs), and regional mechanisms (RMs) have played a key role as first responders in past decades. However, as will be highlighted with the African Union Mission in Somalia (AMISOM), considerable strategic, political, operational, and tactical challenges remain which continue as obstacles on the road to lasting peace. Collaborating to fight terrorism in the Sahel is likely to see greater cooperative partnerships, but here sequencing will be paramount to ensuring smooth transitions. The politics and strategic interests underpinning the regional intervention brigade model will be highlighted, looking at the example of the FIB in MONUSCO. The evolving models of partnership and cooperation are discussed, taking into consideration the various challenges and opportunities presented by greater burden-sharing. Responding to complex threats that require more robust use of force will demand a pragmatic division of labor, playing to the competitive advantages of each organization.

© The Author(s) 2018
J. Karlsrud, *The UN at War*,
https://doi.org/10.1007/978-3-319-62858-5_6

A CONTINENT IN RAPID CHANGE

Since the turn of the century and until 2015, sub-Saharan GDP has been growing at an average rate of 5.2% (World Bank 2016: 6), with many countries making good progress on a range of health, social, educational, and economic indicators. However, the continent is also facing considerable challenges. It is not yet sufficiently integrated into the global trade and value chain: African countries are still heavily reliant on their natural resources—and are reeling under the rapid decline in prices for oil, copper, and other resources (IMF 2015). In the course of the next 15 years, some 435 million Africans will be entering the workforce, representing two-thirds of the growth in the global workforce (African Economic Outlook: xii)—and if there are no jobs, unrest and crises are certain to continue to erupt. Young people form the core of any movement for change, also those willing to use political violence and terrorism as tools.

For decades, Africa has been the main area of deployment for international peace operations—due to instability and fragility, but also because the Security Council P5 have fewer conflicting interests than in the case of other regions and countries (e.g., the Middle East), enabling the Security Council to reach agreement on mandating and deploying peace operations. Central Africa has been the center of gravity of these operations, but with the increasing instability in the Cameroon, Chad, Libya, Mali, Niger, and northern Nigeria in recent years, operations are moving north. Concurrently, there has been a trend toward more "robust" operations—increasingly at odds with the core principles of UN peace operations, as detailed in previous chapters. While the UN missions in Côte d'Ivoire, DRC, and Liberia are likely to be downscaled over the next years, operations in Libya, Mali, and the Lake Chad basin are likely to remain for many years to come.

New theatres come with new threats and challenges. In Nigeria, Boko Haram has pledged allegiance to the IS, and in Mali the current UN mission is faced with groups like AQIM, Ansar Dine and the Movement for Unity and Jihad in West Africa (MUJAO), al-Mourabitoun, and the Macina Liberation Front. Individuals are moving between the groups, which shows that they are cooperating (ISS 2015). Al-Mourabitoun and the Macina Liberation Front claimed responsibility for the bombing of the Radisson Blu Hotel in Bamako on November 20, 2015. The threats of violent extremists are changing, mirroring societal and technological changes. Groups are becoming more interconnected, sharing ideologies, techniques, and strategies across borders in real time. Moreover, violent extremist groups are also engaged in organized crime, which in turn is interlinked with the governing elite in many countries across Africa.

African member states are increasingly developing their policies for participation in multilateral peace operations, whether in the context of the UN, the AU, or in coalitions of the willing. Key among these countries are Ethiopia, Nigeria, and South Africa. Ethiopia has risen to become the largest contributor of troops to UN peacekeeping operations, and is the largest contributor also to AU peace operations, with its 4395-strong contingent in AMISOM in Somalia (AMISOM 2014). Nigeria was the main contributor to the ECOWAS Cease-fire Monitoring Group (ECOMOG) in Liberia and successive ECOWAS operations, and is one of the main contributors to the MNJTF fighting Boko Haram. South Africa has pursued national interests through troop deployment to UN and AU-led peace operations, as in Burundi and more recently with the FIB in the DRC. South Africa is closely aligned with the AU on the increasing role of regional organizations in conflict management.

African Responses

African countries are increasingly contributing troops to peace operations. Since the mid-1990s, the AU and the RECs/RMs have generally been the first in responding to emerging crises in Africa. The ECOMOG interventions in Liberia (1990–1997 and again in 2003), Sierra Leone (1997–2000), and Guinea-Bissau (1998–1999) accentuated the need to build African capacity for dealing with crises on the continent.[1] Building capacity to maintain peace and security was a core part of the mandate for the AU, founded in 2001, replacing the Organisation of African Unity (OAU). Although the AU and RECs/RMs have been able to deploy troops swiftly to peace operations across the continent, there have been continued gaps in the planning and management capacity at AU headquarters in Addis Ababa as well as in the field (see, e.g., Holt and Shanahan 2005; de Coning et al. 2016). Furthermore, African regional organizations have had to rely on external funding to finance their peace operations. As an example, the AMISOM received EUR 285.5 million in 2015 from the European Union through the African Peace Facility (European Commission 2016: 15).

In Chapter 3, I noted that African countries are increasingly deploying troops to UN peace operations. However, not only are African countries contributing far more troops to UN operations: since 2001, the AU and its sub-regional partners have fielded 11 missions with a combined mandated strength of some 90,000 troops, police, and civilians (de Coning et al. 2016: 8–9).[2] In 2016, the AU participated in three missions in Somalia, Darfur, and the AU-led Regional Cooperation Initiative for the Elimination of the Lord's Resistance Army (AU-led RCI-LRA) (AU 2016a); and in 2015, Benin, Cameroon, Chad, Niger, and Nigeria deployed a MNJTF to fight Boko Haram.

The activity level of African regional and sub-regional organizations reflects the increasing institutional capacity and depth of APSA. APSA originated from the Constitutive Act of the AU, adopted in 2000 (AU 2000), and the establishment of the AU Peace and Security Council, which entered into force on December 26, 2003. APSA consists of the Continental Early Warning System, the Panel of the Wise, the African Standby Force (ASF), the Military Committee, and the Peace Fund.[3] APSA and the Peace and Security Council protocol gave a key role to the RECs and RMs for Conflict Prevention, Management, and Resolution in the promotion of peace and security in Africa (AU 2003). The ASF concept consisted of five regional brigades, developed and provided by the RECs/RMs. The development of the ASF has gone through several stages, and in its current form, it also consists of civilian and police capabilities. In January 2016, full operational capability (FOC) of the ASF was declared by the Specialized Technical Committee on Defence, Safety and Security (STCDSS) and supported by the AU Peace and Security Council (AU 2016b). However, this should not mask the fact that there are still major challenges remaining when it comes to developing capacity to plan and manage peace operations at operational as well as strategic levels.

In the next sections, I will look at four mission contexts that give an impression of how the relationship between the UN, the AU, and sub-regional organizations is developing.

Fighting Al-Shabaab in Somalia: No Exit in Sight?

In Somalia, the AMISOM has been fighting al-Shabaab since 2007, at great human, political, and economic cost (see, e.g., Williams 2015). The mission has been given a Chapter 7 mandate by the UNSC to reduce the threat of al-Shabaab and help the Federal Government of Somalia (FGS) to expand control of national territory; to support the development of key institutions, infrastructure, governance, rule of law, and delivery of basic services; train national security forces; and facilitate elections, humanitarian action, stabilization, and recovery efforts (UN 2014).

The UN Support office for the AMISOM (UNSOA)—replaced in November 2015 by the UNSOS—provides a comprehensive support package to AMISOM.[4] This involves logistical support to a mandated strength of 22,126 uniformed personnel and 70 civilians of AMISOM, and 10,900 Somalia National Army (SNA) troops when these are conducting joint operations with AMISOM, and the United Nations Assistance Mission in Somalia (UNSOM) (UN 2015b). UNSOM is a SPM deployed alongside AMISOM to provide the UN's "'good offices' functions, supporting the Federal Government of Somalia's peace and reconciliation process [and provide] strategic policy advice on peacebuilding and statebuilding" (UN 2013c: 2). This includes a range of support activities in the areas of governance, security sector reform, rule of law, disengagement of combatants, DDR, maritime security, human rights, the development of a federal system, and others (ibid.).

Main troop contributors are Burundi, Djibouti, Ethiopia, Kenya, and Uganda. Because of the extremely challenging security environment, these countries maintain direct control over their troops, and so AMISOM leadership has significantly less strategic control over the troops than what is common in UN peace operations. However, it is natural to assume that there is an inverse relationship between the level of force a mission is expected to apply, and the willingness of TCCs to delegate the command and control of their forces to the operation. Member states that deploy forces to highly insecure areas are usually not willing to place the control of their troops entirely in the hands of an international organization. In these cases, as seen with NATO in Afghanistan and the EU in CAR and Chad, member states will maintain strong liaison functions and some form of command and control over their forces. This can be expressed in negative terms, by emplacing caveats as to what kind of operations the troops can participate in—or in positive terms, by actively providing operational guidance to the troops on the ground.

The particular composition and structure of the international effort in Somalia, led by the AU, requires considerable work to coordinate and align efforts on the political, strategic, operational, and tactical levels. AMISOM is the lead in what is probably the most complicated and challenging peace operation deployed today. The levels of command and control that is delegated on the political, strategic, and operational levels may not be equal, leading to challenges on the ground. The Special Representative of the Chairperson (SRCC)/Head of AMISOM risks falling between two stools, as member states may be willing to signal strong political interest at the political level while also maintaining a firm hand on the operational level. A strategic gap may open, bringing significant challenges for the SRCC in aligning the efforts of the various military troop contributors, and among the military, police, and civilian components.

Furthermore, there is a challenge in maintaining a unified and integrated strategy with the SNA, who are at the center of AMISOM operations, as per the current concept of operations, but are not under the direct command of the SRCC. This necessitates a strong and constant working relationship on all levels between AMISOM and its counterparts in the SNA, the national police, and other security forces, as well as civilian administration. Following the recommendation of the Joint AU–UN Review to set up Joint Operations Coordination Centers in the regional capitals to ensure "cohesive action between national and international military, paramilitary and police forces and deconflicting tasks and responsibilities during operations" would be one step in the right direction (UN 2015c: 19).

The challenges of command and control in AMISOM are further compounded by the complex structure of the mission(s). Aside from the military, police, and civilian components of AMISOM, UNSOA provides a logistical support package and UNSOM provides various substantive functions, including support to political processes and reconciliation. Referring to UNSOA, the 2015 Joint AU–UN Review noted "clear shortfalls in the integrated provision of logistical support to front line AMISOM and SNA troops, which hampered the continued pace of offensive operations" (AU 2015a: 7). As pointed out in the 2013 AMISOM review:

> AMISOM lacks a fully functional multi-dimensional headquarters. This shortcoming has negatively affected the ability of the mission to ensure full complementarity and coherence of efforts in the implementation of its mandate. The structure and capacity of the civilian component needs to be addressed, including; (a) activation of the Senior Leadership Team and related mission coordination structures, (b) increased staffing to enable civilian support for the military consolidation and stabilization efforts in areas recovered from Al Shabaab, addressing governance, reconciliation and socio-economic recovery at local community level. (AU 2013b: 21)

Since the 2013 review, AMISOM has made some progress. The mission has been staffed with more police and civilian officers. However, more needs to be done. The 2015 AU–UN Joint Review recommended the reconfiguration of the AMISOM forces to enhance the police component, and the deployment of quick reaction and special forces (UN 2015d). It also recommended the deployment of joint civilian teams of AMISOM and UNSOM to help establish "sufficient civilian presences at the capital level" (AU 2015a: 23). However, the real challenges will remain on the local level, as regards enabling the mission to develop and implement a stabilization approach that is not about controlling hearts and minds, but providing security, state support, and services to local populations.

AMISOM has during the last few years been able to take control over large areas previously controlled by al-Shabaab, but together with the FGS it is struggling to provide the "liberated" areas with security, service delivery, and peace dividends. Due to the difficult security circumstances, the AU and UN have been reluctant to deploy civilians and police who could start implementing the range of activities mandated by the UNSC. If al-Shabaab continues to be able to collect taxes and provide security, access to services and freedom of movement in return, local populations may see it as a better alternative. That means that the AU and the UN must begin to provide real and long-term peace dividends to local populations. However, they must also carefully consider the potential backlashes and retaliations that may be inflicted upon local populations if areas that are "liberated" return to the control of al-Shabaab.

Fighting Terrorism in the Sahel

Mali had long been a country of relative stability and development in the Sahel, but the situation took a turn for the worse in 2012. On March 22, President Amadou Toumani Touré was overthrown by a young officer in the Malian army, Captain Amadou Sanogo, in a *coup d'état*. The coup-makers were dissatisfied with the country's weak and corrupt leadership and the inability of the president to counter an armed rebellion in the North, led by the Movement for the National Liberation of Azawad (MNLA). However, the coup quickly proved counterproductive, and the MNLA, allied with several armed Islamist groups, took advantage of the confusion. On April 6, the rebels proclaimed the independence of the Republic of Azawad and the imposition of sharia law in northern Mali. Some 412,000 persons had fled their homes and become internally displaced or moved across the border to Burkina Faso, Mauritania, or Niger (UN 2012a).

With the rapid development of events in Mali, and the advance of the MNLA and Islamist elements toward the south, the situation quickly rose to prominence on the international agenda. The ECOWAS sent a mediation team to Mali to support political dialogue between armed groups and the military junta. However, the humanitarian situation continued to worsen. Fighting broke out between the various rebel groups; and the MNLA was quickly sidelined by its Islamist allies and soon lost control of Timbuktu, Gao, and Kidal. By November 2012, AQIM had taken control of Timbuktu and Tessalit; the MUJAO had taken control of Douentza, Gao, Menaka, Ansongo, and Gourma; and Kidal was under the control of the Islamist group Ansar Dine ("defenders of the faith") (ibid.).

International non-governmental organizations reported that war crimes were being committed by the Islamist groups, and ECOWAS and the AU prepared to intervene. The AU PSC called upon the UNSC to endorse the ECOWAS Force, and asked for a "support package funded by UN-assessed contributions" (AU 2012: 3). A few months later, the AU PSC requested a Security Council mandate for an "African military force" that would "support the authorities in their primary responsibility to protect the population" (UN 2012b: 14), but progress was slow, for several reasons. There was reluctance to help the coup-makers, and disagreement on the political strategy between ECOWAS and the AU (Lacher and Tull 2013). On November 28, the SG presented the concept of operations developed with ECOWAS and endorsed by the AU on November 13 (UN 2012c: 12–18), and the UNSC finally endorsed the operation on December 20, 2012 (UN 2012d). The resolution authorized the deployment of the African-led International Support Mission in Mali (AFISMA) and reflected the statements by ECOWAS and the AU that AFISMA should be given a strong mandate to respond to the atrocities unfolding on the ground and "to defend the unity and territorial integrity of Mali" (UN 2012b: 3).[5] AFISMA was mandated, inter alia,

(b) To support the Malian authorities in recovering the areas in the north of its territory under the control of terrorist, extremist and armed groups and in reducing the threat posed by terrorist organizations, including AQIM, MUJWA [MUJAO] and associated extremist groups, while taking appropriate measures to reduce the impact of military action upon the civilian population;

(d) To support the Malian authorities in their primary *responsibility to protect* the population (UN 2012d: 4; my italics)

However, events on the ground again overtook the planning and deployment of the force. In early January 2013, the Islamist groups rapidly moved south; fearing to lose Bamako, the government of Mali requested France to intervene. The French *Opération Serval* was deployed on January 11, 2013, and started to move north, retaking cities and population centers. Chad, not an ECOWAS member, provided a large contingent that fought alongside *Serval* (2400 men as of March 13, 2013), sustaining heavy losses. In February, AFISMA started to deploy with ECOWAS troops; the Chadian contingent was gradually included in this force. By March, *Serval*, Chadian troops, and AFISMA had, together with Malian forces, established control of most of the territory, and the Islamist forces had withdrawn northward to the *Adrar des Ifoghas massif* (UN 2013d).

The mandate for the transfer of authority from AFISMA to MINUSMA was provided by Security Council Resolution 2100 on April 25, 2013 (UN 2013b). The mandate scheduled the transfer of authority for July 1 the same year, at the request of the transitional government (Lotze 2015). The idea was that the AU would enforce the peace, and the UN would keep it once established. This division of labor was strongly opposed by the AU and ECOWAS, both of which preferred a strengthened UN presence that would focus primarily on political and developmental activities, with AFISMA continuing to engage in the stability-oriented tasks until agreed security benchmarks had been achieved (Lotze 2015; UN 2013d). Only hours before UN SCR 2100 was adopted, the AU protested that "Africa was not appropriately consulted in the drafting and consultation process that led to the adoption of the UN Security Council Resolution [2100] authorizing the deployment of a UN Multidimensional Mission for Stabilization in Mali (MINUSMA) to take over AFISMA" (AU 2013a).

The transition to a UN peacekeeping mission was rushed—the Security Council was unwilling to fund the continuation of AFISMA—and without consideration for the medium- and long-term implications. Although AFISMA was indeed struggling, the division of work that has developed between the UN, the AU, and sub-regional organizations on the African continent suggests that another approach could have been followed. Instead of replacing AFISMA, more efforts should have been made to strengthen the operation, by providing more troop training, increasing logistical support, and ensuring a robust funding base. Since most AU missions are handed over to the UN within 6 to 18 months, more work should be done to ensure smooth transitions in terms of doctrine, training of troops to be re-hatted, equipment, logistical support, etc., drawing on the lessons from the transitions in Mali and in CAR (de Coning et al. 2016: 139). Furthermore, it could be argued that the deployment of the UN peacekeeping mission was premature: as there was no peace to keep, MINUSMA has since lost 70 troops through suicide actions and other hostile acts (UN 2016a). Already in 2014, the then head of UN peacekeeping, Hervé Ladsous, declared that UN in Mali is "no longer in the context of maintaining peace" (*Mail & Guardian* 2014).

FIB in MONUSCO

Faced with the crisis in the DRC in November 2012, when the M23 captured Goma, 11 regional countries agreed in February 2013 on a Peace, Security, and Cooperation Framework for the DRC, and the establishment of a brigade-strength Neutral Intervention Force. The force should be under the aegis of the Southern African Development Community (SADC), but the funding estimated at USD 100 million was not forthcoming from the contributing countries, the UN or donors. After intense political pressure, the UNSC mandated the inclusion of a FIB in MONUSCO in March 2013 (UN 2013a). The FIB was mandated to "take all necessary measures" to "neutralize" and "disarm" groups posing a threat to "state authority and civilian security" (ibid.: 7–8). The mandate was given on "on an exceptional basis and without creating a precedent or any prejudice to the agreed principles of peacekeeping" with strong reservations from Pakistan and Russia, among others (UN 2013e). The FIB was initially successful in fighting the M23, but political support from the sending countries of South Africa and Tanzania waned when the FIB was asked by the mission leadership to take on other armed groups, including the *Forces démocratiques de libération du Rwanda* (FDLR) (see, e.g., ISS 2015).

For many African countries, the FIB concept fused several strategic interests and provided an opportunity to equip UN missions with the necessary capabilities to tackle armed insurgents and violent extremists. When national interests and mission objectives align, African TCCs are generally less beholden to classic peacekeeping principles and more willing to use force and be partial actors than some other major traditional troop-contributing countries (Curran and Holtom 2015; Gowan 2015a: 18). Troops that would be provided to such

FIBs in UN missions can also expect to be supported by relatively strong logistics and medical capabilities, and with much higher reimbursement rates than what could be expected in an AU or sub-regional peace support operation. These may be among the reasons why African countries have pushed for the inclusion of a FIB in MINUSMA in Mali (AU 2015b), for a robust mission to be deployed in Libya (Lagneau 2014), and for a regional protection force to be included in UNMISS in South Sudan.

Boko Haram and the MNJTF

The fight against Boko Haram has intensified in recent years, particularly after the kidnapping of 276 girls from a school in Chibok, Borno State, Nigeria, in April 2014. In 2015, the AU Peace and Security Council mandated the MNJTF to fight Boko Haram. The MNJTF consists of troops from the Lake Chad Basin Commission (LCBC)—Benin, Cameroon, Chad, Niger, and Nigeria—with headquarters in N'Djamena, the capital of Chad. The constellation of countries, including members from ECOWAS as well as the Economic Community of Central African States (ECCAS), shows that although RECs/RMs are key constitutive parts of the ASF, the AU–REC/RM relationship can and must also embrace flexible solutions adjusted to specific security challenges that cross their boundaries and lines of authority.

The MNJTF has been able to weaken Boko Haram, but much work remains (AU 2016c). The AU has been receiving considerable bilateral support from France, the EU, the UK, and the USA, but continues to lack key enablers and equipment (ibid.). During 2016, the conflict moved north, increasing in intensity in the Lake Chad area and in Niger; by June 2016, a major humanitarian catastrophe was imminent, with 2.5 million people displaced (Reliefweb 2016). Tull (2015) has warned that the Boko Haram was strengthening its foothold in Cameroon, and that the state had far less capacity to deal with the threat than commonly thought. Chad is viewed as the strong state in the region, but the regime is dependent on oil money to keep control over the military forces and various allegiances. With rapidly dwindling dividends from oil from 2014 and onward, stability was threatened, and the regime chose a militarized and securitized response, spiraling the country toward further insecurity and instability (see, e.g., ICG 2016).

AN EVOLVING PARTNERSHIP

By June 2016, 9 out of 16 UN peacekeeping operations and 6 out of 11 UN SPMs were located in Africa (UN 2016b, 2016c). African troops are increasingly deployed to UN and non-UN peace operations (more than 70,000 deployed in 2014), and about 50% of peacekeepers in UN operations are African (Gowan 2015a: 19). This is a sharp increase over the past ten years, from 27% in January 2006 (UN 2006a).

The UN has come to recognize that the AU is gaining institutional capacity and depth. With the growing participation of African troops also in UN peace operations, the AU is increasingly becoming a partner in the sphere of peace and security. This is reflected in the institutionalization of the partnership in recent years, at operational and strategic levels. At the strategic level, the UN and AU agreed on a *Ten-Year Capacity Building Programme (TYCBP) for the African Union* in 2006 (UN 2006b). The aim was to build capacity and strengthen cooperation between the UN, AU, and RECs, inter alia, in the area of peace and security. The cooperation framework has resulted in a gradual increase of institutional staff exchange, capacity development, and the establishment of the UN Office to the AU in Addis Ababa in 2010. Since 2007, the UNSC and the AU Peace and Security Council have had annual meetings, now held twice a year. The DPA has institutionalized senior-level interaction through a bi-annual Joint Task Force on peace and security, and working-level interaction through annual Desk-to-Desk meetings with AU counterparts. In the area of peace operations, the cooperation was initially driven by the deployment of the joint operation in Darfur—African Union–United Nations Mission in Darfur (UNAMID)—and then the deployment of AMISOM and the UN support mission UNSOA. These operations required a deepening and strengthening of the relationship between the two organizations. In recent years, the AU has handed over several missions to the UN—like AFISMA to MINUSMA in Mali and African-led International Support Mission to the Central African Republic (MISCA) to MINUSCA in CAR.

Four types of cooperation are discernable in the field: (1) integrated operations (UNAMID); (2) partially integrated operations (AMISOM-UNSOA); (3) parallel operations (AMISOM-UNSOM); and (4) sequential operations (MISCA-MINUSCA).[6] The evolving burden-sharing of operations requires further strengthening of the relationship. This was also noted by the HIPPO Report, which said that the UN–AU partnership should "provide more predictable financing" and that the partnership should be based on the following principles of cooperation:

> ... consultative decision-making and common strategy; the division of labour based on respective comparative advantage; joint analysis, planning, monitoring and evaluation; integrated response to the conflict cycle, including prevention; and transparency, accountability and respect for international standards. (UN 2015a: 77)

Looking forward, if AU operations are to be readied to assume the robust part of the mission spectrum, it will be necessary to develop a fit-for-purpose mission support concept; to strengthen the strategic leadership dimension; to improve financial and human rights accountability; and to develop a holistic stabilization approach that can encompass security, political, development, and humanitarian dimensions. In the medium term, AU peace operations should aim at transitioning into UN peace-keeping or peacebuilding missions, but in the longer term, African capacity should be built to enable also the AU to take on these missions, when necessary.

Intervention Brigades or Delegating Authority?

When MINUSMA was mandated to replace the AFISMA in 2013, the AU was not pleased with what it saw as a rushed transition (AU 2013a; Lotze 2015). To enable African troops that were being re-hatted to continue to fight against the terrorist threat in the North of Mali, it asked the UNSC to provide a robust mandate to the UN mission, "including the fight against criminal and terrorist networks operating in the North of Mali" (AU 2013c: 3). In April 2013, the Security Council authorized MINUSMA in Mali "[i]n support of the transitional authorities of Mali, to stabilise the key population centres, especially in the north of Mali and, in this context, to deter threats and take active steps to prevent the return of armed elements to those areas" (UN 2013b: 7). Although this was a very offensive mandate for a UN mission, effectively giving the mission enforcement tasks, the mandate did not explicitly task MINUSMA to fight criminal and terrorist networks as the AU had wanted. Nevertheless, Chad, despite significant losses among its mission troops deployed to northern Mali, as well as other African states, continued to press for a more robust mission and mandate.

Alongside MINUSMA, two cooperation mechanisms have been developed in the sub-region—the Group of Five Sahel (G-5 Sahel) consisting of Burkina Faso, Chad, Niger, Mali and Mauritania—was formed at a summit in February 2014 (Le Sahel 2014) to strengthen security coordination and cooperation and formulate a joint strategy for fighting terrorism in the region. France sees the G-5 Sahel is seen as the main partner of *Operation Barkhane* in the fight against terrorism in the Sahel-Saharan region (Ministère de la Défense 2016). The G-5 Sahel was eminently placed to become an FIB within MINUSMA. In 2014, after MINUSMA had suffered high losses, Mali asked for the establishment of "a rapid intervention force capable of effectively combating terrorists" (What's in Blue 2014), but the request was not approved by the Security Council.

Along a parallel track, member states of the sub-region have sought to strengthen their security cooperation under the aegis of the AU *Nouakchott Process*, starting with a meeting at the ministerial level in Nouakchott in March 2013. Following further meetings, the AU has outlined three alternatives for dealing with the challenges of terrorism in Mali, each based on existing operational models (AU 2015b: 16–22):

1. an intervention brigade integrated in MINUSMA, based on the FIB in MONUSCO;
2. a separate AU mission, but with logistical support from the UN, based on the AMISOM/UNSOM model in Somalia;
3. a fully fledged AU mission with an integrated support element, based on the model of the MNJTF fighting Boko Haram.

The fact that the AU has requested the inclusion of intervention brigades/protection forces in Mali, South Sudan, and Libya testifies to the popularity of the model, but so far the UNSC has only been forthcoming in the case of South Sudan. The reluctance to include FIBs in other UN missions stems from the same reasons that Pakistan, Russia, and some other states were reluctant to include the FIB in MONUSCO in the first place (UN 2013e). UN missions have traditionally been supposed to have the consent of the main parties, be impartial, and use a minimum of force except in self-defense and defense of the mission's mandate. As explained earlier, the HIPPO panel drew the line at UN peacekeeping missions being used for counter-terrorism purposes.

For African states, there are several incentives for providing troops to intervention brigades rather than African-led operations. While both types of operations are likely to bring bilateral training and equipment support from states like the USA and France, the reimbursement rates, logistical support, medical and casualty evacuation are stronger and more dependable in UN peace operations. This points to the need to strengthen these dimensions in African-led operations, to enable them to conduct missions that the UN cannot take upon itself, for principled and practical reasons, such as peace enforcement and counter-terrorism operations (see also Karlsrud 2017).

Burden-Sharing and Financing

Over time, a form of burden-sharing has been developed between the UN and African regional and sub-regional organizations, where the more robust tasks have been either delegated by the UNSC or operations have been deployed at the request of the host country. However, while progress has been made, these operations depend on financial, logistical, equipment, and training support from bilateral and multilateral partners. With the number and scope of African peace operations on the rise, there is a need to further develop the international cooperation framework for these operations, which are becoming an essential part of the international peace and security toolbox.

The UN and key partners like the EU, the UK, and the USA have borne most of the costs of the AU and sub-regional peace operations so far. These partners have put pressure on the AU to cover a greater share of the financial costs of AU peace operations. In 2015, African member states pledged "to assume responsibility for up to 25% of all AU peace and security activities, including peace support operations [by 2020], while the other 75% of the cost of such missions would be provided by UN through assessed contributions" (AU 2015c: 3). The document noted that UN-assessed contributions would in particular be for peace enforcement and/or counter-terrorism mandates. The decision also detailed that operationalization of this financing arrangement would be predicated on the following principles and actions:

1. African ownership, as a key factor to the success of peace efforts on the continent;
2. reaffirmation of the primary role of the UNSC in the maintenance of international peace and security, and of the role of regional arrangements as elaborated in Chap. 8 of the UN Charter;
3. acknowledgment that support by the UN to regional organizations in matters relating to the maintenance of international peace and security is an integral part of collective security as provided for in the UN Charter;
4. enhanced strategic partnership with the UN, including the development of a framework outlining the steps necessary to activate authorization by the UNSC of AU-led missions to be supported by UN assessed contributions;
5. strengthening of the AU's capacity to plan and manage peace support operations;
6. enhancement of AU financial oversight mechanisms; and
7. strengthening of the AU's Human Rights Due Diligence capabilities, including preventing and combating sexual exploitation and abuses in AU-led peace support operations. (Ibid.: 3–4).

This amounts to an ambitious program for strengthening and institutionalizing the UN–AU relationship. First and foremost, it hinges on the ability of African member states to show the political will and ability to define and fulfill the 25% financing goal by 2020. In line with this, Donald Kaberuka, a former president of the African Development Bank, was in 2016 appointed as High Representative for the AU Peace Fund and tasked by the AU with devising a plan for reaching this goal. In June 2016, the member states at the AU Summit in Kigali approved his model for funding the AU, which is based on a 0.2% levy on eligible imports. According to the model, such a levy should generate approximately USD 325 million that would cover the AU's regular budget, 70% of its program budget and 25% of its peace operations (AU 2016d). If all parties keep their part of the bargain, the AU will be able to access UN-assessed contributions within the next few years, and become a more permanent partner shouldering efforts situated at the harder end of the peace operations spectrum.

TWO OPPOSING BUT MUTUALLY SUPPORTIVE TRENDS?

The APSA was declared operational in January 2016, during the AU Summit (AU 2016b). The ASF and its regional building blocks have progressed far, and in most regions the ASF has been declared operational. However, the ASF still remains work in progress.

In 2013, the AU decided to develop an African Immediate Crisis Response Capacity (ACIRC), consisting of 1500 military troops deployed by a lead nation or a group of AU member states. These troops should be self-sustaining for a minimum of 30 days, and were to conduct stabilization and enforcement operations, neutralize terrorist groups, and provide emergency assistance to member states. According to de Coning (2016), the ACIRC was developed because of frustrations with the French intervention in Mali and the short-lived AFISMA mission. As such, the concept filled an apparent gap, given the rapidly unfolding crises in CAR, Mali, and northern Nigeria. However, as the ACIRC could represent a potential challenge to the validity and centrality of the ASF, strong resistance was discernable among several African member states. The concept was initially supported by South Africa and to some extent Ethiopia, while Nigeria was among the more skeptical, reflecting traditional power dynamics on the continent. In January 2016, as full operational capacity was declared for the ASF, the STCDSS also recommended that the ACIRC be dissolved. The recommendation was subsequently supported by the AU PSC (2016a: 2), but the AU General Assembly took a more guarded approach: it decided to continue the ACIRC and await further evaluation of the readiness of the Regional Standby Forces during 2016 (AU 2016e: 4). According to de Coning et al. (2016), the ASF is likely to remain the main framework for African peace operations. However, the ASF as such will probably not be utilized in actual operations. These will take a more ad hoc character, drawing on the institutionalized competence put in place with the development of the ASF, but most often under a lead-nation concept (ibid.: 138, see also Darkwa 2017 and Reykers and Karlsrud 2017).

The UN has repeatedly asked the EU whether it could deploy its Battlegroups as a quick reaction force to crises in Africa, but so far they have not been utilized. In addition to the requirement for unanimous support from all its member states, the EU is wary of creating a precedent for the use of the Battlegroups, in terms of costs and activation of the instrument, and prefers the use of ad hoc solutions that do not create precedents and place costs along with national interests. Financial constraints and lack of interest in committing troops to the African continent also play a role (see, e.g., Reykers 2016a). Reykers (2016b) argues that France, a key penholder on the UNSC, did not even consider the Battlegroups as a credible option when devising the mandate for the intervention in Mali, as it was aware of the long decision-making process that this would entail, and with the outcome uncertain. France and the UK are wary about endorsing the use of the EU Battlegroups, which might prove costlier for them, as EU member states, than authorizing the deployment of regional organizations or a UN mission. Nevertheless, it has also been held that "the battlegroups are important drivers for European defence transformation and regional military cooperation, regardless of whether they have seen action or not" (Andersson 2015: 1). On the other hand, critics like the USA argue that the EU Battlegroups tie up personnel, are extremely costly, and have never been deployed (Power 2015). In this respect, the EU Battlegroups hold several lessons that are applicable to the African context, for the further development of the ASF, the future of the ACIRC, and utility of ad hoc arrangements complementing formal institutionalization of security arrangements (see also Reykers 2017).

In Africa, there has been a mushrooming of sub-regional security initiatives crisscrossing the boundaries of existing sub-regional organizations, such as the MNJTF and the G-5 Sahel. Engaging in robust counterterrorism operations requires strong national interest, and will necessarily be geographically limited in scope to those countries who feel their national security may be in danger. These two trends may actually not be in competition, but mutually supportive. The development of the ASF has contributed to capacity development and to gradual institutionalization of cooperation frameworks on the sub-regional level. This provides a platform for engagement when ad hoc coalitions are formed in order to deal with specific challenges.

Cooperation, Representation, and Taxation

The AU has come to enjoy increasing respect and legitimacy, for the endurance of its mission in Somalia and its ability to gain control over increasing amounts of the territory in the face of stiff resistance from al-Shabaab. Through this and other missions, the AU has demonstrated its capacities for planning and deploying peace support operations to situations where there is no peace to keep and where force must be employed in order to create stability and protect civilians. A de facto division of labor has evolved between the UN and the AU on the African continent, driven by pragmatic considerations (Williams and Boutellis 2014): the AU deploys its troops to the most difficult situations, while the UN deploys where there are greater chances of achieving stability and sustained peace. We should also bear in mind that the AU has engaged in mediation and preventive efforts across the continent: further support is also needed in this area (see, e.g., Gebrehiwot and de Waal 2016).

With the situation in Libya in 2011, the AU–UN relations took a turn for the worse. The AU established an ad hoc high-level committee composed of five African heads of state and the head of the African Commission to mediate between Libyan President Gaddafi and rebels in the east of the country. However, with the situation on the ground developing rapidly, the UNSC adopted Resolution 1973 authorizing the use of all necessary measures to protect civilians (UN 2011),[7] and a NATO-led coalition began air-strikes the next day—thereby moving the AU to the margins on Libya.

This had repercussions for how the UN, the AU, and ECOWAS came to interpret the situation in Mali. ECOWAS and the AU expressed their readiness to intervene during the spring of 2012, but the Security Council did not endorse the deployment of a regional support operation (Lotze 2015), and requested further information on what shape the intervention should take and its key objectives (UN 2012b). When the go-ahead to intervene was finally given, it was without the necessary support package from the UN to enable speedy deployment. And adding insult to injury, the mandate for the follow-on UN mission was given only months later: AFISMA was never given a chance to prove its worth on the ground. However, relations improved somewhat with the deployment of the MISCA and the transition to MINUSCA. These showed "that the UN, the AU and the RECs can through consultations learn from previous experiences and adapt to new realities" (de Coning et al. 2016: 139).

It should also be noted that, with stronger representation, and the fact that most UN peace operations are deployed to African countries, African proposals for policy shifts are now accorded more weight. There is strong pressure on the UN from African member states for more robust peace operations being deployed, moving the UN away from the principle of impartiality: "African officials are critical of the UN's caution and have heartily supported France's robust military responses to the crises in Mali and the Central African Republic. There is likely to be a further blurring between peacekeeping, stabilization missions, and counter-terrorism operations in Africa—most likely under a mix of UN and regional mandates, whatever the UN's qualms" (Gowan 2015b). There is greater willingness to use troops from neighboring countries who may have a national interest, and to give these a more robust mandate, siding with the government of the day.

The AU–UN relationship is likely to be increasingly important for African peace and security. The AU and sub-regional organizations have demonstrated their relevance and importance, and will continue to shoulder the more dangerous part of the mission spectrum in the years to come. The burden-sharing of peace and security tasks will need to be reflected in the financial arrangements and institutional support and capacity-building activities of the AU's multilateral and bilateral partners. There must be a move from ad hoc solutions to a more structured and long-term relationship, where the AU is acknowledged for its central role in the maintenance of peace and security in Africa. That being said, as they continue to develop economically and institutionally, African states should take on a larger share of the tab for peace operations on the continent.

The increase in cooperation has developed during a period of overall growth for peace operations in Africa. Although the picture is a mixed one, it is not clear that this trend will continue. For some within the UN and the AU, this may mean a decreasing market for their services, resulting in a zero-sum logic. We have seen how some parts of the UN system may be willing to stretch beyond the principles of peacekeeping to take on new tasks in the areas of countering violent extremism and counter-terrorism. This could indicate a fear of a possible decline in the overall "market share" of the UN of international peace operations in the future, as the AU gains competence, funding, and legitimacy to maintain peace and security on the African continent.

NOTES

1. The OAU deployment of a Pan-African Peacekeeping Force in Chad in 1981 is generally considered the first deployment of a peace operation by an African regional organization.
2. This includes UNAMID in Darfur, a joint UN–AU operation, and the MNJTF deployed by the Lake Chad Basin Commission to fight Boko Haram.
3. Here, I examine only the ASF.
4. UNSOA was established in 2009.

5. Annex 1 of the letter contains letter from ECOWAS "Letter dated 5 April 2012 from the President of the Commission of the Economic Community of West African States addressed to the Secretary-General."
6. This is an expansion of the typology developed by Koops and Tardy (2015: 61–62). Some of these examples of forms of cooperation should be considered as ideal types, i.e., not actually having achieved the agreed type of cooperation in practice. As for UNAMID, the AU has influence over senior appointments, but the mission is managed and run by the UN.
7. All African members of the Security Council supported the resolution at the time, while Brazil, China, Germany, India, and the Russian Federation abstained.

REFERENCES

AMISOM (2014) "Ethiopia - ENDF," January 1, 2014. Available at: http://amisom-au.org/ethiopia-endf/. Accessed July 21, 2016.

Andersson, Jan J. (2015) *If Not Now, When? The Nordic EU Battlegroup.* Paris: European Union Institute for Security Studies.

AU (2000) *Constitutive Act of the African Union.* Addis Ababa: African Union.

AU (2003) *Protocol Relating to the Establishment of the Peace and Security Council of the African Union.* Addis Ababa: African Union.

AU (2012) *Communiqué* (PSC/PR/COMM. (CCCXXIII), June 12, 2012). Addis Ababa: African Union.

AU (2013a) *Communiqué* (PSC/PR/COMM. (CCCLXXI), April 25, 2013). Addis Ababa: African Union.

AU (2013b) *Report of the African Union Commission on the Strategic Review of the African Union Mission in Somalia (AMISOM), PSC/PR/2.(CCCLVI).* Addis Ababa: African Union Commission.

AU (2013c) *PSC/PR/COMM(CCCLVIII),* March 7, 2013. Addis Ababa: African Union.

AU (2015a) *Report of the Joint African Union–United Nations Mission on the Benchmarks for a United Nations Peacekeeping Operation in Somalia and recommendations on the next steps in the military campaign,* June 30, 2015. Addis Ababa: African Union.

AU (2015b) *Report of the Commission of the African Union on the Follow-up to the Relevant Provisions of the Declaration of the Summit of the Member Countries of the Nouakchott Process of 18 December 2014.* Addis Ababa: African Union.

AU (2015c) *PSC/AHG/COMM/2(DXLVII) Peace and Security Council 547[th]Meeting at the Level of Heads of State and Government,* September 26, 2015. Addis Ababa: African Union.

AU (2016a) "Peace Operations conducted by the African Union and Partners," November 20, 2015. Available at: http://www.peaceau.org/en/page/72-peace-ops. Accessed January 6, 2016.

AU (2016b) *PSC/PR/BR.(DLXX)*. Addis Ababa: African Union.

AU (2016c) *PSC/PR/COMM.(DLXVII)*, January 14, 2016. Addis Ababa: African Union.

AU (2016d) *Press Release: The African Union Adopts the AU Peace Fund*. Addis Ababa: African Union. Available at: http://www.peaceau.org/uploads/auc-pr-peacefund-18.07.2016.pdf. Accessed August 26, 2016.

AU (2016e) *Assembly/AU/Dec.589(XXVI)*. Addis Ababa: African Union.

de Coning, Cedric (2016) "Adapting the African standby force to a just-in-time readiness model," in de Coning, Cedric, Linnea Gelot, and John Karlsrud (eds.), *The future of African peace operations: From the Janjaweed to Boko Haram*. London: Zed Books.

de Coning, Cedric, Linnea Gelot, and John Karlsrud (eds.) (2016) *The future of African peace operations: From the Janjaweed to Boko Haram*. London: Zed Books.

Curran, David and Paul Holtom (2015) "Resonating, Rejecting, Reinterpreting: Mapping the Stabilization Discourse in the United Nations Security Council, 2000–14," *Stability: International Journal of Security & Development*, 4(1): pp. 1–18. https://doi.org/10.5334/sta.gm.

Darkwa, Linda (2017) "The African Standby Force: The African Union's tool for the maintenance of peace and security," Contemporary Security Policy, 38(3): pp. 1–12. doi: https://doi.org/10.1080/13523260.2017.1342478.

European Commission (2016) *African Peace Facility: Annual Report 2015*. Brussels: European Commission. Available at: http://www.africa-eu-partnership.org/sites/default/files/documents/apf-report-2015-en.pdf. Accessed July 7, 2016.

Gowan, Richard (2015a) "Ten Trends in UN Peacekeeping," in Jim Della-Giacoma (ed.), *Global Peace Operations Review: Annual Compilation 2015*. New York: Center on International Cooperation, New York University, pp. 17–26.

Gowan, Richard (2015b) "Can U.N. peacekeepers fight terrorists?," *Global Peace Operations Review*, June 30, 2015. Available at: http://peaceoperationsreview.org/commentary/can-u-n-peacekeepers-fight-terrorists/. Accessed January 11, 2016.

Holt, Victoria K. and Moira K. Shanahan (2005) *African Capacity-Building for Peace Operations: UN Collaboration with the African Union and ECOWAS*. Washington, DC: The Henry L. Stimson Center. Available at: file:///C:/Users/Karljoh/Downloads/doc_10936_290_en.pdf. Accessed July 7, 2016.

ICG (2016) "Chad: Between Ambition and Fragility," *Africa Report No. 233,* March 30, 2016. Available at: https://d2071andvip0wj.cloudfront.net/233-chad-between-ambition-and-fragility.pdf. Accessed August 26, 2016.

IMF (2015) *Regional Economic Outlook: Sub-Saharan Africa. Navigating Headwinds,* April 2015. Washington, DC: International Monetary Fund.

ISS (2015) "Kinshasa government attacks FDLR rebels without the UN," *ISS Peace and Security Council Report,* March 3, 2015. Available at: https://www.issafrica.org/pscreport/situation-analysis/kinshasa-government-attacks-fdlr-rebels-without-the-un. Accessed May 4, 2016.

Karlsrud, John (2017) "Towards UN counter-terrorism operations?," *Third World Quarterly,* 38 (6): pp. 1215–1231. doi: http://dx.doi.org/10.1080/01436597.2016.1268907.

Koops, Joachim A. and Thierry Tardy (2015) "The United Nations' Inter-Organizational Relations in Peacekeeping," in J. A. Koops, N. Macqueen, T. Tardy, and P. D. Williams (eds.), *The Oxford Handbook of United Nations Peacekeeping Operations.* Oxford: Oxford University Press, pp. 61–77.

Lacher, Wolfram and Denis M. Tull (2013) *Mali: Beyond Counterterrorism. SWP Comments 7.* Berlin: German Institute for International and Security Affairs (SWP).

Lagneau, Laurent (2014) "Le G5 Sahel demande une intervention de l'ONU en Libye, en accord avec l'Union africaine," December 20, 2014. Available at: http://www.opex360.com/2014/12/20/le-g5-sahel-demande-intervention-de-lonu-en-libye-en-accord-avec-lunion-africaine/. Accessed January 8, 2016.

Le Sahel (2014) "Communiqué final du Sommet des Chefs d'Etat du G5 du Sahel : Création d'un cadre institutionnel de coordination et de suivi de la coopération régionale dénommé G5 du Sahel," *Le Sahel.* Available at: http://www.lesahel.org/index.php/component/k2/item/5054-communiqu%C3%A9-final-du-sommet-des-chefs-detat-du-g5-du-sahel--cr%C3%A9ation-dun-cadre-institutionnel-de-coordination-et-de-suivi-de-la-coop%C3%A9ration-r%C3%A9gionale-d%C3%A9nomm%C3%A9-g5-du-sahel. Accessed January 8, 2016.

Lotze, Walter (2015) "United Nations Multidimensional Integrated Stabilization Mission in Mali (MINUSMA)," in J. A. Koops, N. Macqueen, T. Tardy, and P. D. Williams. (eds.), *The Oxford Handbook of United Nations Peacekeeping Operations.* Oxford: Oxford University Press, pp. 854–864.

Mail & Guardian (2014) "Jihadists announce blood-soaked return to northern Mali," *Mail & Guardian,* October 9, 2014. Available at: http://mgafrica.com/article/2014-10-09-jihadists-announce-blood-soaked-return-to-northern-mali. Accessed May 4, 2016.

Ministère de la Défense (2016) "Opération Barkhane," November 30, 2016. Available at: http://www.defense.gouv.fr/operations/sahel/dossier-de-presentation-de-l-operation-barkhane/operation-barkhane. Accessed January 8, 2017.

Power, Samantha (2015) "Remarks on Peacekeeping in Brussels," *United States Mission to the United Nations,* March 9, 2015. Available at: http://usun.state.gov/remarks/6399. Accessed January 8, 2016.

Reliefweb (2016) "Lake Chad Basin: Forced Displacement," June 16, 2016. Available at: http://reliefweb.int/report/nigeria/lake-chad-basin-forced-displacement-echo-ngos-un-government-echo-daily-flash-16-june. Accessed June 17, 2016.

Reykers, Yf (2016a) "Hurry Up and Wait: EU Battlegroups and a UN Rapid Reaction Force," January 21, 2016. Available at: http://peaceoperationsreview.org/thematic-essays/hurry-up-and-wait-eu-battlegroups-and-a-un-rapid-reaction-force/. Accessed June 21, 2016.

Reykers, Yf (2016b) "Waiting for Godot: A Rational-Institutionalist Analysis of the Absence of the EU Battlegroups in Recent Crises." Paper presented at The European Union in International Affairs V Conference, May 11–13, 2016, Brussels.

Reykers, Yf (2017) "High Costs, No Benefits," Contemporary Security Policy, 38(3): pp. 1–14. doi: https://doi.org/10.1080/13523260.2017.1348568.

Reykers, Yf and John Karlsrud (2017) "Multinational rapid response mechanisms: Past promises and future prospects," Contemporary Security Policy, 38(3): pp. 1–7. doi: https://doi.org/10.1080/13523260.2017.1348567.

Tull, Denis M. (2015) "Cameroon and Boko Haram: Time to Think beyond Terrorism and Security," *SWP Comments 42.* Berlin: German Institute for International and Security Affairs.

UN (2006a) "Monthly Summary of Contributions," as of January 31, 2006. Available at: http://www.un.org/en/peacekeeping/resources/statistics/contributors_archive.shtml. Accessed May 4, 2016.

UN (2006b) *A/61/630,* December 12, 2006. New York: United Nations.

UN (2011) *S/RES/1973,* March 17, 2011. New York: United Nations.

UN (2012a) *S/2012/894,* November 28, 2012. New York: United Nations.

UN (2012b) *S/2012/439. Letter dated 13 June 2012 from the Secretary-General to the President of the Security Council,* June 13, 2012. New York United Nations.

UN (2012c) *S/2012/894. Report of the Secretary-General on the Situation in Mali,* November 28, 2012. New York: United Nations.

UN (2012d) *S/RES/2085,* December 20, 2012. New York: United Nations.

UN (2013a) *S/RES/2098,* March 28, 2013. New York: United Nations.

UN (2013b) *S/RES/2100,* April 25, 2013. New York: United Nations.

UN (2013c) *S/RES/2102,* May 2, 2013. New York: United Nations.

UN (2013d) *S/2013/189. Report of the Secretary-General on the Situation in Mali,* March 26, 2013. New York: United Nations.

UN (2013e) "'Intervention Brigade' Authorized as Security Council Grants Mandate Renewal for United Nations Mission in Democratic Republic of Congo," March 28, 2013. Available at: http://www.un.org/press/en/2013/sc10964.doc.htm. Accessed September 27, 2016.

UN (2014) *S/RES/2182*, October 24, 2014. New York: United Nations.

UN (2015a) *A/70/95-S/2015/446. Report of the High-level Independent Panel on Peace Operations on Uniting our Strengths for Peace: Politics, Partnership and People* ("HIPPO Report"). New York: United Nations.

UN (2015b) *S/RES/2245*, November 9, 2015. New York: United Nations.

UN (2015c) *S/2015/567*, July 24, 2015. New York: United Nations.

UN (2015d) *S/PV.7487*, July 16, 2015. New York: United Nations.

UN (2016a) "(4a) Fatalities by Mission, Year and Incident Type," *United Nations Peacekeeping*, October 30, 2016. Available at: http://www.un.org/en/peacekeeping/fatalities/documents/stats_4a.pdf. Accessed February 7, 2017.

UN (2016b) "UN Peacekeeping Operations Fact Sheet: 30 June 2016." Available at: http://www.un.org/en/peacekeeping/documents/bnote0616.pdf. Accessed September 16, 2016.

UN (2016c) "United Nations Political and Peacebuilding Missions: 30 November 2015." Available at: http://www.un.org/undpa/sites/www.un.org.undpa/files/ppbm_November_2015.pdf. Accessed September 16, 2016.

de Waal, Alex (2016) "South Sudan's corrupt elite have driven a debt-free and oil-rich country to ruin," *International Business Times,* July 15, 2016. Available at: http://www.ibtimes.co.uk/south-sudans-corrupt-elite-have-driven-debt-free-oil-rich-country-ruin-1570845?utm_source=yahoo&utm_medium=referral&utm_campaign=rss&utm_content=%2Frss%2Fyahoous%2Fnews&yptr=yahoo. Accessed July 21, 2016.

What's in Blue (2014) "Informal Interactive Dialogue on UN Mission in Mali's Mandate," November 10, 2014. Available at: http://www.whatsinblue.org/2014/11/informal-interactive-dialogue-on-un-mission-in-malis-mandate.php#. Accessed January 8, 2016.

Williams, Paul D. (2015) "Special Report: How Many Fatalities Has the African Union Mission in Somalia Suffered?," *IPI Global Observatory*, September 10, 2015. Available at: http://theglobalobservatory.org/2015/09/amisom-african-union-somalia-peacekeeping/. Accessed January 11, 2016.

Williams, Paul D. and Arthur Boutellis (2014) "Partnership peacekeeping: Challenges and opportunities in the United Nations–African Union Relationship," *African Affairs,* 113 (451): pp. 254–278.

World Bank (2016) *Global Economic Prospects,* June 2015. Washington, DC: World Bank. Available at: https://www.worldbank.org/content/dam/Worldbank/GEP/GEP2015a/pdfs/GEP2015a_chapter2_regionaloutlook_SSA.pdf. Accessed June 13, 2016.

CHAPTER 6

People-Centered Reform at the UN? UN Peace Operations at a Crossroads

INTRODUCTION

With all the discussions on institutional challenges and the inner workings of the UN at headquarters in New York, it is too easy to lose sight of the real issue at hand: the millions of people who suffer during and after conflicts. We should never forget that the UN Charter was motivated by the desire "to save succeeding generations from the scourge of war [and] to promote social progress and better standards of life in larger freedom" (UN 1945: 3).

Recent reviews, like the HIPPO Report (UN 2015a), the 2015 review of the UN peacebuilding architecture (UN 2015b), and the 2030 agenda for sustainable development (UN 2015c), have reaffirmed this principle and put *people* at the front and center of the international community's efforts to bring about peace, security, and development. These reports focus on the need for responsive, inclusive, participatory, and representative political settlements to achieve sustained peace.

All this has followed in the wake of increasing criticism that the UN and other international peacebuilders focus more on placating national elites and their masters at headquarters in New York, Brussels, and Washington, rather than on the needs of the people they are mandated to protect. The international engagement in fragile states has been based on top–down approaches, assuming hierarchy in formal and informal, or neo-patrimonial, systems. Critics of international peace operations and peacebuilding interventions argue that strategies are devised on a normative basis—looking for what is lacking, rather than what is there. In other words—when a

© The Author(s) 2018
J. Karlsrud, *The UN at War*,
https://doi.org/10.1007/978-3-319-62858-5_7

...untry is deemed to be "failing" or "fragile" due to its lack of institutions, or the presence of weak ones, it may well be that we, as international interveners, fail to discern the informal structures of power present and operating (see, e.g., Eriksen 2011). The violence and parasitic behavior of rebel groups and sometimes government security forces may display "patterns of violence already embedded in society" (see, e.g., Bøås and Jennings 2012: 124). In many countries, current policies focus on propping up illegitimate regimes—while, as noted by Dörrie (2015), "militant groups provide social services and navigate local politics expertly. For many locals, that makes them no better or worse than central governments that have seldom provided any tangible benefit for the people living in the remote areas." This makes it essential to have a clear understanding of the political economy and the nature of the interplay between formal and informal governance structures, at national and local levels.

The UN should be in the business of protecting civilians, not governments. As the UN, the AU, and other multilateral organizations are state-centric organizations, this becomes a central challenge for interventions intended to halt conflict, and preserve and build peace. UN peacekeeping operations are normally supplied with a mandate to extend state authority, but there has not been enough emphasis on the quality, content, and direction of the authority being exercised. Although the objective is to support people in need, support is given through state structures that may not have the best interests of those people in mind, but may instead be intent on manipulating the resources of international partners—be they military, economic, or political—to perpetuate their own grip on power, legitimate or not. Further, Séverine Autesserre and other scholars argue that international peacebuilders are more intent on following their professional prescripts than responding to local needs (Autesserre 2010; Mac Ginty and Richmond 2013; de Coning 2013), focusing on tangible outputs like buildings, institutions, laws, and technical assistance: and the result is a top–down approach (Haider 2011). These critics argue that the UN needs to focus on helping establish states that are more accountable, inclusive, and responsive, capable of responding to the needs and views of their people (see, e.g., Schia et al. 2013, 2014). These must be articulated by the people through formal as well as informal political institutions (Pouligny 2010). In order to help—really help—people and the states they live in, UN peace operations must respond to the challenges facing fragile states by fostering societies that are more inclusive and more responsive (OECD 2015). Moreover, we cannot ignore the reports of peacekeepers who violate the trust of vulnerable groups, taking advantage of the very people they are meant to protect. The scandals involving peace-keepers in sexual abuse on a massive scale in the DRC and CAR have shown that there is still a long way to go.

To highlight the challenges that UN peacekeeping missions are facing and some of the best practices that have been generated, I take the case of the UNMISS and the MINUSCA, with a special focus on their ability (or not) to respond to the needs of people on the ground. Next, I ask how the UN can better respond to the needs of people affected by conflict, drawing on one of the central recommendations of the HIPPO Report: for peace operations to be successful, it is necessary to strengthen practices of UN peace operations for engaging with local people. Some concrete suggestions are offered as to how such commitments can be operationalized. In the context of potential reform, it is important not to lose sight of the UN's core mandate, which is to serve and protect the people on the ground. Political solutions must have their basis in the needs of the people, not those of self-serving elites, if they are to be sustainable and lay the foundations for long-term stability and peace.

Nowhere to Go? Protection of Civilians in South Sudan

On July 9, 2011, South Sudan gained independence from Sudan and became the world's 193rd country. The UN mission in Sudan was at the same time succeeded by the UNMISS, mandated with a broad statebuilding agenda (UN 2011). Although the country was debt-free and had income from oil, the struggle for liberation from Sudan was soon replaced with renewed internal struggle over money, resources, and land. The 20-year civil war had not only been between the north and south but also between various factions in the south (see, e.g., da Costa and de Coning 2015). These rivalries were rekindled by an economic crisis started by the shut-down of oil production in 2012. On December 15, 2013, violence broke out between the factions following President Salva Kiir and those following former Vice-President Riek Machar (who was dismissed from office on July 23, 2013).

As the country descended into violence, UNMISS struggled with providing protection to civilians seeking refuge. 85,000 internally displaced people fled to UNMISS camps, which eventually became permanent "protection of civilians sites" or "PoC sites" (Lilly 2014). The number of IDPs housed within the PoC sites increased continuously and exceeded 200,000 at one point (UNMISS 2015).[1] UNMISS bases were not set up to house such large number of IDPs, and because of the crammed conditions, it has been very difficult to maintain minimum humanitarian standards and the civilian character of the camps (UN 2016a). The PoC sites have since become a central task of the UN in South Sudan, at the expense of fulfilling mandated tasks including protection of civilians outside of the camps. The camps have also been attacked several times. On April 17, 2014, more than 50 civilians who had sought refuge in the UNMISS base in Bor were killed (Lilly 2014); and in February 2016, troops in SPLA uniforms entered the UNMISS protection site in Malakal, and killing 40 people and wounding many more (Lynch 2016).

A Board of Inquiry was set up to look into the Malakal incident, and found that UNMISS troops had failed to protect civilians. According to a UN official, "Ethiopian peacekeepers abandoned their posts during the attack" and "Rwandan peacekeepers asked for permission in writing to fire their weapons as the base was under attack, even though peacekeepers are obligated to use force to protect civilians" (cited in Lynch 2016). Hervé Ladsous, the then head of UN peacekeeping operations, vowed that this inaction would have consequences for the troops concerned: "I will not name names but there will be repatriations of units and of individual officers" (Al-Jazeera 2016). The Board of Inquiry that looked into the Malakal incident noted that "there were unrealistic expectations as to the level of protection that UNMISS could feasibly provide to the 48,000 internally displaced persons in Malakal at the time of the incident" (UN 2016b). Of the 48,000 IDPs, 32,719 were inside the base, while the rest were residing outside the base. This reflects an overall trend in South Sudan—UNMISS simply did not have the capacity to provide shelter and minimum physical protection for the rising numbers of IDPs in their bases, much less in the country at large.

When first mandated in 2011, the mission embarked on an ambitious program to support the extension of state authority and build national capacities to provide local-level service delivery by establishing County Support Bases (CSBs) in 35 counties (da Costa and de Coning 2013). These CSBs were planned as hubs for UN agencies, humanitarian actors, and others, facilitating peacebuilding and statebuilding on the local level. However, progress in establishing and running the bases was slow, and with the outbreak of violence in 2013, statebuilding was toned down. The new mandate adopted in 2014 focused on protection of civilians, human rights monitoring, and support to the delivery of humanitarian aid (UN 2014a). The HIPPO Report reflects this in recommending sequenced and phased mandates, adapting the mission to the political situation on the ground, and prioritizing core tasks like protection of civilians when the situation is unstable (see also Gorur and Sharland 2016; Johnstone 2016).

In August 2015, the main parties signed a peace agreement, but the peace was fragile, as the Malakal incident showed. In July 2016, as the country was getting ready to celebrate the fifth anniversary of its independence, fighting broke out again in Juba. Two UNMISS compounds in Juba were "caught in the cross-fire and sustained mortar and heavy artillery fire" and many thousands were displaced (UN 2016c). The then SG Ban Ki-moon was sharp in his criticism of Salva Kiir and Riek Machar: "the leaders of South Sudan have failed their people" (ibid.). As the violence escalated, UNMISS troops from Ethiopia, China, and Nepal were accused of standing by while a woman was raped outside their camp in clear view of about 30 troops (Kennedy 2016; Burke and Pilkington 2016), and the Terrain compound only minutes away from UNMISS bases housing international humanitarian workers was attacked for four long hours (Burke and Pilkington 2016). In a joint call to the international community at the end of July 2016, many of the humanitarian agencies in South Sudan deplored the "inability of UNMISS to protect civilians" and asked the international community to give the necessary support for UNMISS to implement its mandate and "protect civilians and humanitarian personnel and facilitate humanitarian assistance" (Oxfam International 2016).

To respond to the gap in providing civilian protection, IGAD and the AU have been advocating for a more robust force to be deployed to South Sudan. In July 2016, the AU Summit adopted the proposal of IGAD to include a 4000-strong African force in UNMISS, to be named a "Regional Protection Force" (RPF), modeled on the FIB in the DRC (Fabricius 2016). However, the situation confronting a possible RPF was more challenging than that facing the FIB when it was mandated in 2013. While President Joseph Kabila was supportive of the FIB, as it would help him to remove the M23 and reduce Rwandan influence in eastern DRC, President Salva Kiir remained strongly against proposals by the AU to intervene militarily in the conflict, including the RPF in July 2016. The USA is the penholder on South Sudan; it pushed for a robust mandate to be given to

UNMISS and the RPF. Since the beginning of the Civil War, President Salva Kiir has had a very difficult relationship with UNMISS—accusing it of being a "parallel government" (BBC 2014), and only reluctantly accepted the force after the UNSC threatened an arms embargo *(The Nation Mirror)*. On August 12, 2016, the RPF was included in UNMISS by the adoption of a new mandate for UNMISS (UN 2016d). The RPF would be under the command of the UNMISS Force Commander and tasked with "the responsibility of providing a secure environment in and around Juba," and deployed "*in extremis* in other parts of South Sudan as necessary" (ibid.: 4).

The attackers at the Terrain compound were eventually stopped by the South Sudanese government, after pressure from the US Embassy (Burke and Pilkington 2016). The Terrain incident thus shows the limits of the use of force. The mission is faced with an exceedingly difficult dilemma when the threat against civilians comes from the host government, or militia groups affiliated with or supporting the government. If it intervenes against a strategic level actor, the UN risks the withdrawal of consent, the immediate stop of freedom of movement, and eventually the end of the mission. However, if it does not act, the mission will be accused of standing idly by while civilians are raped and murdered. For the greater good of being able to retain its presence on the ground, the mission might choose the latter option.[2] This highlights the need for the UN to be a central player in the political negotiations, which is unfortunately not the case in South Sudan.

To understand South Sudanese politics, we must take into consideration the long history of violence and war and the patchwork of ethnic militias that have been kept in check by a constant supply of oil money. As Alex de Waal argues, "President Kiir's strategy for remaining on top of his diverse, fractious and quarrelsome generals, and other members of a kleptocratic elite, was a 'big tent' policy: he paid them all off by allowing them to steal from state coffers" (de Waal 2016). When the state coffers ran empty in 2013, it was only a matter of time before unrest and violence would begin. The peace deal that was reached in 2015 did not change the situation: it simply maintained the status quo, dividing the responsibility for providing security in Juba between the security forces of the two opponents (ibid.). At every level, South Sudan has been moving toward greater, not less insecurity for people on the ground. Militias have been extracting bribes and payments on every road in the country (ibid.).

These trends indicate several thorny dilemmas. First, at the political level, has enough been done to come to a political solution to the conflict, to avoid further displacement and bloodshed, but also establish more transparent control of the finances of the country? IGAD, the AU, and bilateral partners have been taking the lead in the political mediation process, giving UNMISS a weak political role. Commenting on the missions in the DRC, Darfur, and South Sudan, the HIPPO Report lamented that "the United Nations and its partners have been unable to marshal the political effort necessary to provide solutions to these conflicts and ultimately to facilitate a responsible exit strategy" (UN 2015a: 5).

Second, South Sudan also reveals that there is an enduring gap between increasingly robust mandates and the ability and willingness to use force on the ground. In part, the gap reflects the lack of political will among many of the troop contributing countries to expose their troops to danger, when push comes to shove. This should be addressed through at least three different actions. First, there needs to be greater pre-mission awareness of general caveats that TCCs may have, by including these caveats "not only in the MoU signed with DPKO but also in the concept of operations and the operational plan" (Novosseloff 2016). This will enable greater clarity for the Force Commander and staff when planning troop deployment, and the caveats to be accommodated if the UN Secretariat accepts troops from a particular country. Second, if the lack of action is a result not of an announced caveat, but rather an act of disobedience or a "hidden" or "sudden" caveat, strict enforcement measures should be enacted, with the SG naming and shaming and repatriating non-performing contingents. Third, the improvement of the sourcing of TCC contingents and pledges needs to be further strengthened by deeper dialogue between Western states and TCCs on the limits of "robust peacekeeping" (ibid.).

Third, to what extent has the UNSC enabled and resourced the mission to execute its task according to its mandate? Is it realistic to expect UNMISS to be able to protect civilians across the country when conflict is raging? In South Sudan, even if all the troops had been ready and able to use force to protect civilians, they would not have been able to cover the protection needs. There are and will continue to be large gaps between the mandates given by the UNSC and the ability of the UN to implement these, as long as missions are deployed with a conflict management role, and not a peacekeeping one.

The Central African Republic: On a Treadmill to Oblivion?

On April 10, 2014, the UNSC mandated the UN peacekeeping operation in the CAR, the MINUSCA, to replace the existing SPM known as the UN Integrated Peacebuilding Office in the Central African Republic (BINUCA) (UN 2014b).[3] The crisis was the last in a long string of violence, coups, and upheavals, stretching back for more than a decade. The country is one of the least developed in the world, and being land-locked and with only 4.9 million inhabitants (World Bank 2016), it has managed to retain the attention of the international community for only a few years at the time. In 2014, CAR ranked 187 out of 188 on the Human Development Index. The country has had serious challenges in extending its authority even to the outskirts of Bangui, the capital (UNDP 2015: 237).

In 2013, the country again descended into internal conflict, with Muslims (Séléka) pitted against Christian (anti-Balaka) populations. In March 2013, President Francois Bozizé was ousted by the Séléka rebels who installed Michel Djotodia as the leader of the CAR for the next ten months. The crisis lingered on with unrest and violence continuing. In December 2013, the UNSC authorized the MISCA and a French-backed peacekeeping force *(Opération Sangaris)* (UN 2013).[4] MISCA deployed about 5000 troops and *Sangaris* 2000 troops in the next months. Soon after, on February 10, 2014, with the support of the UNSC, the EU mandated the deployment of the operation EUFOR RCA, to consist of another 700 troops (UN 2014c; EU 2016). The international troops were able to keep matters in check at least partially, but the situation on the ground remained volatile, with recurring outbursts of violence. In March 2014, the UN Special Adviser on the Prevention of Genocide, Adama Dieng, warned, "that crimes against humanity are being committed and that the risk of genocide remains high" (UN 2014d). With Resolution 2149, adopted by the UNSC on April 10, 2014, the UN mission MINUSCA was mandated to replace MISCA on September 15, 2014, and "include in MINUSCA as many MISCA military and police personnel as possible and in line with United Nations standards" (UN 2014b: 8).

MINUSCA was given a broad mandate to stabilize and support various peace- and statebuilding tasks in the CAR, including protection of civilians, mediation and reconciliation efforts at national and local levels, the political transition and preparations for elections, DDR of combatants, and the rapid extension of state authority. For several years prior to MINUSCA's deployment, the UN had, through various agencies and BINUCA, been running peacebuilding programs including in the area of DDR, with little progress. An independent evaluation undertaken for the UN Peacebuilding Fund found that programs implemented between 2008 and 2012 lacked an inclusive and participatory approach in design and implementation; suffered from a lack of strategic coherence between the various agencies implementing the programs; lacked a theory of change and how the individual program should contribute to peacebuilding, and lack of monitoring and evaluation (Vinck et al. 2012: 9). Furthermore, the report argued that key dimensions of the domestic conflict dynamics, such as the exploitation of natural resources and the conflict between farmers and herders, had not been addressed. This was confirmed by the descent into renewed chaos only months after the evaluation report was published.

Unfortunately, for the CAR, the international community have not been able to sustain its attention for long enough to support lasting peace. Although it is generally agreed that the relatively rapid deployment of MISCA and *Sangaris* contributed to averting large-scale massacres and a reduction in violence where peacekeepers have been deployed, the follow-on mission MINUSCA has been stretched thin and not seen as able to respond to and prevent attacks against civilians, particularly outside of Bangui (see, e.g., Barbelet 2015: 11). However, MINUSCA has also generated some new practices that should be noted. Its joint police and military task force in Bangui have received praise for the "arrest of 'high-value' targets who were involved in violence against predominantly Muslim neighborhoods and international security forces" (Sebastián 2015: 20). As an "urgent temporary measure" (UTM), MINUSCA was in 2015 with Resolution 2217 given semi-executive authority "to arrest and detain in order to maintain basic law and order and fight impunity" (UN 2015d: 11). While this offered the mission the option of arresting and detaining individuals, it also gave rise to familiar dilemmas about how to handle possible prisoners and whether they can be handed back to national authorities to an unknown fate.

MINUSCA was mandated to support the redeployment of "[s]tate administration in the provinces, including through the effective restoration of the administration of the judiciary and the criminal justice system throughout the country" (ibid.: 7). That was a tall order, as in many places it is not a question of redeploying state authorities, but of establishing the

presence of state authorities for the very first time, challenging local traditional and other forms of governance. This has become a familiar dilemma
in UN peace operations, and over time the organization has developed
practices and guidelines for grappling with center-periphery governance
tensions in war-torn countries. Civil Affairs officers are usually at the center of this effort. The Civil Affairs team in the CAR has underscored its
"support to local level efforts and bottom up approaches to protection,
political dialogue and the promotion of social cohesion" (MINUSCA
2016). It has also emphasized its role in gauging local perceptions and
providing early warning about local conflict dynamics (ibid.). The bottom–up approach of the Civil Affairs section in MINUSCA is mirrored in
many other UN peace operations, and often stands in stark contrast to the
top–down focus of the UNSC and the UN Secretariat.

The support of the international community to the crisis in the CAR
has also been marred by repeated revelations of sexual exploitation and
abuse by international peacekeepers. A leaked UN report in 2014 revealed
sexual abuse of boys down to nine years of age by French, Chadian, and
Equatorial Guinean troops (Code Blue 2015). Anders Kompass, a Swedish
UN employee who passed details of the report to French authorities, was
first suspended and investigated by the UN for leaking information, but
was later exonerated after massive pressure on the UN to deal more force-
fully with these issues and not sweep them under the carpet. On June 3,
2015, the SG commissioned an external review to examine the issue. Only
two months later, Babacar Gaye, the SRSG and head of MINUSCA, was
forced to resign, after revelations of new abuses involving UN peacekeepers (BBC 2015). The external review, released in December 2015, docu-
mented "gross institutional failure" in the UN's handling of the allegations
of sexual exploitation and abuse by UN peacekeepers (Deschamps et al.
2015: v). Unfortunately, the story did not end there—on March 25,
2016, the UN announced that it had received new allegations of sexual
exploitation and abuse, this time committed by troops from Burundi and
Gabon (UN 2016e). The SG vowed to improve performance and underscored the UN's zero tolerance policy on sexual exploitation and abuse
(UN 2016f). Adding to this, Human Rights Watch had previously
reported that MISCA troops from the Republic of Congo had committed
serious crimes against anti-Balaka prisoners, including forced disappear-
ances, torture, and extrajudicial killings (Human Rights Watch 2014).

On September 15, 2016, EUFOR RCA ended its mission. France also
pulled out the remainder of *Sangaris*, about 900 troops, during 2016.

Unfortunately, it is conceivable that the CAR will receive diminishing attention in the years to come, with a corresponding decline in member-state support, troop numbers, and funding. The international community has a limited attention span and the CAR does not spark the same strategic interests as Mali, South Sudan, or the DRC (and even these countries do not easily grab the headlines). The result is likely to be a limited reach of MINUSCA beyond Bangui and the main population centers, and insufficient attention to the necessary reforms, reconciliation, and disarmament measures that need to be implemented by President Faustin Archange Touadera, who was elected president in 2016 (and who was prime minister under President François Bozizé). Sustained attention to the root causes of the conflict—including elite kleptocracy, marginalization of the Muslim population, illegal natural resource extraction, and lack of support to build up a more inclusive and responsive governance apparatus—is sorely needed if the country is to avoid falling into another spiral of violence and turmoil (see, e.g., Day 2016).

RESPONDING TO THE NEEDS OF PEOPLE IN CONFLICT

Concerning the strategic level, the HIPPO Report argued for "a renewed resolve on the part of UN peace operations personnel to engage with, serve and protect the people they have been mandated to assist" (UN 2015a: viii). Conflict-affected countries often struggle with center–periphery tensions, along with self-serving elites who know how to engage with and influence international actors, but who neither necessarily represent the general populace, or have its best interests in mind. The HIPPO Report is in line with the recommendations of the UNSG in his 2014 report on *Peacebuilding in the Aftermath of Conflict*, where he

> stressed the importance of mechanisms for inclusive politics in post-conflict transitions. […] Promoting inclusivity can involve difficult choices and trade-offs regarding urgency, representativeness, effectiveness and legitimacy. […] Yet, in order to sustain peace and uphold basic rights of political participation, subsequent mechanisms for broad participation need to be embraced, with the goal of increasing inclusivity over time. (UN 2014e: 7)

The Sustainable Development Goals build on the Millennium Development Goals and follow up on the recommendations of the UNSG. Goal 16 emphasizes the need to "promote peaceful and inclusive societies"; and "effective, accountable and inclusive institutions at all levels" (UN 2015c: 14).

However, truly engaging with local populations will necessarily involve difficult trade-offs and negotiations. The main interlocutor in peacekeeping and peacebuilding is the host state, and states are the primary units of the UN. The focus on strengthening state authority is thus built into the system itself. Host states may view any efforts to consult more broadly and deeply with the local population as infringing on their sovereignty. For peacebuilding and peacekeeping efforts to succeed, however, it is essential to build more inclusive and participatory states that are responsive and accountable to their people. In tandem, it is crucial to build institutions, and to build trust in those institutions. Missions should support inclusive politics, but also more inclusive economics. As the former SRSG in Liberia, Karin Landgren, convincingly points out, it is important to move away from an enclave economy that benefits only a small elite (2015).

The key tenet of the HIPPO Report and the SG's peacebuilding report (2014e) is the primacy of politics—and politics grounded in the will and needs of the people of conflict-affected countries, on the national and local levels. The engagement of external peacebuilders—focusing their efforts on building national capacity and extending state authority—can add tension rather than build peace: "in a context of fragmentation, it is possible that an attempt to rebuild or extend central authority could lead not to peace but to deepening conflict" (UN 2015a: 16). Looking at the practices of the UNSC and in the field, Johnstone argues that there may be a normative shift ongoing, where protection mandates are merged with "proactive public order mandates for peace operations" (2010: 197). This can result in a dilemma between the mandate to extend state authority and the need to obtain the consent of the main parties of the conflict.

In his follow-up report to HIPPO, the then SG Ban Ki-moon argued that the UN should be "more responsive and more accountable to the needs of countries and people in conflict" (UN 2015e: 3)—as he also singled out as one of three key priorities when launching the report (UN 2015f). The follow-up report went on to deal with expectation management and strategic communications to "foster public support," but this is only part of the picture. To achieve inclusive political settlements, the people need to be consulted and feel consulted, not merely informed. However, there was little in the report on how UN peace operations should be made more accountable to people's needs. This is disappointing, as the HIPPO Report raised expectations for a more reflective stance on the topic.

The examples of South Sudan and CAR have showed the need to focus on political solutions that are grounded in the needs of the people and not the elite. A fast-tracked political solution may be successful in bringing the situation and the country out of the international community spotlight— but unless underlying grievances and insecurities of local populations are addressed, tensions will linger on and violence is likely to resume. UN peace operations need to engage with local communities and facilitate the communication of their needs into a broad and inclusive peace process (UN 2016g; Rupesinghe 2016a, b).

To move from conflict to peace consolidation, "genuine deliberation among internal and external actors" is required (Johnstone 2007: 14). Deliberative democracy is not the same as liberal democracy, but to pre-vent external actors from imposing their statebuilding prescripts of elec-toral democracies and market-based economies, deliberation on the form and function of the state is needed on all levels. Deliberation should be guided by the principles of reciprocity, participation, and publicity—sig-naling mutual respect, inclusion, and accountability for decisions taken (ibid.). UN peace operations can foster engagement and support for key processes to move on, such as transitional governance on national levels; the provision of security by state actors, international interveners, and rebel groups; and transitional justice that can balance between justice and retribution, and between formal and customary law (ibid.). Promising practices are being generated in several missions today, for example, in CAR, but there is still reluctance among many member states to start to make the needed change in the mandates from "extend state authority" to "enhance state-society relations and social cohesion".

What Has the UN Been Doing?

People-oriented peace operations will have to respond to the protection needs of people in vulnerable situations, but also be sufficiently equipped and supported to mediate a long-term political solution that can put the country on a more peaceful path. This will require the full support of key member states, regional organizations, and the membership of the UNSC. The focus on PoC has undoubtedly had a positive impact on the willingness and ability of UN peacekeeping to take a more people-centered approach during the last 15 years. However, as Jean Arnault (2015) con-vincingly argues, one effect has been that missions have been mandated to protect civilians in a robust manner, often without a corresponding long-term political strategy. While the PoC strategy has three pillars, the main focus has been on protecting civilians from physical violence, with an emphasis on military capabilities and the willingness to use them. Protecting civilians in situations of ongoing conflict is an insurmountable task if the parties have not agreed to stop fighting and missions are deployed in a "conflict management" mode.

On the positive side, this has brought heightened attention at UN headquarters to what peace operations do at local levels. For instance, it has led to the inclusion of new capacities for better understanding local conflict dynamics and perceptions. One example here could be the Community Liaison Assistants and the Community Alert Networks first deployed by the UN stabilization mission in the Democratic Republic of Congo and now being rolled out in several other missions (UN 2015g). Another example is the set of guidelines on understanding and integrating local perceptions issued by the UN DPKO in 2014 (UN 2014f). DPKO has also been working on a set of guidelines for supporting and enhancing state–society relations at the local level.

A third example is the Country Support Bases UNMISS started to establish before the crisis in 2013 (da Costa and de Coning 2013). These bases were intended to enable improved state presence and service delivery on the local level. UNMIL in Liberia serves as a fourth example, with its Justice and Security Hubs and County Security Councils that boosted the presence of national authorities on local levels and facilitated the transition and exit of the peacekeeping mission (Caparini 2014; Landgren 2015; Schia 2015). Together, these examples show that there is indeed momentum for a more people-centered approach in UN peace operations, but this must be matched with an understanding that this is not only an issue for civil affairs officers in the field, but should guide the overall strategy of the mission if it is to be successful.

HOW SHOULD PEACE OPERATIONS BECOME MORE PEOPLE-ORIENTED?

The conflicts in eastern DRC, northern Mali and South Sudan are "messy"—it is not a question of one single conflict in each of these countries, but of multiple larger and smaller conflicts that overlap and intersect, each with their complex set of actors and interests. These conflicts concern land, power, material, and economic resources but may also relate to historical disputes over identity, social status, and exclusion. To understand the political economy and how to manage some of these conflicts, and thereby set them on the path from violent confrontation to peaceful resolution, peace operations must become better at engaging with and understanding local communities and their conflict dynamics.

UN peacekeeping operations have long had significant presence outside of the capitals of the countries to which they are deployed. Their civil affairs officers have often been the only presence in remote locations; indeed, in some places, such as Kosovo and Timor-Leste, the UN missions have *been* the government on the ground. Civil affairs officers, military liaison officers, gender advisors, and, more recently, community liaison assistants can all reach out and talk with local communities and their representatives. However, missions need to take care to identify credible voices among youth, women, and civil society, as well as traditional, religious, and academic leaders. A frequent challenge is that one and the same person may be a traditional leader, a businessman, and a member of an armed group. Officials may not be the most influential members of society, and could have much to gain from the legitimacy that external peacebuilders can confer. Extra care should be taken not to appear partial solely to the local authorities. It is vital to reach out to minorities and others who may not be represented.

Missions should use experts, social anthropologists, and others with in-depth knowledge of the country, as has been done in Liberia (Landgren 2015). Community liaison assistants and community alert networks are useful new innovations. National professional officers have always been a valuable source of knowledge and analysis, and may be able to serve as brokers between the mission and local communities (da Costa and Karlsrud 2013). Surveys should be carried out at regular intervals to establish baselines for monitoring of opinions and progress, and appropriate plans should be developed on the results (for an example of surveys on Liberia, see Afrobarometer 2016). New tools and technologies have made it easier to conduct quick opinion polls; they offer a way toward better understanding the needs and challenges of affected populations.

The Civil Affairs Section of the DPKO has been working on a set of guidelines to improve engagement with local communities. Reflecting the concern highlighted in the above-mentioned reviews of peace operations and peacebuilding, the language in Security Council mandates should be shifted from the standard mandate of "extending state authority" to "enhancing and supporting local-level state/society relations." As Cedric de Coning, Paul Troost, and I have argued elsewhere (de Coning et al.

2015), this work needs further support from member states, civil society, and other stakeholders if peace operations are to succeed in states emerging from conflict. Should UN peace operations address issues of state–society relations, such as inequality, marginalization, and lack of social cohesion? Some member states would probably say "no." However, if the UN is to succeed in sustaining peace, the answer is undoubtedly "yes."

The task is far from easy. Exclusion, discrimination, elite kleptocracy, and instrumentalized politics are often at the root of a conflict, with powerful interests seeking to keep things that way. Leadership may be under duress because of prolonged resource and capacity constraints—which also increase the chance of leaders falling prey to corruption, collusion with organized crime, and self-serving maintenance of the status quo.

NOTES

1. The total number of IDPs reached 180,000 by December 2013 and rapidly increased during the conflict, reaching about 1,600,000 in July 2016 (OCHA 2016).
2. I would like to thank Cedric de Coning for highlighting this point.
3. BINUCA was a peacebuilding mission without police and military components.
4. MISCA stands for *Mission Internationale de Soutien à la Centrafrique sous Conduite Africaine.*

REFERENCES

Afrobarometer (2016) "Liberia data," *Afrobarometer.* Available at: http://afrobarometer.org/data/320. Accessed January 12, 2016.

Al-Jazeera (2016) "UN to send peacekeepers home over South Sudan inaction," *Al-Jazeera,* June 23, 2016. Available at: http://www.aljazeera.com/news/2016/06/send-peacekeepers-home-south-sudan-inaction-160623060004340.html. Accessed July 25, 2016.

Arnault, Jean (2015) "A background to the report of the high-level panel on peace operations," *Global Peace Operations Review.* Available at: http://peaceoperationsreview.org/thematic-essays/a-background-to-the-report-of-the-high-level-panel-on-peace-operations/. Accessed January 8, 2016.

Autesserre, Séverine (2010) *The Trouble with the Congo: Local Violence and the Failure of International Peacebuilding.* New York: Cambridge University Press.

Barbelet, Veronique (2015) *Central African Republic: addressing the protection crisis.* London: Humanitarian Policy Group, Overseas Development Institute.

Available at: https://www.odi.org/publications/10103-central-african-republic-addressing-protection-crisis. Accessed August 17, 2016.

BBC (2014) "South Sudan President Salva Kiir hits out at UN," January 21, 2014. Available at: http://www.bbc.com/news/world-africa-25826598. Accessed September 6, 2016.

BBC (2015) "UN's CAR envoy Gaye sacked over peacekeeper abuse claims," August 12, 2015. Available at: http://www.bbc.com/news/world-africa-33890664. Accessed August 17, 2016.

Burke, Jason and Ed Pilkington (2016) "UN under pressure over 'failure to act' during South Sudan rampage," *The Guardian*, August 17, 2016. Available at: https://www.theguardian.com/world/2016/aug/17/un-under-pressure-over-failure-to-act-during-south-sudan-rampage. Accessed September 16, 2016.

Bøås, Morten and Kathleen M. Jennings (2012) "Rebellion and warlordism: The spectre of neopatrimonialism," in Daniel C. Bach and Mamoudou Gazibo (eds.), *Neopatrimonialism in Africa and Beyond*. Abingdon: Routledge, pp. 124–131.

Caparini, Marina (2014) *Extending State Authority in Liberia: The Gbarnga Justice and Security Hub*. Oslo: Norwegian Institute of International Affairs (NUPI).

Code Blue (2015) "The UN's Dirty Secret: The untold story of child sexual abuse in the Central African Republic and Anders Kompass," May 29, 2015. Available at: http://www.codebluecampaign.com/carstatement/. Accessed August 17, 2016.

de Coning, Cedric (2013) "Understanding Peacebuilding as Essentially Local," *Stability* 2 (1): pp. 1–6.

de Coning, Cedric, John Karlsrud, and Paul Troost (2015) "Towards More People-Centric Peace Operations: From 'Extension of State Authority' to 'Strengthening Inclusive State-Society Relations,'" *Stability: International Journal of Security & Development*, 4 (1): pp. 1–13.

da Costa, Diana Felix and Cedric de Coning (2013) "UNMISS County Support Bases: peacekeeping–peacebuilding nexus at work?," *Policy Brief 4, 2013*. Oslo: Norwegian Institute of International Affairs (NUPI).

da Costa, Diana Felix, and Cedric de Coning (2015) "United Nations Mission in the Republic of South Sudan (UNMISS)," in J. A. Koops, N. Macqueen, T. Tardy and P. D. Williams (eds.), *The Oxford Handbook of United Nations Peacekeeping Operations*. Oxford: Oxford University Press, pp. 830–841.

da Costa, Diana Felix, and John Karlsrud (2013) "'Bending the rules': the space between HQ policy and local action in UN Civilian Peacekeeping," *Journal of International Peacekeeping*, 17 (3–4), pp. 293–312.

Day, Christopher (2016) "The Bangui Carousel: How the recycling of political elites reinforces instability and violence in the Central African Republic," *The Enough Project*. Available at: http://www.enoughproject.org/files/TheBanguiCarousel_080216.pdf. Accessed August 19, 2016.

Deschamps, Marie, Hassan B. Jallow, and Yasmin Sooka (2015) *Taking Action on Sexual Exploitation and Abuse by Peacekeepers: Report of an Independent Review on Sexual Exploitation and Abuse by International Peacekeeping Forces in the Central African Republic.* New York: United Nations. Available at: http://www.un.org/News/dh/infocus/centafricrepub/Independent-Review-Report.pdf. Accessed August 17, 2016.

Dörrie, Peter (2015) "France's Overstretched Military Not Enough to Stabilize the Sahel," *World Politics Review,* December 15, 2015. Available at: http://www.worldpoliticsreview.com/articles/17460/france-s-overstretched-military-not-enough-to-stabilize-the-sahel. Accessed January 11, 2016.

Eriksen, Stein S. (2011) "'State failure' in theory and practice: the idea of the state and the contradictions of state formation," *Review of International Studies* 37 (1): pp. 229–247.

EU (2016) "EUFOR RCA," European Union External Action. Available at: http://www.eeas.europa.eu/archives/csdp/missions-and-operations/eufor-rca/index_en.htm. Accessed July 27, 2016.

Fabricius, Peter (2016) "The AU's silver bullet to end fighting in South Sudan?," July 20, 2016. Pretoria: Institute for Security Studies. Available at: https://www.issafrica.org/iss-today/the-aus-silver-bullet-to-end-fighting-in-south-sudan. Accessed August 11, 2016.

Gorur, Aditi and Lisa Sharland (2016) *Prioritizing the Protection of Civilians in UN Peace Operations: Analyzing the Recommendations of the HIPPO Report.* Washington DC: The Henry L. Stimson Center. Available at: https://www.stimson.org/sites/default/files/file-attachments/PCIC-HIPPO-REPORT-FINAL-WEB.pdf. Accessed July 23, 2016.

Haider, Huma (2011) *State–Society Relations and Citizenship in Situations of Conflict and Fragility.* Birmingham: Governance and Social Development Resource Centre, University of Birmingham.

Human Rights Watch (2014) "Central African Republic: Peacekeepers Tied to Abuse," June 2, 2014. Available at: https://www.hrw.org/news/2014/06/02/central-african-republic-peacekeepers-tied-abuse. Accessed August 17, 2016.

Johnstone, Ian (2007) "Consolidating Peace: Priorities and Deliberative Processes," in Ian Johnstone (ed.) *Annual Review of Global Peace Operations.* Boulder, CO: Lynne Rienner. Available at: https://www.dropbox.com/s/9y88xwb1g7qfefu/2007_annual_review.pdf. Accessed July 7, 2016.

Johnstone, Ian (2010) "Normative Evolution at the UN: Impact on Operational Imperatives," in Bruce D. Jones, Shepard Forman, and Richard Gowan (eds.), *Cooperating for Peace and Security: Evolving Institutions and Arrangements in a Context of Changing U.S. Security Policy.* Cambridge: Cambridge University Press, pp. 187–214.

Johnstone, Ian (2016) "Between Bureaucracy and Adhocracy: Crafting a Spectrum of Peace Operations," *Global Peace Operations Review,* March 31, 2016.

Available at: http://peaceoperationsreview.org/thematic-essays/from-bureau-cracy-to-adhocracy-crafting-a-spectrum-of-un-peace-operations/.   Accessed April 27, 2016.

Kennedy, Merrit (2016) "Witnesses: U.N. Peacekeepers Did Nothing As South Sudanese Soldiers Raped Women," *NPR*, July 27, 2016. Available at: http://www.npr.org/sections/thetwo-way/2016/07/27/487625112/report-u-n-peacekeepers-did-nothing-as-south-sudanese-soldiers-raped-women. Accessed August 14, 2016.

Landgren, Karin (2015) "Reflections on a career in peace operations," *Global Peace Operations Review*. Available at: http://peaceoperationsreview.org/interviews/karin-landgren-reflections-on-a-career-in-peace-operations/. Accessed January 12, 2016.

Lilly, Damian (2014) "Protection of Civilians sites: a new type of displacement settlement?" *Humanitarian Exchange* No 62, November 2014: pp. 31-33. Available at: http://odihpn.org/wp-content/uploads/2014/09/HE_62_web2_FINAL.pdf. Accessed July 23, 2016.

Lynch, Justin (2016) "UN failed to protect civilians in South Sudan: report," *Al-Jazeera*, June 22, 2016. Available at: http://www.aljazeera.com/news/2016/06/failed-protect-civilians-south-sudan-report-160622060607406.html. Accessed July 25, 2016.

Mac Ginty, Roger and Oliver Richmond (2013) "The local turn in peace building: a critical agenda for peace," *Third World Quarterly*, 34 (5): pp. 763–783.

MINUSCA (2016) "Civil Affairs." Available at: http://minusca.unmissions.org/en/civil-affairs. Accessed August 17, 2016.

Novosseloff, Alexandra (2016) "No Caveats Please?: Breaking a Myth in UN Peace Operations," September 12, 2016. Available at: http://peaceoperation-sreview.org/thematic-essays/no-caveats-please-breaking-a-myth-in-un-peace-operations/. Accessed September 14, 2016.

OCHA (2016) "South Sudan," OCHA. Available at: http://www.unocha.org/south-sudan. Accessed July 25, 2016.

OECD (2015) *States of Fragility 2015: Meeting Post-2015 Ambitions*. Paris: OECD Publishing.

Oxfam International (2016) "Violence fuels South Sudan's humanitarian crisis," July 28, 2016. Available at: https://www.oxfam.org/en/pressroom/pressre-leases/2016-07-28/violence-fuels-south-sudans-humanitarian-crisis. Accessed August 14, 2016.

Pouligny, Béatrice (2010) *State–Society Relations and Intangible Dimensions of State Resilience and State Building: A Bottom–Up Perspective*. Florence: European University Institute.

Rupesinghe, Natasja (2016a) "Community Engagement: softening the hard edge of stabilization," *Conflict Trends*, 2016 (3): pp. 20–26.

Rupesinghe, Natasja (2016b) "Strengthening Community Engagement in United Nations Peace Operations: Opportunities and Challenges in the Field," *Policy Brief 30· 2016.* Oslo: Norwegian Institute of International Affairs (NUPI).

Schia, Niels N. (2015) *Peacebuilding, Ownership, and Sovereignty from New York to Monrovia: A Multi-sited Ethnographic Approach.* Department of Social Anthropology, University of Oslo: Academia.

Schia, Niels N., Ingvild, M. Gjelsvik, and John Karlsrud (2013) "What people think does matter: Understanding and integrating local perceptions into UN peacekeeping." *Policy Brief 13 · 2013.* Oslo: Norwegian Institute of International Affairs (NUPI).

Schia, Niels N., Ingvild M. Gjelsvik, and John Karlsrud (2014) "Connections and disconnections: understanding and integrating local perceptions in United Nations peacekeeping," *Conflict Trends* 2014 (1): pp. 28–34.

Sebastián, Sofía (2015) "The Role of Police in UN Peace Operations: Filling the Gap in the Protection of Civilians from Physical Violence," *Civilians in Conflict: Policy Brief No. 3.* Washington DC: Stimson Center. Available at: https://www.stimson.org/sites/default/files/file-attachments/CIC-Policy-Brief_3_Sept-2015-Web-REVISED_Jan2016_0.pdf. Accessed August 17, 2016.

UN (1945) *Charter of the United Nations and Statute of the International Court of Justice.* New York: United Nations.

UN (2011) *S/RES/1996,* July 8, 2011. New York: United Nations.

UN (2013) *S/RES/2127,* December 5, 2013. New York: United Nations.

UN (2014a) S/RES/2155, May 27, 2014. New York: United Nations.

UN (2014b) S/RES/2149, April 10, 2014. New York: United Nations.

UN (2014c) S/RES/2134, January 28, 2014. New York: United Nations.

UN (2014d) "Meeting of the Security Council in Arria format on Inter-communities dialogue and prevention of crimes in Central African Republic: Statement of Under Secretary-General/Special Adviser on the Prevention of Genocide Mr. Adama Dieng," March 14, 2014. Available at: http://www.un.org/en/preventgenocide/adviser/pdf/2014-03-12%20Statement%20of%20USG%20Adama%20Dieng%20to%20the%20Security%20%20Council.%20FINAL.pdf. Accessed July 27, 2016.

UN (2014e) *A/69/399-S/2014/694. Peacebuilding in the Aftermath of Conflict.* New York: United Nations.

UN (2014f) Guidelines on Understanding and Integrating Local Perceptions in UN Peacekeeping. New York: United Nations.

UN (2015a) *A/70/95-S/2015/446. Report of the High-level Independent Panel on Peace Operations on Uniting our Strengths for Peace: Politics, Partnership and People* ("HIPPO Report"). New York: United Nations.

UN (2015b) *The Challenge of Sustaining Peace: Report of the Advisory Group of Experts for the 2015 Review of the United Nations Peacebuilding Architecture.* New York: United Nations.

UN (2015c) *Transforming Our World: The 2030 Agenda for Sustainable Development*. New York: United Nations. Available at: https://sustainabledevelopment.un.org/post2015/transformingourworld. Accessed June 14, 2016.

UN (2015d) *S/RES/2217*, April 28, 2015. New York: United Nations.

UN (2015e) *A/70/357–S/2015/682. The future of United Nations peace operations: implementation of the recommendations of the High-level Independent Panel on Peace Operations*. New York: United Nations.

UN (2015f) "Statement by the Secretary-General on the release of his report, *The Future of UN Peace Operations*," September 11, 2015. Available at: http://www.un.org/sg/statements/index.asp?nid=8964. Accessed January 12, 2016.

UN (2015g) "MONUSCO's Civil Affairs," *MONUSCO*. Available at: http://monusco.unmissions.org/LinkClick.aspx?fileticket=sbKJDmIIJWQ%3D&tabid=10715&mid=13709&language=en-US. Accessed January 12, 2016.

UN (2016a) *Report of the Secretary-General on South Sudan*, 13 April 2016. New York: United Nations.

UN (2016b) "South Sudan: UN peacekeeping chief says action will be taken on probe into Malakal violence," June 22, 2016. Available at: http://www.un.org/apps/news/story.asp?NewsID=54300#.V5XhROOO7M5. Accessed July 25, 2016.

UN (2016c) "Secretary-General's press encounter on South Sudan," July 11, 2016. Available at: http://www.un.org/sg/offthecuff/index.asp?nid=4616. Accessed July 25, 2016.

UN (2016d) S/RES/2304, August 12, 2016. New York: United Nations.

UN (2016e) "Note to Correspondents on allegations of sexual exploitation and abuse in the Central African Republic," March 30, 2016. Available at: https://www.un.org/sg/en/content/sg/note-correspondents/2016-03-30/note-correspondents-allegations-sexual-exploitation-and. Accessed August 17, 2016.

UN (2016f) "Probe into sexual abuse in Central African Republic must 'leave no stone unturned' – UN rights chief," March 31, 2016. Available at: http://www.un.org/apps/news/story.asp?NewsID=53583#.V7RZauOO7M4. Accessed August 17, 2016.

UN (2016g) *Practice note: Community engagement*. New York: Policy and Best Practices Service, Department of Peacekeeping / Department of Field Support, United Nations.

UNDP (2015) *Human Development Report 2015*. New York: United Nations Development Programme. Available at: http://hdr.undp.org/sites/default/files/2015_human_development_report.pdf. Accessed July 27, 2016.

UNMISS (2015) "Update," August 31, 2015. Available at: http://reliefweb.int/sites/reliefweb.int/files/resources/15-8-%20Update%20%2089.pdf. Accessed August 11, 2016.

Vinck, Patrick, Léonard D. Gotoas and Anthony H. Yavala (2012) *Fonds de Consolidation de la Paix en République Centrafricaine: Evaluation Externe de la Mise en Œuvre des Projets* (2008–2012). New York: UN Peacebuilding Fund. Available at: http://www.unpbf.org/wp-content/uploads/Central-African-Republic_2012.pdf. Accessed July 27, 2016.

de Waal, Alex (2016) "South Sudan's corrupt elite have driven a debt-free and oil-rich country to ruin," *International Business Times,* July 15, 2016. Available at: http://www.ibtimes.co.uk/south-sudans-corrupt-elite-have-driven-debt-free-oil-rich-country-ruin-1570845?utm_source=yahoo&utm_medium=referral&utm_campaign=rss&utm_content=%2Frss%2Fyahoous%2Fnews&yptr=yahoo. Accessed July 21, 2016.

World Bank (2016) "Central African Republic," The World Bank. Available at: http://data.worldbank.org/country/central-african-republic. Accessed July 27, 2016.

CHAPTER 7

Serving the People

THE SUPPLY AND DEMAND OF UN PEACE OPERATIONS

The topic of this book has been UN peace operations—and UN peace-keeping operations in particular. Western and African member states want to make peace operations more effective and more robust, so that they can be deployed to conflicts where there is insufficient interest in deploying a coalition of the willing, and to replace or be deployed instead of a regional organization. However, there are several problems with this approach. First, there is a persistent gap between increasingly robust mandates and the ability and willingness to use force on the ground, and attempts have been made to deal with this by bringing in regional member states in coalitions of the willing deployed as part of the UN mission. However, a regional force may be willing to engage militarily with only some of the parties that can be a threat to civilians, as the experience with the FIB in the DRC has shown.

Second, equipping missions with new tools and equipment may be a good step forward—provided that they are used in accordance with the principles and guidelines of UN peace operations. However, bringing on board Western troops and equipment can create an expectations gap for host governments and parts of the local population that has proved difficult to close. Third, moving UN peace operations toward enforcement operations entails the distinct risk that the UN will lose it legitimacy and credibility as an impartial arbiter of conflicts, undermining its most essen-

© The Author(s) 2018
J. Karlsrud, *The UN at War*,
https://doi.org/10.1007/978-3-319-62858-5_8

tial political role, as well as its work to facilitate and implement humanitarian action, peacebuilding, and development.

On the demand side, UN peace operations should not serve elite kleptocracies with short-term goals: they must be relevant to and support enduring peace for people who live in daily fear. The crisis in South Sudan stands as a stark example of the challenges facing UN peace operations today. When the UN last stood at a crossroads, it was the failures to protect civilians in Bosnia and Rwanda that led to reform and change. Similarly, the focus of reform efforts today should be motivated by the UN's inability to provide sufficient protection to civilians in South Sudan.

The literature on local ownership and UN peace operations has long focused on the host state and its leaders, and not enough on the host populations that these leaders should represent, with some notable exceptions (e.g., Pouligny 2006; Autesserre 2010). The missions in the CAR and the DRC, as just two examples, are mandated to support the extension of state authority, when this authority is disputed at best on the local level. Johnstone has formulated the dilemma this way:

> …on the one hand, the more proactive the external role, the harder it is for local state structures to gain legitimacy and effectiveness; on the other hand, rigid adherence to "local ownership" can mean deferring to local power brokers that may lack the legitimacy and capacity to deliver sustainable peace. (2007: 15)

UN peace operations need to nurture the ownership of local populations by ensuring that their voice is heard, regardless of their ethnicity, tribe, or religious conviction: "…aside from the bargain with local elites, the UN is also in an implicit 'social compact' with the population as a whole: this is what makes the UN dilemma particularly difficult" (Piccolino and Karlsrud 2011: 466; see also Johnstone 2011). The move to make UN peace operations more supportive to inclusive and representative governance on national as well as local levels is essential to enable sustained peace to take hold.

Moving Toward Chapter 7½?

The FIB in the DRC was mandated to "take all necessary measures" to "neutralize" and "disarm" groups that posed a threat to "state authority and civilian security" (UN 2013: 7–8). In Mali, the Chadian troops may be seen as the robust spear end of MINUSMA, although not equipped with the same high-end technology and massive firepower as the European troops.

They are joined by troops from other regional member states, inter alia from Niger and Mauretania.[1] In South Sudan, the RPF has been tasked to

> [p]romptly and effectively engage any actor that is credibly found to be preparing attacks, or engages in attacks, against United Nations protection of civilians sites, other United Nations premises, United Nations personnel, international and national humanitarian actors, or civilians. (UN 2016)

The tasks specified for the RPF in UNMISS are not different from those that fall under the regular tasks of the existing UNMISS troops. Likewise, the MONUSCO troops could, and have already in several previous incidents, used preemptive force to protect civilians. However, the trend of using force on not only the tactical but also the operational and strategic levels, and specifying "enemies," effectively taking sides in the conflict, may in the longer term render the role of the UN as an impartial arbiter of conflicts impossible to carry out in a legitimate manner (Karlsrud 2015) and lead to an "existential crisis in UN peace operations" (Hunt 2016: 2).

In effect, what we are seeing is a move toward Chapter 7½ mandates, delegating the task of enforcement action to regional actors, but keeping the force under the UN banner, providing logistics, per diems, and the legitimacy of the UN. This is an uneasy compromise that marries several strategic considerations. As detailed in Chapter 5, many member states and the UN Secretariat are unwilling to follow a path where peace operations are increasingly delegated to regional organizations. Worries about lack of training and equipment, possible human rights violations, as well as the longer-term prospect of increasing professionalization of African peace operations leading to a decline in the overall "market share," are among the motives that can be discerned. However, regional member states with an interest in the outcome are more willing to put troops in harm's way. Furthermore, UN peace operations generally offer stronger economic incentives in terms of UN reimbursements and bilateral training and equipment programs. Mandating a separate force, but including it in the UN mission, marries these considerations, but may undermine the overall legitimacy of UN peace operations.

MAINTAINING RELEVANCE, BUT HOW?

The calls for updating UN peace operations originate from the increasingly strong perception that violent extremism and terrorism is becoming a feature of today's and tomorrow's conflicts, and that the UN will have to adapt in order to deal with these challenges. The UNSC increasingly mandates

UN peace operations to be deployed in extremely challenging theatres, facing threats of violent extremists and terrorist networks. As a knee-jerk response, some are arguing for a more robust posture of UN peace operations, updating doctrines, tools, and troops to enable them to counter violent extremism and terrorism. In this environment, clarity is needed: what are UN peacekeepers, and what will they be capable of dealing with? Jean-Marie Guéhenno, the former head of UN peacekeeping, argues that

> [e]very U.N. force is a sort of ad hoc assembly of different military forces. It is not configured to really wage war. What the U.N. peacekeepers can do better is deter and crush marginal spoilers. That's what they can and should do, but beyond that it is setting itself up for failure. (cited in Coleman 2015)

Furthermore, when peacekeepers are under the constant threat of attack in an asymmetric threat environment like Mali, they tend to bunker down and limit the risks. However, this severely restricts the ability of the mission to interact with and establish the trust of local populations, leading the mission onto a downward spiral. Including new technologies in peace operations can have the same effect—leading to remote surveillance of sentiments and perceptions, instead of actively and personally engaging with local populations. Ideally, these tools should rather complement and strengthen existing practices of engagement and interaction.

The Primacy of Politics

The threats of violent extremism and terrorism can be addressed and UN peace operations are part of the spectrum of tools that can be used. However, approaching this problem set will require an honest assessment of the level of political inclusion in the country in question, and how to deal with possible legitimate grievances of marginalized populations. We simply need to get better at understanding the various sources of radicalization, and here more research is needed. Without acceptance from the host state and other key member states for such an approach, little progress can be made. The current trend of militarizing and securitizing what are essentially development challenges will continue to bring more recruits to these organizations.

The HIPPO Report noted a broader trend, whereby conflict management is being relegated to the UN, while other actors take the lead in political negotiations. As argued by de Coning et al.

...there is an inverse relationship between the level of force that needs to be used to achieve and maintain stability and the degree to which a UN stabilization mission will be perceived as an impartial mediator in a peace process. As stabilization operations slide towards the more robust end of the scale, the ability to provide good offices and mediate in the crisis will decrease as the UN is increasingly considered, and effectively is, a party to the conflict. (2017: 39)

When the UN is marginalized by the international community, national leaders will also pay less heed to the advice and impartiality of a UN peace operation, and consent will gradually wither (Piccolino and Karlsrud 2011, see also Johnstone 2011). The government will seek to exploit the political, financial, military, and logistical resources of the mission to retain and strengthen its own grip on power, while limiting the influence that the mission has on the political process. The missions in Darfur, the DRC, and South Sudan have all found themselves in this situation, and the UNSC has to decide whether the benefits of keeping the mission on the ground outweighs the political, moral, and financial costs. As Richard Gowan asks: "At what point do efforts to maintain relations with abusive leaders and regime become morally and politically unsustainable?" (Gowan 2016, see also Stearns 2015).

BETTER UNDERSTAND CAUSES OF RADICALIZATION

Who will become a terrorist? Research is still struggling to come up with convincing answers (see, e.g., Wolffe and Moorhead 2014; UN 2015b; Appuzzo 2016). Here, it is essential to take into account the complex political economy on the ground. Today's winners can be tomorrow's losers and families may hedge their bets by participating in the various forms of formal and informal governance and security mechanisms that crisscross and overlap each other in geographic, economic, and social space. The same family in Somalia can send off one son to the al-Shabaab, one to the Somali National Army, one to a refugee camp across the border in Kenya and possible employment in Europe, and one to stay and take part in local and traditional governance structures. To better understand these multiple, and, from a Western viewpoint, at times contradictory logics underpinning radicalization and recruitment to extremist groups, we need more local knowledge, also at the neighborhood level. Some broad contextual factors can be drivers of radicalization, such as lack of effective and good governance, lack of inclusion, mobility, and representation (IEP 2015). Efforts to stop radicalization should focus on removing these barriers to human fulfillment, and "enable a positive alternative vision for the future to emerge" (Lindberg and Rothkopf 2015). But this also points to the limits of UN peace operations in this endeavor. Even though UN peace operations may claim that they are good at understanding local contexts, this does not make them the spearhead or even a major part in the effort to counter violent extremism. Only in a limited set of cases will UN peace operations be the right actor for providing relevant and necessary support to deal with these challenges. Furthermore, it would be counterproductive, as well as serving to alienate those in danger of radicalization, if existing early peacebuilding projects within and outside of UN peace operations were to be relabeled as "deradicalization" and "countering and preventing violent extremism" (see also Karlsrud 2017).

Practice Dictating Principles?

The most relevant cases are Mali, where the UN has a peacekeeping operation, and Somalia, where the UN is supporting the AU peace enforcement mission. Some argue that the UN needs new policy to guide the organization when facing violent extremism and terrorism (Cockayne and O'Neil 2015; Boutellis and Fink 2016), although the guidelines would have to build on a very limited sample of practices. In Mali, the UN supports the government's lead on DDR, while in Afghanistan and Somalia the UN is providing support to other lead actors. For better or worse, this is how peacekeeping guidance has developed over the last two decades. Policy development and organizational learning in the area of UN peace operations have always been characterized by a certain degree of inductiveness to them (see, e.g., Benner et al. 2011). It was not until 1995 that UN DPKO got its first Lessons Learned Unit, and practices have preceded policy guidelines on a range of issues, from protection of civilians to DDR, to engaging with local communities and engaging in dialogue with terrorist groups (da Costa and Karlsrud 2013; Karlsrud 2013). Johnstone has studied how practices can precede norm- and law-making activities in international organizations (2008), I have elsewhere examined bottom–up innovation and learning in UN peacekeeping (Karlsrud 2016).

Max Weber and the sociology of professions show us how bureaucracies have a natural tendency to expand and want to define and control new policy spaces (Weber et al. 1946; Karlsrud 2016). The push to develop guidelines for UN peace operations and countering violent extremism ignores that this was explicitly proscribed by the HIPPO Report. The current eagerness to occupy the counter-terrorism and PCVE policy space is not to be taken lightly, and can have real and detrimental consequences for the work of UN peace operations in both the short and the long term.

Toward People-Centered Peacekeeping?

To a large degree, the success of a peace operation is measured by the extent it is able to maintain stability and implement its mandated tasks. Most of these tasks are state-centric in nature, formulated in a state-centric manner, or executed with state institutions as the main counterpart even when they are supposed to promote the extension of state authority and services, and explicitly include civil society actors. However, the main objective will be military: to maintain stability and protect civilians, if necessary by force.

Better engagement with local communities can strengthen the understanding of a mission's objectives, what it can and cannot do. Managing expectations not only at the strategic level but also at the local level can give peace operations the chance to respond to local needs, and to be considered successful also by local populations. UN peace operations can provide security, and facilitate and support early peacebuilding activities.

But how to go about this? Drawing on complexity theory, de Coning has argued that "sustaining peace should be about stimulating and facilitating the capacity of societies to self-organise, so that they can increase their ability to absorb and adapt to stress, to the degree necessary to sustain peace" (2016: 8). From this perspective, ambitions as to the changes that international actors may be able to achieve in fragile states may be lower, but also more transformative: aimed not solely at achieving institutional change, but also thinking about how to support a transition from violence to peaceful conflict solution. This must be undertaken in cooperation with local communities and authorities, civil society, and other international actors.

Peacebuilding activities require a good grasp of local dynamics, if undesired effects are to be avoided. UN peace operations and other international actors must be equipped with real expertise about local dynamics, as well as flexibility in funding and the willingness to start and stop funding as required in response to local dynamics. However, this form of dynamic support stands in direct contradiction to the requirements for long-term planning, disbursement, and accountability stipulated by host states and implementing agents such as peace operations and donors alike.

Here let me quote from the HIPPO Report:

> [c]ountries emerging from conflict are not blank pages and their people are not "projects." They are the main agents of peace. However, the international approach is often based on generic models that ignore national realities. It often overlooks social mechanisms or informal institutions and networks of mutual assistance that deliver services and enjoy trust at the community level, where women play an important role. Efforts to sustain peace must build upon those institutions and the resilience and reconciliation processes of local communities, and not undermine them. (UN 2015a: 48)

In continuing the work on reforming UN peace operations, member states should acknowledge and respond to the challenges identified by the HIPPO Report and the SG's peacebuilding review, and their proposals for properly including the needs and aspirations of people affected by conflict.

The then SG's follow-up report to the HIPPO Report mentioned the obligation to heed the needs and aspirations of the people. The list of issues to be covered is long indeed, and other important dimensions of peace operations have fared no better. Nevertheless, the fact that the report picked up on this component indicated the will to improve in this particular area. To help the UN succeed, it is necessary to continue to push and support UN peacekeepers and peacebuilders in their pursuit of more people-oriented peace operations—not only by developing guidelines but also by putting these into practice. This will greatly improve the chances of success for peacekeeping operations, and provide more value for money for their funders as well.

In this world, there are too many people who still await peace on the ground. UN peace operations cannot continue to be the option of last resort, muddling through on a minimum of resources and responding to the needs of key members of the UNSC rather than the people in war-torn countries. UN peace operations must be recognized as achieving something, responding to and dealing with the root causes of conflict and the everyday needs of those who live in fear.

NOTES

1. Also Benin, Cameroon, and Guinea provide about one battalion each.

REFERENCES

Appuzzo, Matt (2016) "Who Will Become a Terrorist? Research Yields Few Clues," *The New York Times,* March 27, 2016. Available at: http://www. nytimes.com/2016/03/28/world/europe/mystery-about-who-will-become-a-terrorist-defies-clear-answers.html?emc=edit_th_20160328&nl=tod aysheadlines&nlid=33162912&_r=0. Accessed 9 July, 2016.

Autesserre, Séverine (2010) *The Trouble with the Congo: Local Violence and the Failure of International Peacebuilding.* New York: Cambridge University Press.

Benner, Thorsten, Stephan Mergenthaler, and Philipp Rotmann (2011) *The New World of UN Peace Operations: Learning to Build Peace?* Oxford: Oxford University Press.

Boutellis, Arthur and Naureen C. Fink (2016) *Mind the Gap: UN Peace Operations and Terrorism and Violent Extremism Between Policy and Practice, Opportunities and Risks.* New York: International Peace Institute.

Cockayne, James and Siobhan O'Neil (eds.) (2015) *UN DDR in an Era of Violent Extremism: Is It Fit for Purpose?* Tokyo: United Nations University.

Coleman, Michael (2015) "Ex-U.N. Peacekeeping Chief: Do Less, Do It Better," *The Washington Diplomat,* October 29, 2015. Available at: http://washdiplomat.com/index.php?option=com_content&view=article&id=12590:ex-un-peacekeeping-chief-do-less-do-it-better&catid=1537&Itemid=428. Accessed August 19, 2016.

de Coning, Cedric (2016) "From peacebuilding to sustaining peace: Implications of complexity for resilience and sustainability," *Resilience*: pp. 1–16. https://doi.org/10.1080/21693293.2016.1153773.

de Coning, Cedric, Chiyuki Aoi and John Karlsrud (eds.) (2017) *UN Peacekeeping Doctrine in a New Era Adapting to Stabilisation, Protection and New Threats.* Abingdon: Routledge.

da Costa, Diana Felix, and John Karlsrud (2013) "'Bending the rules': the space between HQ policy and local action in UN Civilian Peacekeeping," *Journal of International Peacekeeping*, 17 (3–4), pp. 293–312.

Gowan, Richard (2016) "When should blue helmets walk away from a conflict?" *Global Peace Operations Review,* August 16, 2016. Available at: http://peaceoperationsreview.org/thematic-essays/when-should-blue-helmets-walk-away-from-a-conflict/. Accessed August 24, 2016.

Hunt, Charles T. (2016) "All necessary means to what ends? the unintended consequences of the 'robust turn' in UN peace operations," *International Peacekeeping.* https://doi.org/10.1080/13533312.2016.1214074

IEP (2015) *Global Terrorism Index 2015.* Sydney: Institute of Economics and Peace.

Johnstone, Ian (2007) "Consolidating Peace: Priorities and Deliberative Processes," in Ian Johnstone (ed.) *Annual Review of Global Peace Operations.* Boulder, CO: Lynne Rienner. Available at: https://www.dropbox.com/s/9y88xwb1g7qfefu/2007_annual_review.pdf. Accessed July 7, 2016.

Johnstone, Ian (2008) "Law-Making through the Operational Activities of International Organizations," *George Washington International Law Review,* 40 (1): pp. 87–122.

Johnstone, Ian (2011) "Managing Consent in Contemporary Peacekeeping Operations," *International Peacekeeping* 18 (2): pp. 168–182.

Karlsrud, John (2013) "SRSGs as Norm Arbitrators? Understanding Bottom–Up Authority in UN Peacekeeping," *Global Governance,* 19 (4), pp. 525–544.

Karlsrud, John (2015) "The UN at War: Examining the Consequences of Peace Enforcement Mandates for the UN Peacekeeping Operations in the CAR, the DRC and Mali," *Third World Quarterly* 36 (1): pp. 40–54.

Karlsrud, John (2016) *Norm Change in International Relations: Linked Ecologies in UN Peacekeeping Operations.* Abingdon: Routledge.

Karlsrud, John (2017) "Towards UN counter-terrorism operations?," *Third World Quarterly,* 38 (6): pp. 1215–1231. doi: http://dx.doi.org/10.1080/01436597.2016.1268907.

Lindberg, Nancy and David Rothkopf (2015) 'Four Lessons for Fighting Violent Extremists – Without Guns," *Foreign Policy,* September 29. Available at: https://foreignpolicy.com/2015/09/29/four-lessons-for-fighting-extremists-without-guns-obama-united-nations-summit/?utm_content=buffer93351&utm_medium=social&utm_source=twitter.com&utm_campaign=buffer. Accessed January 12, 2016.

Piccolino, Giulia and John Karlsrud (2011) "Withering consent, but mutual dependency: UN peace operations and new African assertiveness," *Conflict, Security and Development,* 11 (4): pp. 447–471.

Pouligny, Béatrice (2006) *Peace Operations Seen from Below.* London: Kumarian Press.

Stearns, Jason (2015) "Can Force be Useful in the Absence of a Political Strategy? Lessons from the UN Missions to the DR Congo." Available at: http://peaceoperationsreview.org/thematic-essays/can-force-be-useful-in-the-absence-of-a-political-strategy-lessons-from-the-un-missions-to-the-dr-congo/. Accessed January 11, 2016.

UN (2013a) *S/RES/2098,* March 28, 2013. New York: United Nations.

UN (2015a) *A/70/95-S/2015a/446. Report of the High-level Independent Panel on Peace Operations on Uniting our Strengths for Peace: Politics, Partnership and People* ("HIPPO Report"). New York: United Nations.

UN (2015b) *A/70/674. Plan of Action to Prevent Violent Extremism*. New York: United Nations.

UN (2016b) *S/RES/2304*, August 12, 2016. New York: United Nations.

Weber, Max, Hans Heinrich Gerth, and C. Wright Mills (1946) *From Max Weber: Essays in Sociology*. New York: Oxford University Press.

Wolffe, John and Gavin Moorhead (2014) *Religion, Security and Global Uncertainties*. Milton Keynes: The Open University. Available at: http://www.open.ac.uk/arts/research/religion-martyrdom-global-uncertainties/sites/www.open.ac.uk.arts.research.religion-martyrdom-global-uncertainties/files/files/ecms/arts-rmgu-pr/web-content/Religion-Security-Global-Uncertainties.pdf. Accessed September 13, 2016.

REFERENCES

Abilova, Olga and Alexandra Novosseloff (2016) *Demystifying Intelligence in UN Peace Operations: Toward an Organizational Doctrine*. New York: International Peace Institute. Available at: https://www.ipinst.org/wp-content/uploads/2016/07/1608_Demystifying-Intelligence.pdf. Accessed August 25, 2016.

Abiola, Seun, Cedric de Coning, Eduarda Hamann, and Chander Prakash (2017) "The large contributors and UN peacekeeping doctrine," in Cedric de Coning, Chiyuki Aoi, and John Karlsrud (eds.), *UN Peacekeeping Doctrine in a New Era Adapting to Stabilisation, Protection and New Threats*. Abingdon: Routledge, pp. 152–185.

AFP (2016) "Chinese peacekeeper killed in Mali attack," June 2, 2016. Available at: http://m.news24.com/news24/Africa/News/chinese-peacekeeper-killed-in-mali-attack-20160602. Accessed September 5, 2016.

AFP (2017) "African leaders agree to new joint counter-terrorism force," February 6, 2017. Available at: http://m.france24.com/en/20170206-african-leaders-agree-new-joint-counter-terrorism-force?ns_campaign=reseaux_sociaux&ns_source=twitter&ns_mchannel=social&ns_linkname=editorial&aef_campaign_ref=partage_user&aef_campaign_date=2017-02-06. Accessed February 8, 2017.

African Economic Outlook (2015) *Measuring the pulse of Africa*. Available at: http://www.africaneconomicoutlook.org/fileadmin/uploads/aeo/2015/PDF_Chapters/Overview_AEO2015_EN-web.pdf. Accessed January 7, 2015.

Afrobarometer (2016) "Liberia data," *Afrobarometer*. Available at: http://afrobarometer.org/data/320. Accessed January 12, 2016.

© The Author(s) 2018   171
J. Karlsrud, *The UN at War*,
https://doi.org/10.1007/978-3-319-62858-5

Alberts, David S., John J. Garstka and Frederick P. Stein (2000) *Network Centric Warfare: Developing and Leveraging Information Superiority*. Washington DC: United States Department of Defense.

Al-Jazeera (2016) "UN to send peacekeepers home over South Sudan inaction," *Al-Jazeera*, June 23, 2016. Available at: http://www.aljazeera.com/news/2016/06/send-peacekeepers-home-south-sudan-inaction-160623060004340.html. Accessed July 25, 2016.

AMISOM (2014) "Ethiopia - ENDF," January 1, 2014. Available at: http://amisom-au.org/ethiopia-endf/. Accessed July 21, 2016.

Andersson, Jan J. (2015) *If Not Now, When? The Nordic EU Battlegroup*. Paris: European Union Institute for Security Studies.

Anna, Cara and Menelaos Hadjicostis (2015) "As UN peacekeeping veers toward counterterror, US steps in," Yahoo! News, September 26, 2015. Available at: https://www.yahoo.com/news/un-peacekeeping-veers-toward-counterterror-us-steps-145304737.html?ref=gs. Accessed September 6, 2016.

Appuzzo, Matt (2016) "Who Will Become a Terrorist? Research Yields Few Clues," *The New York Times*, March 27, 2016. Available at: http://www.nytimes.com/2016/03/28/world/europe/mystery-about-who-will-become-a-terrorist-defies-clear-answers.html?emc=edit_th_20160328&nl=todaysheadlines&nlid=33162912&_r=0. Accessed 9 July, 2016.

Arnault, Jean (2015) "A background to the report of the high-level panel on peace operations," *Global Peace Operations Review*. Available at: http://peaceoperationsreview.org/thematic-essays/a-background-to-the-report-of-the-high-level-panel-on-peace-operations/. Accessed January 8, 2016.

Atwood, Richard (2015) "Violent extremism and crisis management," International Crisis Group, June 4, 2015. Available at: https://www.yahoo.com/news/un-peacekeeping-veers-toward-counterterror-us-steps-145304737.html?ref=gs. Accessed June 30, 2016.

AU (2000) *Constitutive Act of the African Union*. Addis Ababa: African Union.

AU (2003) *Protocol Relating to the Establishment of the Peace and Security Council of the African Union*. Addis Ababa: African Union.

AU (2012) *Communiqué* (PSC/PR/COMM. (CCCXXIII), June 12, 2012). Addis Ababa: African Union.

AU (2013a) *Communiqué* (PSC/PR/COMM. (CCCLXXI), April 25, 2013). Addis Ababa: African Union.

AU (2013b) *Report of the African Union Commission on the Strategic Review of the African Union Mission in Somalia (AMISOM), PSC/PR/2.(CCCLVI)*. Addis Ababa: African Union Commission.

AU (2013c) *PSC/PR/COMM(CCCLVIII)*, March 7, 2013. Addis Ababa: African Union.

AU (2015a) *Report of the Chairperson of the Commission on follow-up steps on the Common African Position on the Review of United Nations Peace Operations, PSC/AHG/3.(DXLVII)*, 26 September 2015. Addis Ababa: African Union.

AU (2015b) *Report of the Joint African Union–United Nations Mission on the Benchmarks for a United Nations Peacekeeping Operation in Somalia and recommendations on the next steps in the military campaign,* June 30, 2015. Addis Ababa: African Union.

AU (2015c) *Report of the Commission of the African Union on the Follow-up to the Relevant Provisions of the Declaration of the Summit of the Member Countries of the Nouakchott Process of 18 December 2014.* Addis Ababa: African Union.

AU (2015d) *PSC/AHG/COMM/2(DXLVII) Peace and Security Council 547ᵗʰ Meeting at the Level of Heads of State and Government,* September 26, 2015. Addis Ababa: African Union.

AU (2016a) "Peace Operations conducted by the African Union and Partners," November 20, 2015. Available at: http://www.peaceau.org/en/page/72-peace-ops. Accessed January 6, 2016.

AU (2016b) *PSC/PR/BR.(DLXX).* Addis Ababa: African Union.

AU (2016c) *PSC/PR/COMM.(DLXVII),* January 14, 2016. Addis Ababa: African Union.

AU (2016d) *Press Release: The African Union Adopts the AU Peace Fund.* Addis Ababa: African Union. Available at: http://www.peaceau.org/uploads/auc-pr-peacefund-18.07.2016.pdf. Accessed August 26, 2016.

AU (2016e) *Assembly/AU/Dec.589(XXVI).* Addis Ababa: African Union.

Autesserre, Séverine (2010) *The Trouble with the Congo: Local Violence and the Failure of International Peacebuilding.* New York: Cambridge University Press.

Avezov, Xenia and Timo Smit (2014) "The consensus on Mali and international conflict management in a multipolar world," *SIPRI Policy Brief,* September 2014. Available at: http://books.sipri.org/files/misc/SIPRIPB1403.pdf. Accessed April 21, 2016.

Barakat, Sultan, Seán Deely, and Steven A. Zyck (2010) "'A tradition of forgetting': stabilization and humanitarian action in historical perspective," *Disasters,* 34 (3): pp. 297–319. https://doi.org/10.1111/j.1467-7717.2010.01207.x.

Barbelet, Veronique (2015) *Central African Republic: addressing the protection crisis.* London: Humanitarian Policy Group, Overseas Development Institute. Available at: https://www.odi.org/publications/10103-central-african-republic-addressing-protection-crisis. Accessed August 17, 2016.

Barluet, Alain (2014) "Au Sahel, l'opération 'Barkhane' remplace 'Serval'," *Le Figaro,* July 13, 2014. Available at: http://www.lefigaro.fr/international/2014/07/13/01003-20140713ARTFIG00097-au-sahel-l-operation-barkhane-remplace-serval.php. Accessed September 19, 2016.

Barnett, Michael N. and Martha Finnemore (2004) *Rules for the World: International Organizations in Global Politics.* Ithaca, NY: Cornell University Press.

Barrera, Alberto (2015) "The Congo trap: MONUSCO islands of stability in the sea of instability," *Stability: International Journal of Security & Development,* 4 (1): pp. 1–16. https://doi.org/10.5334/sta.gn.

BBC (2011) "Governments, IOC and UN hit by massive cyber-attack." August 3, 2011. Available at: http://www.bbc.com/news/technology-14387559. Accessed April 27, 2016.

BBC (2014) "South Sudan President Salva Kiir hits out at UN," January 21, 2014. Available at: http://www.bbc.com/news/world-africa-25826598. Accessed September 6, 2016.

BBC (2015) "UN's CAR envoy Gaye sacked over peacekeeper abuse claims," August 12, 2015. Available at: http://www.bbc.com/news/world-africa-33890664. Accessed August 17, 2016.

Benner, Thorsten, Stephan Mergenthaler, and Philipp Rotmann (2011) *The New World of UN Peace Operations: Learning to Build Peace?* Oxford: Oxford University Press.

Berdal, Mats and David H. Ucko (2014) "The United Nations and the use of force: between promise and peril," *Journal of Strategic Studies*, 37 (5): pp. 665–673, https://doi.org/10.1080/01402390.2014.937803.

Bjørgås, Tove and Vegard Tjørhom (2015) "Vil ha eit meir aggressivt FN i krigs-felten," *NRK*, September 28, 2015. Available at: http://www.nrk.no/urix/vil-ha-eit-meir-aggressivt-fn-i-krigsfelten-1.12574869. Accessed January 11, 2016.

Bode, Ingvild (2016) "How the world's interventions in Syria have normalised the use of force," *The Conversation*, February 17, 2016. Available at: https://the-conversation.com/how-the-worlds-interventions-in-syria-have-normalised-the-use-of-force-54505. Accessed 27 February 2016.

Borger, Julian (2015) "Arming Ukraine army may escalate conflict, west warned." *The Guardian*. February 8, 2015. Available at: http://www.theguardian.com/world/2015/feb/08/arming-ukraine-army-escalate-conflict-ocse. Accessed 27 April 2016.

Boulden, Jane (2001) *Peace Enforcement: The United Nations Experience in Congo, Somalia, and Bosnia*. Westport, CT: Praeger.

Boulden, Jane (2005) 'Mandates Matter: An Exploration of Impartiality in United Nations Operations', *Global Governance* 11 (2): pp. 147–160.

Boutellis, Arthur (2015) "Can the UN stabilize Mali? Towards a UN stabilization doctrine?," *Stability* 4 (1): pp. 1–16.

Boutellis, Arthur and Naureen C. Fink (2016) *Mind the Gap: UN Peace Operations and Terrorism and Violent Extremism Between Policy and Practice, Opportunities and Risks*. New York: International Peace Institute.

Boutros-Ghali, Boutros (1992) *An agenda for peace: preventive diplomacy, peace-making, and peace-keeping: report of the Secretary-General pursuant to the statement adopted by the summit meeting of the Security Council on 31 January 1992*. New York: United Nations.

Boutros-Ghali, Boutros (1995) *A/RES/51/242: Supplement to An Agenda for Peace*. New York: United Nations.

Bratersky, Maxim and Alexander Lukin (2017) "The Russian perspective on UN peacekeeping: today and tomorrow," in Cedric de Coning, Chiyuki Aoi and John Karlsrud (eds.), *UN Peacekeeping Doctrine in a New Era Adapting to Stabilisation, Protection and New Threats.* Abingdon: Routledge, pp. 132–151.

Brosig, Malte (2015) *Cooperative Peacekeeping in Africa: Exploring regime complexity.* Abingdon: Routledge.

Burke, Jason and Ed Pilkington (2016) "UN under pressure over 'failure to act' during South Sudan rampage," *The Guardian,* August 17, 2016. Available at: https://www.theguardian.com/world/2016/aug/17/un-under-pressure-over-failure-to-act-during-south-sudan-rampage. Accessed September 16, 2016.

Bøås, Morten and Kathleen M. Jennings (2012) "Rebellion and warlordism: The spectre of neopatrimonialism," in Daniel C. Bach and Mamoudou Gazibo (eds.), *Neopatrimonialism in Africa and Beyond.* Abingdon: Routledge, pp. 124–131.

Caparini, Marina (2014) *Extending State Authority in Liberia: The Gbarnga Justice and Security Hub.* Oslo: Norwegian Institute of International Affairs (NUPI).

China Military Online (2016) "Hundreds honor Chinese soldier killed in Mali," *China Military Online,* June 11, 2016. Available at: http://english.chinamil.com.cn/news-channels/china-military-news/2016-06/11/content_7095122.htm. Accessed September 5, 2016.

Clapper, James (2016) "Remarks as delivered by The Honorable James R. Clapper, Director of National Intelligence. Senate Armed Services Committee Hearing: IC's Worldwide Threat Assessment Opening Statement," February 9, 2016. Available at: https://fas.org/irp/congress/2016_hr/020916-sasc-ad.pdf. Accessed April 14, 2016.

Cockayne, James and Siobhan O'Neil (eds.) (2015) *UN DDR in an Era of Violent Extremism: Is It Fit for Purpose?* Tokyo: United Nations University.

Code Blue (2015) "The UN's Dirty Secret: The untold story of child sexual abuse in the Central African Republic and Anders Kompass," May 29, 2015. Available at: http://www.codebluecampaign.com/carstatement/. Accessed August 17, 2016.

Coleman, Michael (2015) "Ex-U.N. Peacekeeping Chief: Do Less, Do It Better," *The Washington Diplomat,* October 29, 2015. Available at: http://washdiplomat.com/index.php?option=com_content&view=article&id=12590:ex-un-peacekeeping-chief-do-less-do-it-better&catid=1537&Itemid=428. Accessed August 19, 2016.

de Coning, Cedric (2013) "Understanding Peacebuilding as Essentially Local," *Stability* 2 (1): pp. 1–6.

de Coning, Cedric (2016a) "Adapting the African standby force to a just-in-time readiness model," in de Coning, Cedric, Linnea Gelot, and John Karlsrud (eds.), *The future of African peace operations: From the Janjaweed to Boko Haram.* London: Zed Books.

de Coning, Cedric (2016b) "From peacebuilding to sustaining peace: Implications of complexity for resilience and sustainability," *Resilience*: pp. 1–16. https://doi.org/10.1080/21693293.2016.1153773.

de Coning, Cedric and Karsten Friis (2011) "Coherence and coordination: the limits of the comprehensive approach," *Journal of International Peacekeeping*, 15 (1–2): pp. 43–56.

de Coning, Cedric, John Karlsrud, and Paul Troost (2015) "Towards More People-Centric Peace Operations: From 'Extension of State Authority' to 'Strengthening Inclusive State-Society Relations,'" *Stability: International Journal of Security & Development*, 4 (1): pp. 1–13.

de Coning, Cedric, Chiyuki Aoi and John Karlsrud (eds.) (2017) *UN Peacekeeping Doctrine in a New Era Adapting to Stabilisation, Protection and New Threats*. Abingdon: Routledge.

de Coning, Cedric, Linnea Gelot, and John Karlsrud (eds.) (2016) *The future of African peace operations: From the Janjaweed to Boko Haram*. London: Zed Books.

Convergne, Elodie and Michael R. Snyder (2015) "Making maps to make peace: geospatial technology as a tool for UN peacekeeping," *International Peacekeeping* 22 (5): pp. 565–586.

Cordesman, Anthony H. (2009) *Shape, Clear, Hold and Build: The Uncertain Lessons of the Afghan and Iraq Wars*. Washington, DC: Center for Strategic and International Studies.

da Costa, Diana Felix and Cedric de Coning (2013) "UNMISS County Support Bases: peacekeeping–peacebuilding nexus at work?," *Policy Brief 4, 2013*. Oslo: Norwegian Institute of International Affairs (NUPI).

da Costa, Diana Felix, and Cedric de Coning (2015) "United Nations Mission in the Republic of South Sudan (UNMISS)," in J. A. Koops, N. Macqueen, T. Tardy and P. D. Williams (eds.), *The Oxford Handbook of United Nations Peacekeeping Operations*. Oxford: Oxford University Press, pp. 830–841.

da Costa, Diana Felix, and John Karlsrud (2013) "'Bending the rules': the space between HQ policy and local action in UN Civilian Peacekeeping," *Journal of International Peacekeeping*, 17 (3–4), pp. 293–312.

Cox, W. Robert (1981) "Social forces, states and world orders: beyond international relations theory," *Millennium: Journal of International Studies*, 10 (2): pp. 126–55.

Crisismappers (2016) "CrisisMappers: The Humanitarian Technology Network." Available at: http://crisismappers.net/. Accessed July 8, 2016.

Curran, David and Paul Holtom (2015) "Resonating, Rejecting, Reinterpreting: Mapping the Stabilization Discourse in the United Nations Security Council, 2000–14," *Stability: International Journal of Security & Development*, 4(1): pp. 1–18. https://doi.org/10.5334/sta.gm.

Curran, David and Paul D. Williams (2016a) "The UK and UN Peace Operations: A Case for Greater Engagement." London: Oxford Research Group. Available at: http://www.oxfordresearchgroup.org.uk/publications/briefing_papers_and_reports/uk_and_un_peace_operations_case_greater_engagement. Accessed 6 September 2016.

Curran, David and Paul D. Williams (2016b) "The United Kingdom and United Nations peace operations," *International Peacekeeping* 23 (5): pp. 1–22. https://doi.org/10.1080/13533312.2016.1235098.

Curran, David and Paul D. Williams (2017) "The United Kingdom and UN Peacekeeping," in Cedric de Coning, Chiyuki Aoi and John Karlsrud (eds.), *UN Peacekeeping Doctrine in a New Era Adapting to Stabilisation, Protection and New Threats*. Abingdon: Routledge: pp. 68–89.

Daily Mail (2015) "Military solution 'impossible' in parts of Middle East: CIA chief," *Daily Mail*, October 28, 2015. Available at: http://www.dailymail.co.uk/wires/afp/article-3292855/Military-solution-impossible-parts-Middle-East-CIA-chief.html. Accessed January 11, 2016.

Darkwa, Linda (2017b) "The African Standby Force: The African Union's tool for the maintenance of peace and security," Contemporary Security Policy, 38(3): pp. 1–12. doi: https://doi.org/10.1080/13523260.2017.1342478.

Day, Christopher (2016) "The Bangui Carousel: How the recycling of political elites reinforces instability and violence in the Central African Republic," *The Enough Project*. Available at: http://www.enoughproject.org/files/TheBanguiCarousel_080216.pdf. Accessed August 19, 2016.

defenceWeb (2016) "French UAVs exceed 15 000 flight hours in the Sahel," *defenceWeb*, March 14, 2016. Available at: http://www.uavexpertnews.com/french-uavs-exceed-15-000-flight-hours-in-the-sahel/. Accessed September 19, 2016.

defenceWeb (2015) "Eastern Africa Standby Force, U.S. forge new partnership," *defenceWeb*, November 3, 2015. Available at: http://www.defenceweb.co.za/index.php?option=com_content&view=article&id=41262:eastern-africa-standby-force-us-forge-new-partnership&catid=56:Diplomacy%20&%20Peace&Itemid=111. Accessed January 11, 2016.

Deschamps, Marie, Hassan B. Jallow, and Yasmin Sooka (2015) *Taking Action on Sexual Exploitation and Abuse by Peacekeepers: Report of an Independent Review on Sexual Exploitation and Abuse by International Peacekeeping Forces in the Central African Republic*. New York: United Nations. Available at: http://www.un.org/News/dh/infocus/centafricrepub/Independent-Review-Report.pdf. Accessed August 17, 2016.

Dörrie, Peter (2015) "France's Overstretched Military Not Enough to Stabilize the Sahel," *World Politics Review*, December 15, 2015. Available at: http://www.worldpoliticsreview.com/articles/17460/france-s-overstretched-military-not-enough-to-stabilize-the-sahel. Accessed January 11, 2016.

Dorn, A. Walter (2011). *Keeping Watch: Monitoring, Technology & Innovation in UN Peace Operations*. Tokyo: United Nations University Press.

Dorn, A. Walter (2016) *Smart Peacekeeping: Toward Tech-Enabled UN Operations.* New York: International Peace Institute. Available at: https://www.ipinst. org/2016/07/smart-peacekeeping-tech-enabled. Accessed July 21, 2016.

Dorn, A. Walter and Christoph Semken (2015) "Blue Mission tracking: real-time location of UN peacekeepers," *International Peacekeeping* 22 (5): pp. 545–564.

Doucet, Lyse (2010) "Afghanistan: A job half done," BBC News, December 4, 2006. Available at: http://news.bbc.co.uk/2/hi/south_asia/6205220.stm. Accessed June 30, 2016.

Duffield, Mark (2012) "Challenging environments: Danger, resilience and the aid industry," *Security Dialogue* 43 (5): pp. 475–492.

Duffield, Mark (2013) *Disaster Resilience in the Network Age: Access-Denial and the Rise of Cyber-Humanitarianism.* Copenhagen: Danish Institute for International Studies.

EIA (2014) "Country Analysis Brief: Sudan and South Sudan," September 3, 2014. Washington DC: U.S. Energy Information Administration. Available at: https://www.eia.gov/beta/international/analysis_includes/countries_long/ Sudan_and_South_Sudan/sudan.pdf. Accessed June 20, 2016.

Elgin, Ben and Vernon Silver (2012) "Syria crackdown gets Italy firm's aid with U.S.-Europe spy gear," *Bloomberg News.* http://www.bloomberg.com/ news/2011-11-03/syria-crackdown-gets-italy-firm-s-aid-with-u-s-europe-spy-gear.html. Accessed February 25, 2016.

Eriksen, Stein S. (2011) "'State failure' in theory and practice: the idea of the state and the contradictions of state formation," *Review of International Studies* 37 (1): pp. 229–247.

EU (2016) "EUFOR RCA," European Union External Action. Available at: http://www.eeas.europa.eu/archives/csdp/missions-and-operations/eufor-rca/index_en.htm. Accessed July 27, 2016.

European Commission (2016) *African Peace Facility: Annual Report 2015.* Brussels: European Commission. Available at: http://www.africa-eu-partnership.org/ sites/default/files/documents/apf-report-2015-en.pdf. Accessed July 7, 2016.

Fabricius, Peter (2016) "The AU's silver bullet to end fighting in South Sudan?," July 20, 2016. Pretoria: Institute for Security Studies. Available at: https:// www.issafrica.org/iss-today/the-aus-silver-bullet-to-end-fighting-in-south-sudan. Accessed August 11, 2016.

Fortna, Page (2008) Does Peacekeeping Work? Shaping Belligerents' Choices after Civil War. Princeton, NJ: Princeton University Press.

Friis, Karsten (2010) "Peacekeeping and Counter-insurgency – Two of a Kind?," *International Peacekeeping* 17 (1): pp. 49–66. https://doi.org/10.1080/ 1353331100358919.

Gebrehiwot, Mulugeta and Alex de Waal (2016) *African Politics, African Peace.* Boston, MA: The World Peace Foundation, The Fletcher School of Law and Diplomacy, Tufts University. Available at: http://africanpeacemissions.org/. Accessed July 21, 2016.

German Federal Government (2016) "More soldiers for Mali," February 26, 2017. Available at: https://www.bundesregierung.de/Content/EN/Artikel/2017/01_en/2017-01-11-minusma-mali_en.html. Accessed February 7, 2017.

German Federal Government (2017) "More soldiers for Mali," February 26, 2017. Available at: https://www.bundesregierung.de/Content/EN/Artikel/2017/01_en/2017-01-11-minusma-mali_en.html. Accessed February 7, 2017.

Gilman, Daniel (2014) "Unmanned aerial vehicles in humanitarian response," *OCHA Policy and Studies Series, June 2014, 10*. New York: OCHA.

Gilman, Daniel and Leith Baker (2014) *Humanitarianism in the Age of Cyberwarfare: Towards the Principled and Secure Use of Information in Humanitarian Emergencies*. New York: OCHA.

Glazzard, Andrew and Marthine Zeuthen (2016) *Violent extremism*. GSDRC Professional Development Reading Pack no. 34. Birmingham, UK: University of Birmingham. Available at: http://www.gsdrc.org/wp-content/uploads/2016/02/Violent-extremism_RP.pdf. Accessed September 13, 2016.

Global Peace Operations Review (2015) "Leaders' Summit on Peacekeeping," *Global Peace Operations Review*. Available at: http://peaceoperationsreview.org/wp-content/uploads/2015/10/un_2015_peakeeping_summit_pledges.jpg. Accessed January 11, 2016.

Global Peace Operations Review (2016) "Those who pay, do not play..." *Global Peace Operations Review*. Available at: http://peaceoperationsreview.org/infographic/top-10-financial-contributors-to-un-peacekeeping-budget-aug-2016/. Accessed September 5, 2016.

Goldberg, Mark Leon (2015) "Why President Obama is Hosting a Summit on UN Peacekeeping," *UN Dispatch*, September 28, 2015. Available at: http://www.undispatch.com/why-president-obama-is-hosting-a-summit-on-un-peacekeeping/. Accessed January 11, 2016.

Gordon, Robert and Peter Loge (2015) "Strategic Communication: A Political and Operational Prerequisite for Successful Peace Operations," *Occasional Papers* No. 7, November 2015. Stockholm: International Forum for the Challenges of Peace Operations. Available at: http://www.challengesforum.org/en/Reports--Publications/CF/Occasional-Paper-No-7/?retUrl=/Templates/Public/Pages/PublicReportList.aspx?id%3D962%26epslanguage%3Den. Accessed July 8, 2016.

Gorur, Aditi and Lisa Sharland (2016) *Prioritizing the Protection of Civilians in UN Peace Operations: Analyzing the Recommendations of the HIPPO Report*. Washington DC: The Henry L. Stimson Center. Available at: https://www.stimson.org/sites/default/files/file-attachments/PCIC-HIPPO-REPORT-FINAL-WEB.pdf. Accessed July 23, 2016.

Gowan, Richard (2015a) "Ten Trends in UN Peacekeeping," in Jim Della-Giacoma (ed.), *Global Peace Operations Review: Annual Compilation 2015*. New York: Center on International Cooperation, New York University, pp. 17–26.

Gowan, Richard (2015b) "How the UN Can Help Create Peace in a Divided World," *Huffington Post*, October 7, 2015. Available at: http://www.huffingtonpost.ca/centre-for-international-policy-studies/un-world-powers_b_8248628.html. Accessed January 11, 2016.

Gowan, Richard (2015c) *European Military Contributions to UN Peace Operations in Africa: Maximizing Strategic Impact*. New York: Global Peace Operations Review. Available at: http://peaceoperationsreview.org/wp-content/uploads/2015/12/european_military_contributions_gowan_dec_2015.pdf. Accessed July 23, 2016.

Gowan, Richard (2015d) "Can U.N. peacekeepers fight terrorists?," *Global Peace Operations Review*, June 30, 2015. Available at: http://peaceoperationsreview.org/commentary/can-u-n-peacekeepers-fight-terrorists/. Accessed January 11, 2016.

Gowan, Richard (2016) "When should blue helmets walk away from a conflict?" *Global Peace Operations Review*, August 16, 2016. Available at: http://peaceoperationsreview.org/thematic-essays/when-should-blue-helmets-walk-away-from-a-conflict/. Accessed August 24, 2016.

Guéhenno, Jean-Marie (2015) *The Fog of Peace*. Washington, DC: Brookings Institution Press.

Haider, Huma (2011) *State–Society Relations and Citizenship in Situations of Conflict and Fragility*. Birmingham: Governance and Social Development Resource Centre, University of Birmingham.

Harvard Humanitarian Initiative. *Disaster Relief 2.0: The Future of Information Sharing in Humanitarian Emergencies*. Washington, DC, and Newbury, UK: UN Foundation & Vodafone Foundation Technology Partnership, 2011.

Henke, Marina E. (2017) "UN fatalities 1948–2015: A new dataset," *Conflict Management and Peace Science*: pp. 1–17.

Hirono, Miwa and Marc Lanteigne (2012) "Introduction: China and UN Peacekeeping," in Miwa Hirono and Marc Lanteigne (eds.) *China's Evolving Approach to UN Peacekeeping*. Abingdon: Routledge.

Holt, Victoria K. and Moira K. Shanahan (2005) *African Capacity-Building for Peace Operations: UN Collaboration with the African Union and ECOWAS*. Washington, DC: The Henry L. Stimson Center. Available at: file:///C:/Users/Karljoh/Downloads/doc_10936_290_en.pdf. Accessed July 7, 2016.

Howard, Lise M. (2008) *UN Peacekeeping in Civil Wars*. Cambridge: Cambridge University Press.

Howard, Lise M. (2015) "Peacekeeping, Peace Enforcement, and UN Reform," *Georgetown Journal of International Affairs* 16 (2): pp. 6–13.

Human Rights Watch (2014) "Central African Republic: Peacekeepers Tied to Abuse," June 2, 2014. Available at: https://www.hrw.org/news/2014/06/02/central-african-republic-peacekeepers-tied-abuse. Accessed August 17, 2016.

Hunt, Charles T. (2016) "All necessary means to what ends? the unintended consequences of the 'robust turn' in UN peace operations," *International Peacekeeping*. https://doi.org/10.1080/13533312.2016.1214074

Iacucci, Anahi A. (2013) "The conundrum of digital humanitarianism: when the crowd does harm," November 15, 2013. Available at: https://anahiayala. com/2013/11/15/the-conundrum-of-digital-humanitarianism-when-the-crowd-does-harm/. Accessed July 8, 2016.

IASC (2010) *IASC Guidelines: Common Operational Datasets (CODs) in Disaster Preparedness and Response*. Geneva: Inter-Agency Standing Committee.

ICG (2016) "Chad: Between Ambition and Fragility," *Africa Report No. 233*, March 30, 2016. Available at: https://d2071andvip0wj.cloudfront.net/233-chad-between-ambition-and-fragility.pdf. Accessed August 26, 2016.

IEP (2015) *Global Terrorism Index 2015*. Sydney: Institute of Economics and Peace.

IMF (2015) *Regional Economic Outlook: Sub-Saharan Africa. Navigating Headwinds*, April 2015. Washington, DC: International Monetary Fund.

International Conference on Protection of Civilians (2015) *The Kigali Principles on the Protection of Civilians*. Kigali: International Conference on Protection of Civilians.

Internet Society (2015) *Global Internet Society Report 2015*. Washington DC: Internet Society. Available at: http://www.internetsociety.org/globalinternetreport/assets/download/IS_web.pdf. Accessed June 16, 2016.

IRIN (2014) "NGOs against MONUSCO drones for humanitarian work." July 23, 2014. Available at: http://www.irinnews.org/report/100391/ngos-against-monusco-drones-for-humanitarian-work. Accessed April 27, 2016.

ISS (2015) "Kinshasa government attacks FDLR rebels without the UN," *ISS Peace and Security Council Report*, March 3, 2015. Available at: https://www. issafrica.org/pscreport/situation-analysis/kinshasa-government-attacks-fdlr-rebels-without-the-un. Accessed May 4, 2016.

ITU (2015) "Key ICT indicators for developed and developing countries and the world (totals and penetration rates)." Available at: http://www.itu.int/en/ITU-D/Statistics/Pages/stat/default.aspx. Accessed April 27, 2016.

Johnstone, Ian (2007) "Consolidating Peace: Priorities and Deliberative Processes," in Ian Johnstone (ed.) *Annual Review of Global Peace Operations*. Boulder, CO: Lynne Rienner. Available at: https://www.dropbox.com/s/9y88xwb1g7qfefu/2007_annual_review.pdf. Accessed July 7, 2016.

Johnstone, Ian (2008) "Law-Making through the Operational Activities of International Organizations," *George Washington International Law Review*, 40 (1): pp. 87–122.

Johnstone, Ian (2010) "Normative Evolution at the UN: Impact on Operational Imperatives," in Bruce D. Jones, Shepard Forman, and Richard Gowan (eds.), *Cooperating for Peace and Security: Evolving Institutions and Arrangements in a Context of Changing U.S. Security Policy*. Cambridge: Cambridge University Press, pp. 187–214.

Johnstone, Ian (2011) "Managing Consent in Contemporary Peacekeeping Operations," *International Peacekeeping* 18 (2): pp. 168–182.

Johnstone, Ian (2016) "Between Bureaucracy and Adhocracy: Crafting a Spectrum of Peace Operations," *Global Peace Operations Review,* March 31, 2016. Available at: http://peaceoperationsreview.org/thematic-essays/from-bureaucracy-to-adhocracy-crafting-a-spectrum-of-un-peace-operations/.   Accessed April 27, 2016.

Joint Chiefs of Staff (USA) (2011) *Joint Publication 3-07 Stability operations.* September. Available at: http://www.dtic.mil/doctrine/new_pubs/jp3_07.pdf. Accessed March 1, 2016.

Jones, Bruce (2015) "Why the U.S. needs U.N. peacekeeping," *Brookings,* December 10, 2015. Available at: http://www.brookings.edu/blogs/order-from-chaos/posts/2015/12/10-un-peacekeeping-serves-us-strategic-interests-jones. Accessed January 11, 2015.

Karlsrud, John (2013) "SRSGs as Norm Arbitrators? Understanding Bottom–Up Authority in UN Peacekeeping," *Global Governance,* 19 (4), pp. 525–544.

Karlsrud, John (2014) "Peacekeeping 4.0: Harnessing the Potential of Big Data, Social Media and Cyber Technology," in J.F. Kremer and B. Müller (eds.) *Cyber Space and International Relations. Theory, Prospects and Challenges.* Berlin: Springer, pp. 141–160.

Karlsrud, John (2015) "The UN at War: Examining the Consequences of Peace Enforcement Mandates for the UN Peacekeeping Operations in the CAR, the DRC and Mali," *Third World Quarterly* 36 (1): pp. 40–54.

Karlsrud, John (2016a) "New Tools for Blue Helmets," in Jim Della-Giacoma (ed.), *Global Peace Operations Review: Annual Compilation 2015.* New York: Center on International Cooperation, New York University, pp. 101–107.

Karlsrud, John (2016b) "UN peace operations and counter-terrorism—A bridge too far?" in Jim Della-Giacoma (ed.), *Global Peace Operations Review: Annual Compilation 2015.* New York: Center on International Cooperation, New York University, pp. 118–124.

Karlsrud, John (2016c) "How can the UN move towards more people-centered peace operations?" in Jim Della-Giacoma (ed.), *Global Peace Operations Review: Annual Compilation 2015.* New York: Center on International Cooperation, New York University, pp. 108–11.

Karlsrud, John (2016d) *Norm Change in International Relations: Linked Ecologies in UN Peacekeeping Operations.* Abingdon: Routledge.

Karlsrud, John (2017) "Towards UN counter-terrorism operations?," *Third World Quarterly,* 38 (6): pp. 1215–1231. doi: http://dx.doi.org/10.1080/01436597.2016.1268907.

Karlsrud, John and Adam Smith (2015) "Europe's Return to UN Peacekeeping in Africa? Lessons-Learned from Mali," *Providing for Peacekeeping,* No. 10. New York: International Peace Institute.

Karlsrud, John and Arthur Mühlen-Schulte (2017) "Quasi-Professionals in the Organisation of Transnational Crisis Mapping," in L. Seabrooke and

L.F. Henriksen (eds.) *Professional Networks in Transnational Governance*. Cambridge: Cambridge University Press.

Karlsrud, John and Kari M. Osland (2016) "Between self-interest and solidarity: Norway's return to UN peacekeeping?," *International Peacekeeping* 23 (5), pp. 1–20. doi: https://doi.org/10.1080/13533312.2016.1235096.

Karlsrud, John and Frederik Rosén (2017) "Lifting the Fog of War? Opportunities and Challenges of Drones in UN Peace Operations," in Maria G. Jumbert and Kristin B. Sandvik (eds.), *The Good Drone*. Abingdon: Routledge: pp. 45–64.

Kennedy, Merrit (2016) "Witnesses: U.N. Peacekeepers Did Nothing As South Sudanese Soldiers Raped Women," *NPR*, July 27, 2016. Available at: http://www.npr.org/sections/thetwo-way/2016/07/27/487625112/report-u-n-peacekeepers-did-nothing-as-south-sudanese-soldiers-raped-women. Accessed August 14, 2016.

Koops, Joachim A. and Thierry Tardy (2015) "The United Nations' Inter-Organizational Relations in Peacekeeping," in J. A. Koops, N. Macqueen, T. Tardy, and P. D. Williams (eds.), *The Oxford Handbook of United Nations Peacekeeping Operations*. Oxford: Oxford University Press, pp. 61–77.

Koops, Joachim A. and Giulia Tercovich (2016) "A European return to United Nations peacekeeping? Opportunities, challenges and ways ahead" *International Peacekeeping*, 23 (5), pp. 1–14. doi: https://doi.org/10.1080/13533312.2016.1236430.

Lacher, Wolfram and Denis M. Tull (2013) *Mali: Beyond Counterterrorism. SWP Comments 7*. Berlin: German Institute for International and Security Affairs (SWP).

Lagneau, Laurent (2014) "Le G5 Sahel demande une intervention de l'ONU en Libye, en accord avec l'Union africaine," December 20, 2014. Available at: http://www.opex360.com/2014/12/20/le-g5-sahel-demande-intervention-de-lonu-en-libye-en-accord-avec-lunion-africaine/. Accessed January 8, 2016.

Landry, Carole (2017) "US envoy eyes cuts to UN peacekeeping," *Yahoo! News*, February 5, 2017. Available at: https://www.yahoo.com/news/us-envoy-eyes-cuts-un-peacekeeping-075524323.html?soc_src=social-sh&soc_trk=tw. Accessed February 8, 2017.

Lanteigne, Marc (2014) "Red and Blue: China's Evolving United Nations Peacekeeping Policies and Soft Power Development," in Chiyuki Aoi and Yee-Kuang Heng (eds.) *Asia-Pacific Nations in International Peace Support and Stability Operations*. New York: Palgrave Macmillan.

Lanteigne, Marc (2016) *Chinese Foreign Policy: An Introduction* (3rd ed.). Abingdon: Routledge.

Landgren, Karin (2015) "Reflections on a career in peace operations," *Global Peace Operations Review*. Available at: http://peaceoperationsreview.org/interviews/karin-landgren-reflections-on-a-career-in-peace-operations/. Accessed January 12, 2016.

Le Sahel (2014) "Communiqué final du Sommet des Chefs d'Etat du G5 du Sahel: Création d'un cadre institutionnel de coordination et de suivi de la coopération régionale dénommé G5 du Sahel," *Le Sahel*. Available at: http://www.lesahel. org/index.php/component/k2/item/5054-communiqu%C3%A9-final-du-sommet-des-chefs-detat-du-g5-du-sahel--cr%C3%A9ation-dun-cadre-institu-tionnel-de-coordination-et-de-suivi-de-la-coop%C3%A9ration-r%C3%A9gionale-d%C3%A9nomm%C3%A9-g5-du-sahel. Accessed January 8, 2016.

Lederer, Edith M. (2016) "Netherlands and Italy agree to split Security Council term," June 28, 2016. Available at: https://www.washingtonpost.com/world/europe/sweden-wins-seat-on-un-security-council-on-first-ballot/2016/06/28/53a306a0-3d4c-11e6-9e16-4cf01a41decb_story.html. Accessed July 1, 2016.

van der Lijn, Jaïr and Timo Smit (2015) *Peacekeepers under Threat? Fatality Trends in UN Peace Operations*. Stockholm: Stockholm International Peace Research Institute.

Lilly, Damian (2014) "Protection of Civilians sites: a new type of displacement settlement?" *Humanitarian Exchange* No 62, November 2014: pp. 31-33. Available at: http://odihpn.org/wp-content/uploads/2014/09/HE_62_web2_FINAL.pdf. Accessed July 23, 2016.

Lindberg, Nancy and David Rothkopf (2015) 'Four Lessons for Fighting Violent Extremists – Without Guns," *Foreign Policy*, September 29. Available at: https://foreignpolicy.com/2015/09/29/four-lessons-for-fighting-extrem-ists-without-guns-obama-united-nations-summit/?utm_content=buffer93351&utm_medium=social&utm_source=twitter.com&utm_campaign=buffer. Accessed January 12, 2016.

Lindboe, Morten and David Nordli (2016) Intelligence in United Nations Peace Operations: A case study of the All Sources Information Fusion Unit in MINUSMA. Oslo: Norwegian Defence Research Establishment (FFI) & Norwegian Defence International Centre (NODEFIC).

Lotze, Walter (2015) "United Nations Multidimensional Integrated Stabilization Mission in Mali (MINUSMA)," in J. A. Koops, N. Macqueen, T. Tardy, and P. D. Williams. (eds.), *The Oxford Handbook of United Nations Peacekeeping Operations*. Oxford: Oxford University Press, pp. 854–864.

Lynch, Colum (2005) "UN Peacekeeping More Assertive, Creating Risk for Civilians," *Washington Post*, August 14, 2005. Available at: http://www.wash-ingtonpost.com/wp-dyn/content/article/2005/08/14/AR2005081400946.html. Accessed September 13, 2016.

Lynch, Justin (2016) "UN failed to protect civilians in South Sudan: report," *Al-Jazeera*, June 22, 2016. Available at: http://www.aljazeera.com/news/2016/06/failed-protect-civilians-south-sudan-report-160622060607406.html. Accessed July 25, 2016.

MacAskill, Ewen (2016) "UK to send more troops to South Sudan," *The Guardian*, September 8, 2016. Available at: https://www.theguardian.com/uk-news/2016/sep/08/uk-to-send-more-troops-to-south-sudan. Accessed September 19, 2016.

Mac Ginty, Roger and Oliver Richmond (2013) "The local turn in peace building: a critical agenda for peace," *Third World Quarterly*, 34 (5): pp. 763–783.

Maïga, Ibrahim (2015) "Strategic shift needed to combat violent extremism in Mali," December 4, 2015. Available at: https://www.issafrica.org/iss-today/strategic-shift-needed-to-combat-violent-extremism-in-mali. Accessed January 7, 2016.

Mail & Guardian (2014) "Jihadists announce blood-soaked return to northern Mali," *Mail & Guardian*, October 9, 2014. Available at: http://mgafrica.com/article/2014-10-09-jihadists-announce-blood-soaked-return-to-northern-mali. Accessed May 4, 2016.

Martin, Ian (2010) "All Peace Operations Are Political: a case for Designer Missions and the Next UN Reform," in Richard Gowan (ed.), *Review of Political Missions 2010*. New York: Center on International Cooperation, New York University. Available at: http://peaceoperationsreview.org/wp-content/uploads/2015/04/political_missions_20101.pdf. Accessed August 20, 2016.

Mason, Rowena (2015) "UK to deploy troops to help keep peace in Somalia and South Sudan," *The Guardian*, September 27, 2015. Available at: http://www.theguardian.com/politics/2015/sep/27/uk-to-deploy-troops-to-help-keep-peace-in-somalia-and-south-sudan. Accessed January 11, 2016.

McGreal, Chris (2015a) "Countries to pledge troops to bolster UN peacekeepers after intense US pressure," *The Guardian*, September 27, 2015. Available at: http://www.theguardian.com/world/2015/sep/27/un-peacekeeping-obama-countries-pledge-troops-counterterror. Accessed January 11, 2015.

McGreal, Chris (2015b) "What's the point of peacekeepers when they don't keep the peace?" *The Guardian*, September 17, 2015. Available at: http://www.theguardian.com/world/2015/sep/17/un-united-nations-peacekeepers-rwanda-bosnia. Accessed January 11, 2016.

MINUSCA (2016) "Civil Affairs." Available at: http://minusca.unmissions.org/en/civil-affairs. Accessed August 17, 2016.

Ministry of Foreign Affairs of the Russian Federation (2013) "Concept of the Foreign Policy of the Russian Federation. Approved by President of the Russian Federation V. Putin on 12 February 2013." Available at: http://www.mid.ru/brp_4.nsf/0/76389FEC168189ED44257B2E0039B16D. Accessed April 20, 2016.

Ministère de la Défense (2016) "Opération Barkhane," November 30, 2016. Available at: http://www.defense.gouv.fr/operations/sahel/dossier-de-presentation-de-l-operation-barkhane/operation-barkhane. Accessed January 8, 2017.

MONUSCO (2013) *International Security and Stabilization Support Strategy.* Kinshasa: MONUSCO. Available at: http://www.unpbf.org/wp-content/uploads/ISSSS-2013-2017-Strategic-Framework-FINAL_EN.pdf.   Accessed March 2, 2016.

The Nation Mirror (2016) "Government Ready For Dialogue Over Protection Forces Deployment," August 15, 2016. Available at: http://www.thenation-mirror.com/news/south-sudan-news/1981-government-ready-for-dialogue-over-protection-forces-deployment. Accessed August 19, 2016.

NATO (2011) "NATO's military concept for defence against terrorism," NATO, January 2, 2011. Available at: http://www.nato.int/cps/en/natohq/top-ics_69482.htm. Accessed January 27, 2016.

The Netherlands Ministry of Defence (2016) "Mali". Available at: https://www.defensie.nl/english/topics/mali. Accessed July 1, 2016.

News24 (2013) "Snipers hit M23 targets 2.2km away," *News24,* August 29, 2013. Available   at: http://www.news24.com/Africa/News/Snipers-hit-M23-targets-22km-away-20130829-2. Accessed June 17, 2016.

Nikitin, Alexander (2013) "The Russian Federation," in Alex Bellamy and Paul Williams (eds.) *Providing Peacekeepers. The Politics, Challenges, and Future of United Nations Peacekeeping Contributions.* Oxford: Oxford University Press.

Norway Mission to the UN (2015) "Norway's priorities for the 70th UN General Assembly," September 21, 2015. Available at: http://www.norway-un.org/NorwayandUN/Norwegian-UN-Politcies/UNGA-Norwegian-priorities/#.V3Z0jeOO5Q4. Accessed July 1, 2016.

Novosseloff, Alexandra (2015) "Triangular Cooperation – Key to All," November 10, 2015. Available at: http://peaceoperationsreview.org/thematic-essays/triangular-cooperation-key-to-all/. Accessed on June 20, 2016.

Novosseloff, Alexandra (2016) "No Caveats Please?: Breaking a Myth in UN Peace Operations," September 12, 2016. Available at: http://peaceoperation-sreview.org/thematic-essays/no-caveats-please-breaking-a-myth-in-un-peace-operations/. Accessed September 14, 2016.

Novosseloff, Alexandra and Thierry Tardy (2017) "France and the evolution of the UN peacekeeping doctrine," in Cedric de Coning, Chiyuki Aoi, and John Karlsrud (eds.), *UN Peacekeeping Doctrine in a New Era Adapting to Stabilisation, Protection and New Threats.* Abingdon: Routledge, pp. 90-108.

OCHA (2012) *OCHA on Message: Humanitarian Principles.* Geneva: UN Office for the Coordination of Humanitarian Affairs. Available at: https://docs.unocha.org/sites/dms/Documents/OOM-humanitarianprinciples_eng_June12.pdf. Accessed July 8, 2016.

OCHA (2013) *Humanitarianism in the Network Age.* New York: OCHA.

OCHA (2016) "South Sudan," OCHA. Available at: http://www.unocha.org/south-sudan. Accessed July 25, 2016.

OECD (2015) *States of Fragility 2015: Meeting Post-2015 Ambitions.* Paris: OECD Publishing.

Oxfam International (2016) "Violence fuels South Sudan's humanitarian crisis," July 28, 2016. Available at: https://www.oxfam.org/en/pressroom/pressre-leases/2016-07-28/violence-fuels-south-sudans-humanitarian-crisis. Accessed August 14, 2016.

Pawlak, Patryk and Andrea Ricci (eds.) (2014) *Crisis Rooms: Towards a Global Network?* Paris: EU Institute for Security Studies.

Piccolino, Giulia and John Karlsrud (2011) "Withering consent, but mutual dependency: UN peace operations and new African assertiveness," *Conflict, Security and Development*, 11 (4): pp. 447–471.

Pouligny, Béatrice (2006) *Peace Operations Seen from Below*. London: Kumarian Press.

Pouligny, Béatrice (2010) *State–Society Relations and Intangible Dimensions of State Resilience and State Building: A Bottom–Up Perspective*. Florence: European University Institute.

Power, Samantha (2014) "Remarks by Ambassador Samantha Power: Reforming peacekeeping in a time of conflict," *American Enterprise Institute*, November 7, 2014. Available at: https://www.aei.org/publication/remarks-ambassador-samantha-power-reforming-peacekeeping-time-conflict/. Accessed April 18, 2016.

Power, Samantha (2015) "Remarks on Peacekeeping in Brussels," *United States Mission to the United Nations*, March 9, 2015. Available at: http://usun.state.gov/remarks/6399. Accessed January 8, 2016.

van der Putten, Frans P. (2015) *China's Evolving Role in Peacekeeping and African Security*. The Hague: Clingendael Institute.

Ray, John (2017) "Britain's contributing 400 troops to South Sudan peacekeeping mission," *ITV*, February 7, 2017. Available at: http://www.itv.com/news/2017-02-07/britains-contribution-to-un-peacekeeping-in-south-sudan/. Accessed February 8, 2017.

Raymond, Nathaniel, Caitlin Howarth, and Jonathan Hutson (2012) "Crisis Mapping Needs an Ethical Compass," *GlobalBrief*, February 6, 2012. Available at: http://globalbrief.ca/blog/2012/02/06/crisis-mapping-needs-an-ethi-cal-compass/. Accessed 27 April 2016.

Reliefweb (2016) "Lake Chad Basin: Forced Displacement," June 16, 2016. Available at: http://reliefweb.int/report/nigeria/lake-chad-basin-forced-dis-placement-echo-ngos-un-government-echo-daily-flash-16-june. Accessed June 17, 2016.

Reykers, Yf (2016a) "Hurry Up and Wait: EU Battlegroups and a UN Rapid Reaction Force," January 21, 2016. Available at: http://peaceoperationsre-view.org/thematic-essays/hurry-up-and-wait-eu-battlegroups-and-a-un-rapid-reaction-force/. Accessed June 21, 2016.

Reykers, Yf (2016b) "Waiting for Godot: A Rational-Institutionalist Analysis of the Absence of the EU Battlegroups in Recent Crises." Paper presented at The

European Union in International Affairs V Conference, May 11–13, 2016, Brussels.

Reykers, Yf (2017) "High Costs, No Benefits," *Contemporary Security Policy*, 38(3): pp. 1–14. doi: https://doi.org/10.1080/13523260.2017.1348568.

Reykers, Yf and John Karlsrud (2017) "Multinational rapid response mechanisms: Past promises and future prospects," *Contemporary Security Policy*, 38(3): pp. 1–7. doi: https://doi.org/10.1080/13523260.2017.1348567.

Reykers, Yf and Niels Smeets (2015) "Losing control: a principal-agent analysis of Russia in the United Nations Security Council's decision-making towards the Libya crisis," *East European Politics*, 31 (4): pp. 369–387. https://doi.org/10.1080/21599165.2015.1070729.

Rhoads, Emily P. (2016) *Taking Sides in Peacekeeping: Impartiality and the Future of the United Nations.* Oxford: Oxford University Press.

Rieker, Pernille (2017) *French Foreign Policy Practices in the Age of Globalization and Regional Integration. Challenging Grandeur.* New York: Palgrave Macmillan.

Rosén, Frederik and John Karlsrud (2014) "The MONUSCO UAVs: The implications for actions and omissions," *Conflict Trends* 2014 (4): 42–48.

Ruggie, John G. (1993) "Wandering in the void: Charting the UN's new strategic role," *Foreign Affairs,* 72, pp. 26–31.

Rupesinghe, Natasja (2016a) "Community Engagement: softening the hard edge of stabilization," *Conflict Trends,* 2016 (3): pp. 20–26.

Rupesinghe, Natasja (2016b) "Strengthening Community Engagement in United Nations Peace Operations: Opportunities and Challenges in the Field," *Policy Brief 30· 2016.* Oslo: Norwegian Institute of International Affairs (NUPI).

Ryan, Missy and Sudarsan Raghavan (2016) "Another Western intervention in Libya looms," April 3, 2016, *Washington Post.* Available at: https://www.washingtonpost.com/world/national-security/another-western-intervention-in-libya-looms/2016/04/03/90386fde-f76e-11e5-9804-537defcc3cf6_story.html. Accessed July 8, 2016.

Sandvik, Kristin B., Maria G. Jumbert, John Karlsrud, and Mareile Kaufman (2014) "Humanitarian Technology: A Critical Research Agenda," *International Review of the Red Cross:* pp. 1–24.

Santora, Marc (2015) "As South Sudan Crisis Worsens, 'There Is No More Country'." *The New York Times,* June 22, 2015. Available at: http://www.nytimes.com/2015/06/23/world/africa/as-south-sudan-crisis-worsens-there-is-no-more-country.html?_r=0. Accessed January 8, 2016.

Satellite Sentinel Project (2016a) "Partner Organizations." Available at: http://satsentinel.org/our-story/partner-organizations#enough. Accessed July 8, 2016.

Satellite Sentinel Project (2016b) "Documenting the Crisis." Available at: http://www.satsentinel.org/our-story. Accessed July 8, 2016.

Schia, Niels N. (2015) *Peacebuilding, Ownership, and Sovereignty from New York to Monrovia: A Multi-sited Ethnographic Approach.* Department of Social Anthropology, University of Oslo: Academia.

Schia, Niels N. (2016a) "'Teach a person how to surf': Cyber security as development assistance." *NUPI Report no. 4.* Oslo: Norwegian Institute of International Affairs. Available at: https://brage.bibsys.no/xmlui/bitstream/id/415569/NUPI_Report_4_16_Nagelhus_Schia.pdf. Accessed June 20, 2016.

Schia, Niels N. (2016b) "Horseshoe and catwalk: Power, complexity and consensus-making in the United Nations Security Council," in Ronald Niezen and Maria Sapignoli (eds.), *The Anthropology of Global Institutions: Palaces of Hope.* Cambridge: Cambridge University Press, pp. 55–77.

Schia, Niels N., Ingvild, M. Gjelsvik, and John Karlsrud (2013) "What people think does matter: Understanding and integrating local perceptions into UN peacekeeping." *Policy Brief 13 · 2013.* Oslo: Norwegian Institute of International Affairs (NUPI).

Schia, Niels N., Ingvild M. Gjelsvik, and John Karlsrud (2014) "Connections and disconnections: understanding and integrating local perceptions in United Nations peacekeeping," *Conflict Trends* 2014 (1): pp. 28–34.

Sebastián, Sofía (2015) "The Role of Police in UN Peace Operations: Filling the Gap in the Protection of Civilians from Physical Violence," *Civilians in Conflict: Policy Brief No. 3.* Washington DC: Stimson Center. Available at: https://www.stimson.org/sites/default/files/file-attachments/CIC-Policy-Brief_3_Sept-2015-Web-REVISED_Jan2016_0.pdf. Accessed August 17, 2016.

Security Council Report (2014) "In Hindsight: Changes to UN Peacekeeping in 2013," January 31, 2014. Available at: http://www.securitycouncilreport.org/monthly-forecast/2014-02/in_hindsight_changes_to_un_peacekeeping_in_2013.php. Accessed July 8, 2016.

Security Council Report (2016) "UN–AU Cooperation on Peace and Security," April 29, 2016. Available at: http://m.securitycouncilreport.org/466255/show/6e751635384540cf26950d835c651c0d/. Accessed May 5, 2016.

Selway, Bianca (2013) "Who Pays for Peace?" *IPI Global Observatory,* November 4, 2013. Available at: https://theglobalobservatory.org/2013/11/who-pays-for-peace/. Accessed August 22, 2016.

Sengupta, Somini (2014) "Unarmed Drones Aid U.N. Peacekeeping Missions in Africa." July 2, 2014. Available at: http://www.nytimes.com/2014/07/03/world/africa/unarmed-drones-aid-un-peacekeepers-in-africa.html?_r=1. Accessed April 27, 2016.

de Soto, Alvaro (2007) "End of Mission Report," *The Guardian.* Available at: http://image.guardian.co.uk/sys-files/Guardian/documents/2007/06/12/DeSotoReport.pdf. Accessed January 11, 2016.

Stamnes, Eli and Kari M. Osland (2016) *Synthesis Report: Reviewing UN Peace Operations, the UN Peacebuilding Architecture and the Implementation of UNSCR 1325.* Oslo: Norwegian Institute of International Affairs (NUPI).

Stearns, Jason (2015) "Can Force be Useful in the Absence of a Political Strategy? Lessons from the UN Missions to the DR Congo." Available at: http://

peaceoperationsreview.org/thematic-essays/can-force-be-useful-in-the-absence-of-a-political-strategy-lessons-from-the-un-missions-to-the-dr-congo/. Accessed January 11, 2016.

Strobel, Warren (2015) "Exclusive: In Niger, U.S. soldiers quietly help build wall against Boko Haram," *Reuters,* September 18, 2015. Available at: http://www.reuters.com/article/us-usa-niger-boko-haram-idUSKCN0RI0C020150918. Accessed January 11, 2016.

Swedish Armed Forces (2016) "Sweden in MINUSMA, Mali and the Sahel – a long-term commitment to peace and progress," June 20, 2016. Available at: http://www.forsvarsmakten.se/en/news/2016/06/sweden-in-minusma-mali-and-the-sahel-a-long-term-commitment-to-peace-and-progress/. Accessed July 1, 2016.

Tardy, Thierry (2014) "The Reluctant Peacekeeper: France and the Use of Force in Peace Operations," *Journal of Strategic Studies* 37 (5): pp. 770–792. https://doi.org/10.1080/01402390.2014.905472.

Tardy, Thierry (2016) "France: The unlikely return to UN peacekeeping," *International Peacekeeping* 23 (5): 1–20. https://doi.org/10.1080/1353331 2.2016.1235091.

Tardy, Thierry and Dominik Zaum (2016) "France and the United Kingdom in the Security Council," in Sebastian von Einsiedel, David M. Malone, and Bruno S. Ugarte (eds.) *The UN Security Council in the 21ˢᵗ Century.* Boulder, CO: Lynne Rienner, pp. 121–138.

Tull, Denis M. (2015) "Cameroon and Boko Haram: Time to Think beyond Terrorism and Security," *SWP Comments 42.* Berlin: German Institute for International and Security Affairs.

UCDP (2016) "Uppsala Conflict Data Program." Available at: http://ucdp.uu.se/. Accessed August 22, 2016.

UK (2015a) "PM pledges UK troops to support stability in Somalia and South Sudan," September 28, 2015. Available at: https://www.gov.uk/government/news/pm-pledges-uk-troops-to-support-stability-in-somalia-and-south-sudan. Accessed April 26, 2016.

UK (2015b) *A Secure and Prosperous United Kingdom: National Security Strategy and Strategic Defence and Security Review 2015.* London: HM Government of the United Kingdom.

UK Stabilisation Unit (2014) The UK Government's Approach to Stabilisation (2014). London: UK Stabilisation Unit. Available at: file:///C:/Users/Karljoh/Downloads/uk-approach-to-stabilisation-2014.pdf. Accessed March 2, 2016.

UN (1945) *Charter of the United Nations and Statute of the International Court of Justice.* New York: United Nations.

UN (2000) *Report of the Panel on United Nations Peace Operations* [Brahimi Report]. New York: United Nations.

UN (2001) *S/RES/1373,* September 28, 2001. New York: United Nations.

UN (2006a) *A/RES/60/288*, September 20, 2006. New York: United Nations.

UN (2006b) "Monthly Summary of Contributions," as of January 31, 2006. Available at: http://www.un.org/en/peacekeeping/resources/statistics/contributors_archive.shtml. Accessed May 4, 2016.

UN (2006c) *A/61/630*, December 12, 2006. New York: United Nations.

UN (2008) *United Nations Peacekeeping Operations: Principles and Guidelines.* New York: United Nations Department of Peacekeeping Operations and Department of Field Support.

UN (2009) *Peacebuilding in the Immediate Aftermath of Conflict.* New York: United Nations.

UN (2011a) *S/RES/1973*, March 17, 2011. New York: United Nations.

UN (2011b) *S/RES/1996*, July 8, 2011. New York: United Nations.

UN (2012a) *S/2012/894*, November 28, 2012. New York: United Nations.

UN (2012b) *S/2012/439. Letter dated 13 June 2012 from the Secretary-General to the President of the Security Council,* June 13, 2012. New York United Nations.

UN (2012c) *S/2012/894. Report of the Secretary-General on the Situation in Mali,* November 28, 2012. New York: United Nations.

UN (2012d) *S/RES/2085*, December 20, 2012. New York: United Nations.

UN (2013a) *S/RES/2098*, March 28, 2013. New York: United Nations.

UN (2013b) *S/RES/2100*, April 25, 2013. New York: United Nations.

UN (2013c) *S/2013/354. United Nations Integrated Strategy for the Sahel,* June 14, 2013. New York: United Nations.

UN (2013d) *S/RES/2102*, May 2, 2013. New York: United Nations.

UN (2013e) *S/2013/189. Report of the Secretary-General on the Situation in Mali,* March 26, 2013. New York: United Nations.

UN (2013f) "'Intervention Brigade' Authorized as Security Council Grants Mandate Renewal for United Nations Mission in Democratic Republic of Congo," March 28, 2013. Available at: http://www.un.org/press/en/2013/sc10964.doc.htm. Accessed September 27, 2016.

UN (2013g) *S/RES/2127*, December 5, 2013. New York: United Nations.

UN (2014a) "Secretary-General's statement on appointment of High-Level Independent Panel on Peace Operations," October 31, 2014. Available at: http://www.un.org/sg/statements/index.asp?nid=8151. Accessed February 25, 2016.

UN (2014b) *Plan Régional de Stabilisation de la Région de Gao.* Bamako: United Nations Multidimensional Integrated Stabilisation Mission in Mali. [Draft] On file with the author.

UN (2014c) *Standard Operating Procedure: Intelligence Cycle Management.* Bamako: United Nations Multidimensional Integrated Stabilisation Mission in Mali.

UN (2014d) *Guidelines on Understanding and Integrating Local Perceptions in UN Peacekeeping.* New York: United Nations.

UN (2014e) *S/RES/2164*, June 25, 2014. New York: United Nations.

UN (2014f) *S/RES/2182*, October 24, 2014. New York: United Nations.

UN(2014g) *S/RES/2155*, May 27, 2014. New York: United Nations.

UN (2014h) *S/RES/2149*, April 10, 2014. New York: United Nations.

UN (2014i) *S/RES/2134*, January 28, 2014. New York: United Nations.

UN (2014j) "Meeting of the Security Council in Arria format on Inter-communities dialogue and prevention of crimes in Central African Republic: Statement of Under Secretary-General/Special Adviser on the Prevention of Genocide Mr. Adama Dieng," March 14, 2014. Available at: http://www.un.org/en/preventgenocide/adviser/pdf/2014-03-12%20Statement%20of%20USG%20Adama%20Dieng%20to%20the%20Security%20%20Council.%20FINAL.pdf. Accessed July 27, 2016.

UN (2014k) *S/RES/2149*, April 10, 2014. New York: United Nations.

UN (2014l) *A/69/399-S/2014/694. Peacebuilding in the Aftermath of Conflict.* New York: United Nations.

UN (2015a) *A/70/95-S/2015/446. Report of the High-level Independent Panel on Peace Operations on Uniting our Strengths for Peace: Politics, Partnership and People* ("HIPPO Report"). New York: United Nations.

UN (2015b) "Security Council Reiterates Sanctions Decision Against Those Undermining Peace, Stability in Central African Republic," 20 October 2015. Available at: http://www.un.org/press/en/2015/sc12086.doc.htm. Accessed January 11, 2016.

UN (2015c) "Conflict-related sexual violence. Report of the Secretary-General," March 23, 2015. Available at: http://www.un.org/en/ga/search/view_doc.asp?symbol=S/2015/203. Accessed January 29, 2016.

UN (2015d) *Global Study: Preventing Conflict, Transforming Justice, Securing the Peace*, October 14, 2015. New York: United Nations. Available at: http://wps.unwomen.org/~/media/files/un%20women/wps/highlights/unw-global-study-1325-2015.pdf. Accessed June 14, 2016.

UN (2015e) *A/70/674. Plan of Action to Prevent Violent Extremism.* New York: United Nations.

UN (2015f) "UN Peacekeeping Operations Fact Sheet," April 30, 2015. Available at: http://www.un.org/en/peacekeeping/archive/2015/bnote0415.pdf. Accessed February 18, February.

UN (2015g) "UN Political Missions and Peacebuilding Fact Sheet," November 20, 2015. Available at: http://www.un.org/undpa/sites/www.un.org.undpa/files/ppbm_November_2015.pdf. Accessed February 18, 2016.

UN (2015h) *The Challenge of Sustaining Peace: Report of the Advisory Group of Experts for the 2015 Review of the United Nations Peacebuilding Architecture.* New York: United Nations.

UN (2015i) *Transforming Our World: The 2030 Agenda for Sustainable Development.* New York: United Nations. Available at: https://sustainabledevelopment.un.org/post2015/transformingourworld. Accessed June 14, 2016.

UN (2015j) "Daily Press Briefing by the Office of the Spokesperson for the Secretary-General," *United Nations,* April 2, 2015. Available at: http://www.un.org/press/en/2015/db150402.doc.htm. Accessed April 21, 2016.

UN (2015k) *S/2015/229. Partnering for peace: moving towards partnership peacekeeping, April 1, 2015.* New York: United Nations.

UN (2015l) *Performance Peacekeeping.* New York: United Nations. Available at: http://www.performancepeacekeeping.org/offline/download.pdf. Accessed June 14, 2016.

UN (2015m) *S/RES/2227,* June 29, 2015. New York: United Nations.

UN (2015n) *S/RES/2245,* November 9, 2015. New York: United Nations.

UN (2015o) *S/2015/567,* July 24, 2015. New York: United Nations.

UN (2015p) *S/PV.7487,* July 16, 2015. New York: United Nations.

UN (2015q) *S/RES/2217,* April 28, 2015. New York: United Nations.

UN (2015r) *A/70/357–S/2015/682. The future of United Nations peace operations: implementation of the recommendations of the High-level Independent Panel on Peace Operations.* New York: United Nations.

UN (2015s) "Statement by the Secretary-General on the release of his report, *The Future of UN Peace Operations,*" September 11, 2015. Available at: http://www.un.org/sg/statements/index.asp?nid=8964. Accessed January 12, 2016.

UN (2015t) "MONUSCO's Civil Affairs," *MONUSCO.* Available at: http://monusco.unmissions.org/LinkClick.aspx?fileticket=sbKJDmIIJWQ%3D&tabid=10715&mid=13709&language=en-US. Accessed January 12, 2016.

UN (2016a) "(4a) Fatalities by Mission, Year and Incident Type," *United Nations Peacekeeping,* October 30, 2016. Available at: http://www.un.org/en/peacekeeping/fatalities/documents/stats_4a.pdf. Accessed February 7, 2017.

UN (2016b) *S/RES/2304,* August 12, 2016. New York: United Nations.

UN (2016c) "(5) Fatalities by Year and Incident Type up to 31 Jan 2016." Available at: http://www.un.org/en/peacekeeping/fatalities/documents/stats_5.pdf. Accessed February 18, 2016.

UN (2016d) "Fresh allegations of sexual abuse made against UN peacekeepers in Central African Republic," January 5, 2016. Available at: http://www.un.org/apps/news/story.asp?NewsID=52941#.VtAZyG1qhM0. Accessed February 26, 2016.

UN (2016e) "Contributors to United Nations peacekeeping operations (Police, UN Military Experts on Mission and Troops," December 31, 2016. Available at: http://www.un.org/en/peacekeeping/contributors/documents/Yearly_Summary.pdf . Accessed February 8, 2017.

UN (2016f) *S/RES/2295,* June 29, 2016. New York: United Nations.

UN (2016g) "Financing peacekeeping" Available at: http://www.un.org/en/peacekeeping/operations/financing.shtml. Accessed April 26, 2016.

UN (2016h) "The 'New Horizon' process." Available at: http://www.un.org/en/peacekeeping/operations/newhorizon.shtml. Accessed April 25, 2016.

UN (2016i) "Ranking of Military and Police Contributions to UN Operations." Available at: http://www.un.org/en/peacekeeping/contributors/2016/jul16_2.pdf. Accessed August 22, 2016.

UN (2016j) *Lessons Learned Report. Sources Information Fusion Unit and the MINUSMA Intelligence Architecture: Lessons for the Mission and a UN Policy Framework. Semi-final draft for USG Ladsous' review, 1 March 2016.* New York: United Nations. On file with the author.

UN (2016k) *S/RES/2301*, July 26, 2016. New York: United Nations.

UN (2016l) "Security Council Counter-Terrorism Committee," *United Nations.* Available at: http://www.un.org/en/sc/ctc/practices.html. Accessed January 11, 2016.

UN (2016m) "UN Counter-Terrorism Implementation Task Force," *United Nations.* Available at: http://www.un.org/en/terrorism/ctitf/. Accessed January 11, 2016.

UN (2016n) "UN Counter-Terrorism Centre," *United Nations.* Available at: http://www.un.org/en/terrorism/ctitf/uncct/. Accessed January 11, 2016.

UN (2016o) "Main Projects," *United Nations.* Available at: https://www.un.org/counterterrorism/ctitf/en/uncct/main-projects. Accessed April 27, 2016.

UN (2016p) *Summary of Concept Note: Countering and preventing violent extremism: role of UN peacekeeping. Proposed areas for DPKO/DFS research and policy development.* New York: United Nations. On file with the author.

UN (2016q) "UN Peacekeeping Operations Fact Sheet: 30 June 2016." Available at: http://www.un.org/en/peacekeeping/documents/bnote0616.pdf. Accessed September 16, 2016.

UN (2016r) "United Nations Political and Peacebuilding Missions: 30 November 2015." Available at: http://www.un.org/undpa/sites/www.un.org.undpa/files/ppbm_November_2015.pdf. Accessed September 16, 2016.

UN (2016s) *Report of the Secretary-General on South Sudan,* 13 April 2016. New York: United Nations.

UN (2016t) "South Sudan: UN peacekeeping chief says action will be taken on probe into Malakal violence," June 22, 2016. Available at: http://www.un.org/apps/news/story.asp?NewsID=54300#.V5XhROOO7M5. Accessed July 25, 2016.

UN (2016u) "Secretary-General's press encounter on South Sudan," July 11, 2016. Available at: http://www.un.org/sg/offthecuff/index.asp?nid=4616. Accessed July 25, 2016.

UN (2016v) "Note to Correspondents on allegations of sexual exploitation and abuse in the Central African Republic," March 30, 2016. Available at: https://www.un.org/sg/en/content/sg/note-correspondents/2016-03-30/note-correspondents-allegations-sexual-exploitation-and. Accessed August 17, 2016.

UN (2016w) "Probe into sexual abuse in Central African Republic must 'leave no stone unturned' – UN rights chief," March 31, 2016. Available at: http://www.un.org/apps/news/story.asp?NewsID=53583#.V7RZauOO7M4. Accessed August 17, 2016.

UN (2016x) *Practice note: Community engagement.* New York: Policy and Best Practices Service, Department of Peacekeeping / Department of Field Support, United Nations.

UNCCT (2015) "Kingdom of Saudi Arabia Donates USD 100 Million for the United Nations Counter-Terrorism Centre," *The Beam*, Winter 2013–Summer 2014. Available at: http://www.un.org/es/terrorism/ctitf/pdfs/The%20Beam%20Vol%208.pdf. Accessed January 11, 2016.

UNDP (2015) *Human Development Report 2015.* New York: United Nations Development Programme. Available at: http://hdr.undp.org/sites/default/files/2015_human_development_report.pdf. Accessed July 27, 2016.

UNDP (2016) "Community security and armed violence reduction," *UNDP.* Available at: http://www.undp.org/content/undp/en/home/ourwork/democratic-governance-and-peacebuilding/rule-of-law--justice-and-security/community-security-and-armed-violence-areduction.html. Accessed January 11, 2016.

UNGA (2014) *A/68/787. Evaluation of the Implementation and Results of Protection of Civilians Mandates in United Nations Peacekeeping Operations. Report of the Office of Internal Oversight Services.* New York: United Nations General Assembly.

UN Global Pulse (2016) "About." Available at: http://www.unglobalpulse.org/about-new. Accessed April 27, 2016.

UNHRC (2015) *A/70/53. Report of the Human Rights Council,* September 9, 2015. New York: United Nations.

UNHCR (2016) *Global Trends: Forced Displacement in 2015.* Geneva: United Nations High Commissioner for Human Rights. Available at: http://www.unhcr.org/576408cd7. Accessed June 21, 2016.

UNMISS (2015) "Update," August 31, 2015. Available at: http://reliefweb.int/sites/reliefweb.int/files/resources/15-8-%20Update%20%2089.pdf. Accessed August 11, 2016.

UN News Centre (2015) "Preventing violent extremism, promoting human rights go hand-in-hand, Ban tells Washington summit," *UN News Centre*, February 19, 2015. Available at: http://www.un.org/apps/news/story.asp?NewsID=50123#.VpOdrcmEr9d. Accessed January 11, 2016.

UN Office of the Spokesperson (2013) "Highlights of the noon briefing. By Martin Nesirky, Spokesperson for Secretary-General Ban Ki-Moon. Tuesday, 3 December 2013," *United Nations.* Available at: http://www.un.org/sg/spokesperson/highlights/index.asp?HighD=12/3/2013&d_month=12&d_year=2013. Accessed January 8, 2016.

United Kingdom (2016) "LIVE WEBCAST - UN Peacekeeping Defence Ministerial: London 2016," September 8, 2016. Available at: https://www.gov.uk/government/news/live-webcast-un-peacekeeping-defence-ministerial-london-2016. Accessed September 8, 2016.

United States Dept. of the Army and United States Marine Corps (2007) *The U.S. Army/Marine Corps Counterinsurgency Field Manual: U.S. Army Field Manual no. 3–24: Marine Corps warfighting publication no. 3–33.5.* Chicago, IL: University of Chicago Press.

Ushahidi (2014) "About Ushahidi." Available at: https://www.ushahidi.com/about. Accessed April 27, 2016.

U.S. Department of State (2013) "African Contingency Operations Training and Assistance (ACOTA) Program," *U.S. Department of State*, February 6, 2013. Available at: http://www.state.gov/r/pa/prs/ps/2013/02/203841.htm. Accessed April 19, 2016.

U.S. Department of State (2016a) "Global Peace Operations Initiative (GPOI)," *U.S. Department of State*. Available at: http://www.state.gov/t/pm/ppa/gpoi/. Accessed April 19, 2016.

U.S. Department of State (2016b) "The Global Coalition to Counter ISIL," *U.S. Department of State*. Available at: http://www.state.gov/s/seci/. Accessed January 11, 2016.

Vilmer, Jean-Baptiste Jeangène and Olivier Schmitt (2015) "Frogs of War: Explaining the New French Interventionism," *War on the Rocks*, October 14, 2015. Available at: http://warontherocks.com/2015/10/frogs-of-war-explaining-the-new-french-military-interventionism/. Accessed January 11, 2016.

Vinck, Patrick, Léonard D. Gotoas and Anthony H. Yavala (2012) *Fonds de Consolidation de la Paix en République Centrafricaine: Evaluation Externe de la Mise en Œuvre des Projets* (2008–2012). New York: UN Peacebuilding Fund. Available at: http://www.unpbf.org/wp-content/uploads/Central-African-Republic_2012.pdf. Accessed July 27, 2016.

Vogel, C. (2014) *Islands of Stability or Swamps of Insecurity? MONUSCO's Intervention Brigade and the Danger of Emerging Security Voids in Eastern Congo.* Brussels: Egmont Institute.

de Vries, Hugo (2015) *Going Around in Circles: The Challenges of Peacekeeping and Stabilization in the Democratic Republic of Congo.* The Hague: Netherlands Institute of International Relations Clingendael.

de Vries, Hugo (2016) "The Ebb and Flow of Stabilization in the Congo," *PSRP Briefing Paper 8.* Nairobi: Rift Valley Institute.

de Waal, Alex (2014) "When kleptocracy becomes insolvent: brute causes of the civil war in South Sudan," *African Affairs,* 113 (452): 347–369. https://doi.org/10.1093/afraf/adu028.

de Waal, Alex (2016) "South Sudan's corrupt elite have driven a debt-free and oil-rich country to ruin," *International Business Times,* July 15, 2016. Available at: http://www.ibtimes.co.uk/south-sudans-corrupt-elite-have-driven-debt-free-oil-rich-country-ruin-1570845?utm_source=yahoo&utm_medium=referral&utm_campaign=rss&utm_content=%2Frss%2Fyahoous%2Fnews&yptr=yahoo. Accessed July 21, 2016.

Wagner, Ben (2012) *After the Arab Spring: New Paths for Human Rights and the Internet in European Foreign Policy*. Brussels: European Union.

Weber, Max, Hans Heinrich Gerth, and C. Wright Mills (1946) *From Max Weber: Essays in Sociology*. New York: Oxford University Press.

Wells, Matt (2016) "The UN has failed its peacekeepers in S Sudan," *al-Jazeera*, September 10, 2016. Available at: http://www.aljazeera.com/indepth/opinion/2016/09/failed-peacekeepers-sudan-160908091206526.html. Accessed September 16, 2016.

What's in Blue (2014) "Informal Interactive Dialogue on UN Mission in Mali's Mandate," November 10, 2014. Available at: http://www.whatsinblue.org/2014/11/informal-interactive-dialogue-on-un-mission-in-malis-mandate.php#. Accessed January 8, 2016.

What's in Blue (2016a) "Renewal of UN Mission in Mali's Mandate," June 28, 2016. Available at: http://www.whatsinblue.org/2016/06/renewal-of-minusmas-mandate.php. Accessed July 8, 2016.

What's in Blue (2016b) "Mandate Renewal of the UN Mission in the Central African Republic," July 25, 2016. Available at: http://www.whatsinblue.org/2016/07/renewal-of-the-central-african-republic-mission-mandate.php. Accessed August 25, 2016.

The White House (1994) *U.S. Policy on Reforming Multilateral Peace Operations*. Washington, DC: The White House. Available at: http://nsarchive.gwu.edu/NSAEBB/NSAEBB53/rw050394.pdf. Accessed June 13, 2016.

The White House (2014) "FACT SHEET: Summit on Peacekeeping," September 26, 2014. Available at: https://www.whitehouse.gov/the-press-office/2014/09/26/fact-sheet-summit-un-peacekeeping. Accessed January 8, 2016.

The White House (2015) *United States Support to United Nations Peace Operations*. Washington, DC: The White House. Available at: http://www.defense.gov/Portals/1/Documents/pubs/2015peaceoperations.pdf. Accessed June 13, 2016.

Wiharta, Sharon, Neil Melvin, and Xenia Avezov (2012) *The New Geopolitics of Peace Operations: Mapping the Emerging Landscape*. Stockholm: Stockholm International Peace Research Institute.

Williams, Paul D. (2015a) "Keeping a Piece of Peacekeeping," *Foreign Affairs*, October 6, 2015. Available at: https://www.foreignaffairs.com/articles/2015-10-06/keeping-piece-peacekeeping. Accessed April 19, 2016.

Williams, Paul D. (2015b) "Special Report: How Many Fatalities Has the African Union Mission in Somalia Suffered?," *IPI Global Observatory*, September 10, 2015. Available at: http://theglobalobservatory.org/2015/09/amisom-african-union-somalia-peacekeeping/. Accessed January 11, 2016.

Williams, Paul D. and Arthur Boutellis (2014) "Partnership peacekeeping: Challenges and opportunities in the United Nations–African Union Relationship," *African Affairs,* 113 (451): pp. 254–278.

Wolffe, John and Gavin Moorhead (2014) *Religion, Security and Global Uncertainties.* Milton Keynes: The Open University. Available at: http://www.open.ac.uk/arts/research/religion-martyrdom-global-uncertainties/sites/www.open.ac.uk.arts.research.religion-martyrdom-global-uncertainties/files/files/ecms/arts-rmgu-pr/web-content/Religion-Security-Global-Uncertainties.pdf. Accessed September 13, 2016.

World Bank (2015) *Migration and Remittances: Recent Developments and Outlook.* Available at: http://siteresources.worldbank.org/INTPROSPECTS/Resources/334934-1288990760745/MigrationandDevelopmentBrief24.pdf. Accessed January 6, 2016.

World Bank (2016a) *Global Economic Prospects,* June 2015. Washington, DC: World Bank. Available at: https://www.worldbank.org/content/dam/Worldbank/GEP/GEP2015a/pdfs/GEP2015a_chapter2_regionaloutlook_SSA.pdf. Accessed June 13, 2016.

World Bank (2016b) "Central African Republic," The World Bank. Available at: http://data.worldbank.org/country/central-african-republic. Accessed July 27, 2016.

Yin, He (2017) "China's Doctrine on UN Peacekeeping," in Cedric de Coning, Chiyuki Aoi, and John Karlsrud (eds.), *UN Peacekeeping Doctrine Towards the Post-Brahimi Era? Adapting to Stabilization, Protection and New Threats.* Abingdon: Routledge, pp. 109–131.

Zhuang, Pinghui (2016) "Two Chinese UN peacekeepers killed, two seriously injured in attack in South Sudan," *South China Morning Post,* July 11, 2016. Available at: http://www.scmp.com/news/china/diplomacy-defence/article/1988348/two-chinese-un-peacekeepers-killed-two-seriously. Accessed September 5, 2016.

Index[1]

[1]Note: Page number followed by 'n' refers to notes.

© The Author(s) 2018
J. Karlsrud, *The UN at War*,
https://doi.org/10.1007/978-3-319-62858-5

Made in the USA
Middletown, DE
26 August 2018